THE SELECTED POEMS OF
William Blake

D0102449

Wordsworth Poetry Library
Series Editor:

KEITH CARABINE
Rutherford College
University of Kent at Canterbury

The Selected Poems of
William Blake

❦

with Introduction, Notes
and Bibliography by
DR BRUCE WOODCOCK
University of Hull

The Wordsworth Poetry Library

For my husband
ANTHONY JOHN RANSON
with love from your wife, the publisher.
Eternally grateful for your unconditional love,
not just for me but for our children,
Simon, Andrew and Nichola Trayler

Readers who are interested in other titles from
Wordsworth Editions are invited to visit our website at
www.wordsworth-editions.com

For our latest list and a full mail-order service contact
Bibliophile Books, 5 Thomas Road, London E14 7BN
TEL: +44 (0) 207 515 9222 FAX: +44 (0) 207 538 4115
E-MAIL: orders@bibliophilebooks.com

This edition published 1994 by Wordsworth Editions Limited
8B East Street, Ware, Hertfordshire SG12 9ET

ISBN 978-1-85326-452-8

Text © Wordsworth Editions Limited 1994
Intoduction and Notes © Dr Bruce Woodcock 2000

Text © Wordsworth Editions Limited 1993
Introduction and notes © Wordsworth Editions 2000

Wordsworth® is a registered trademark of
Wordsworth Editions Limited,
the company founded by Michael Trayler in 1987

All rights reserved. This publication may not be
reproduced, stored in a retrieval system or
transmitted, in any form or by any means, electronic,
mechanical, photocopying, recording or otherwise,
without the prior permission of the publishers.

Typeset by Antony Gray
Printed and bound in Great Britain by
Clays Ltd, St Ives plc

INTRODUCTION

WILLIAM BLAKE: ART, VISION AND REVOLUTION

Life and Ideas

As an artist and poet, William Blake was a revolutionary visionary and a
visionary revolutionary. He literally saw visions: when he was four, God
'put his head to the window' and set the infant Blake screaming. At the
age of eight, he told his mother that he had seen angels in the trees in
Peckham, and she saved him from being cuffed for storytelling by his
less tolerant father.[1] This visionary capacity stayed with Blake and
formed the core of his art: he viewed the political and social upheavals
of his day as a cosmic battle between Life, manifested as energy, and
Death, manifested as restriction. Blake's art works simultaneously at the
levels of the social, political, psychological, imaginative, historical and
spiritual or cosmic. It shows society divided and at war with itself as a
result of inequality and power; it portrays the human psyche as
fractured into competing faculties and capacities; and in visionary terms
it depicts the universe as being fought over by 'Giant forms' (p. 334),[2]
each epitomising some element of society and the psyche, struggling
around and within the sick and sleeping body of Albion, the ancient
name for Britain. At each level, Blake's art seeks to renew, radicalise and
release human potential, energy and imagination from the limits of
laws, inequalities and the 'single vision' (p. 148) of the rational mind,

1 Wilson, p. 3. For full details of this and all other references, see the Bibliography
at the end of this Introduction. Wherever possible, the surname and page number
follow in parentheses after the quotation.
2 All quotations from and references to Blake's texts are to the present edition and
are given as page numbers in brackets following the reference or quotation. Where
the passage is not included in this edition, references are to the editions by Keynes
and Stevenson listed in the Bibliography.

all epitomised by one particular mythological character in Blake's writing – the lawgiver, Urizen: a pun on 'your reason' or 'your horizon'. But far from being anti-intellectual, Blake's writing celebrates the intellect as part of humanity's rich potential: the poem 'The Schoolboy' indicates that the child longs to take delight in his book and 'sit in learning's bower' (p. 87). What prevents this is the elevation of one restrictive form of intellectual activity and the institutionalisation of learning represented by repressive schooling. As *The Marriage of Heaven and Hell* puts it: 'Those who restrain Desire, do so because theirs is weak enough to be restrained; and the restrainer or Reason usurps its place and governs the unwilling' (p. 196). Blake's critique of reason is of the limits of rationalism in the guise of morality, authority and law, which restrict the capacities of the whole human being. For Blake, human life is made up of a fluid mixture of interacting 'contraries': 'Without Contraries is no progression. Attraction and Repulsion, Reason and Energy, Love and Hate, are necessary to Human existence' (p. 196). Problems arrive when one side of the equation usurps its place and tries to dominate the dialectical relationship. The result is repressive tyranny in all its forms.

A challenging example of Blake's desire to release repressed potential appears in a short poem often called 'Eternity':

> He who binds to himself a Joy
> Does the wingèd life destroy;
> But he who kisses the Joy as it flies
> Lives in Eternity's sunrise.   (p. 153)

The poem argues for spontaneity and against the dangers of trying to tie life down, all of which is very subversive if you try to apply it.

Blake's work presents questions that derail conventional thinking, rather than providing the reader with easily assimilated answers. In *Songs of Experience*, 'The Clod and the Pebble' (pp. 80–1) offers two dialectically opposing definitions of love and seems to ask: which are you? One might view the clod as representing the Christian ideal of selfless love, perhaps how we are supposed to be, or might aspire to be; while the pebble is utterly selfish, perhaps a realistic view of how we actually are. Is it cynical then? But if you are a clod and have the chance to be selfless in your relationship, isn't that actually quite selfish? And doesn't a selfless lover need a selfish partner to allow them to be selfless? Imagine two clods together: they'd never get anywhere. A selfish partner, on the other hand, needs a selfless one, otherwise if two pebbles were continually battering together, they'd destroy each other. So perhaps the best relationship is between the clod and the pebble? Or aren't we all made up of both, rather than being one; and don't the problems come when we become fixed as one thing, through the roles we play or adopt? A later liberationist writer from the anti-psychiatry movement of the 1960s, R. D. Laing, was similarly provocative in his book *Knots* (1970), an antidote for anyone caught up in relationship paralysis.

Blake was born in 1757, the son of a nonconformist London hosier. Instead of attending school, he was apprenticed as an engraver and printer, working under James Basire, engraver to the London Society of Antiquaries which took an interest in Republican ideas and idolised John Milton. So, along with his craft, Blake imbibed the emerging politics of his day. From 1779, he was employed by the bookseller Joseph Johnson, who later published works by Blake himself, Tom Paine, Wordsworth and other leading radicals. He married Catherine Boucher in 1782 and, for all his critiques of marriage, apparently had a sublimely contented partnership. He taught her to read and write as well as to paint, while she dedicated herself to her husband's work, helping print and hand-paint his books, and sharing enthusiastically in his visionary experiences. In 1784, Blake set up his own print-shop and from that point onwards survived precariously as an independent tradesman, taking commissions to produce illustrations for books.

One crucial point in Blake's early formation, then, is his class position: he didn't go through university like Wordsworth and Coleridge, and wasn't of independent means like Byron. Rather, he was a tradesman, a worker with his hands, with direct access to the plebeian radicalism of his day, which emerged as a strong and shaping force when the French Revolution broke out in 1789. Yet, given the date of his birth, Blake was also very much of the eighteenth century and shaped by its traditions. His first extensive work, *An Island in the Moon* (1784-5), was a satirical prose piece, full of anarchic humour, that has similarities to Swift's *Gulliver's Travels*. This link between Blake and his predecessors should remind us that the eighteenth century espousal of reason was partly an ideological defence against disorder and chaos. Enthusiasm and unreasonableness were associated with the radicalism of the English Revolution, England's bourgeois revolution, when Cromwell and the Parliamentary forces reluctantly cut off the head of Charles I. That radicalism was epitomised by Parliamentarians like the young John Milton, the Ranters with their belief in free love, or the Diggers and the Levellers with their programmes for popular democracy. For them,

mystical experiences, inspirations and prophecies were the voice of God
manifested through the individual's inner light: their 'Everlasting Gospel'
rejected the orthodoxy of institutionalised religion, and the social
hierarchy which went with it, in favour of a radically literal assertion of
Christ's message of equality, which grounded the mystical visions in a
very practical demand for a political reordering of society. It was against
such 'extremism' that the so-called 'Glorious Revolution' of 1688 was
instituted, and, while this settlement didn't reverse the economic
changes that had taken place and which had been the motor for the
Puritan Revolution, it did recreate a political system founded on
hierarchical power and inequality with its establishment of a
constitutional monarchy. Henceforth, being English was synonymous
with moderation, reserve, gentility – everything Blake hated. In his
energetic enthusiasm, Blake looks back to the utopian projections of the
revolutionary millenarians of the seventeenth century. After 1688, this
politicised visionary tradition went underground.[3] Like theirs, the
vehicle for Blake's vision is a subversive version of Christianity, one in
which the world of orthodox morality and the established churches is
turned upside down: in *The Marriage of Heaven and Hell*, the devils
epitomise the energy of life and have all the best tunes.

In his own lifetime, the renewed surge of popular dissent culminated
in the social and political upheaval of the American and French
Revolutions, which English radicals hoped would also herald change in
Britain. In 1789, Blake was thirty-two years old and in that seemingly
blissful dawn he published, appropriately enough, *Songs of Innocence*. He
also met various leading radicals through Johnson's publishing house,
including William Godwin, Mary Wollstonecraft and, in all probability,
Tom Paine. Blake also began attending meetings of the Swedenborg
Society, based on the writings of Swedish mystic and visionary Emanuel
Swedenborg, another indication that, for Blake, political radicalism and
visionary radicalism went hand in hand. As in the seventeenth century,
radical politics and religious millenarianism were still closely allied in
their nonconformist critiques of hierarchy and power. Blake was not
alone in this: other visionaries such as Richard Brothers, Joanna Southcott
and William Huntington shared his passionate commitment to visionary

3 See John Mee, *Dangerous Enthusiasm: William Blake and the Culture of Radicalism
in the 1790s*, Oxford University Press, Oxford 1992, and E. P. Thompson, *Witness
Against the Beast: William Blake and the Moral Law*, Cambridge University Press,
Cambridge 1993.

change. But he was unique in the vibrant energy and artistic power which shaped the individual character of his work, as he acknowledged in his letters: 'I find more and more that my Style of Designing is a Species by itself, and in this which I send you have been compell'd by my Genius or Angel to follow where he led; if I were to act otherwise it would not fulfill the purpose for which I alone live' (Keynes pp. 791–2).

The course of the French Revolution, however, was far from the blissful dawn that Wordsworth looked back to in *The Prelude* (1805; 1850). In England a divisive intellectual and political debate broke out immediately. Edmund Burke's attack on the Revolution, *Reflections on the Revolution in France* (1790), launched the most famous manifesto of English law-and-order conservatism. Burke argued that hierarchical society was 'natural' and, in his 'Letter to a Member of the National Assembly' of 1791, that

> Society cannot exist, unless a controlling power upon will and appetite be placed somewhere; and the less of it there is within, the more there must be without. It is ordained in the eternal constitution of things, that men of intemperate minds cannot be free. Their passions forge their fetters.   (Glen, p. 213)

Paine answered Burke with his equally famous argument for the natural rights of freedom and liberty in *The Rights of Man* (1791), already stated in his manifesto for the American Revolution in which he views human society as naturally self-organising and government as a fallen state:

> Society is produced by our wants, and government by our wickedness; the former promotes our happiness *positively* by uniting our affections, the latter *negatively* by restraining our vices [. . .] Society is in every state a blessing, but government, even in its best state, is but a necessary evil; in its worst state an intolerable one [. . .] Government, like dress, is the badge of lost innocence; the palaces of kings are built upon the ruins of the bowers of paradise. For were the impulses of conscience clear, uniform, and irresistibly obeyed, man would need no other law giver.[4]

As the overlapping languages of politics and religious vision here suggest, Blake was with Tom Paine, of the radical camp: images of fetters and manacles become for him emblems of tyrannical law and authority in all

4 Tom Paine, *Common Sense* 1776, in Michael Foot and Isaac Kramnick (eds), *Thomas Paine Reader*, Penguin, Harmondsworth 1987, pp. 66–7

forms. But within a few years, the British government had not only clamped down on radicalism, it had banned the works of Paine and declared war on revolutionary France. According to Blake's early biographer Gilchrist, Paine was tipped off about his imminent capture by Blake himself (Wilson, p. 45), an apocryphal story which formed the basis for Jack Shepherd's fascinating play *In Lambeth* (1989). There, poet and politico confront each other angrily: 'Before we can have revolutions,' shouts Blake in the play, 'there must first be *revelations!*'[5] As if to confirm this assertion, soon after Paine escaped across the Channel and arrived in France, the Revolution itself underwent the dark events of the revolutionary Terror under Robespierre (1793). The seeming reverse of revolutionary hopes and the eventual rise of Napoleon meant that, for much of the 1790s, Blake was faced with a viciously reactionary climate in which hostility to radical ideas was matched by indifference or outright hostility to his art. Not surprisingly, the joyful poems of *Innocence* were soon joined by the dark poems of *Songs of Experience* (1794).

The measure of Blake's sense of both frustration and fear can be seen in 1798: in that year, Joseph Johnson, the radical bookseller and publisher for whom Blake had worked, was jailed for stocking an anti-war pamphlet, an event which Whig politician Charles James Fox took as signalling the destruction of press freedom. In an annotation to a diatribe against the works of Tom Paine, Blake invoked the language of the Apocalypse as he wrote: 'To defend the Bible in this year 1798 would cost a man his life. The Beast and the Whore rule without control.' Yet Blake ends his polemic by saying, 'I have been commanded from Hell not to print this, as it is what our Enemies wish' (Keynes, p. 383). After 1795, Blake published no new poems of his own until he printed his long poem *Milton* in 1810.

In the meantime, he worked on commissions for patrons and friends, but his letters chronicle a period of depression in which he felt as though his visionary capacity 'has for exactly twenty years been closed from me as by a door and by window-shutters' (Keynes, p. 852). This sense of individual deprivation coincided with the retreat of radicalism into the dark years of the war against France and the rise of Napoleon, and led Blake to transpose his own personal torments into a vision of the agonies of the contemporary world. In this he shares much with his younger contemporary, Ludwig van Beethoven, whose own dark night of the soul from the onset of his deafness and thoughts of suicide in 1802 was

5 Jack Shepherd, *In Lambeth*, Methuen, London 1990, pp. 40–1

followed by Napoleon's proclamation of himself as Emperor of France in 1804. Beethoven had been composing a heroic symphony, Symphony No. 3 'Eroica', to celebrate the achievements of Napoleon as the saviour of the French Revolution. When Beethoven heard of Napoleon's self-aggrandisement, he 'flew into a rage and exclaimed: "So he is no more than a common man! Now, too, he will tread under foot all the rights of man, indulge only his own ambition; now he will think himself superior to all men, become a tyrant!" ' and with that he tore up the title page of the symphony with its dedication to Napoleon and threw it to the floor.[6]

For Blake, the bleak years of the late 1790s were alleviated in 1800 by an initially idyllic period of rural retreat to a cottage in Felpham loaned by a patron. But Blake's letters show that his blissful response to this disengagement gradually overlapped with his anger at being exploited as an artist by 'the fiends of commerce' (Keynes, p. 849), which left himself and his wife continually harried by poverty and illness. Along with this and his sense of lost vision went a fearful paranoia about the reactionary times, a threat which was manifested visibly when he was accused of sedition for having thrown out of his garden a drunken soldier called Schofield. Blake was put on trial and, while the case was dismissed, its impact on his imagination assumed mythic proportions. As with Beethoven, the result was that Blake transformed this overlap of his own agonies and those of the times into some of his most powerful work. Although written before Napoleon became Emperor, the huge funeral march which forms the second movement of the 'Eroica' symphony seems in retrospect like a dirge for revolutionary aspirations as well as a tragic expression of Beethoven's own personal sense of desolation. In Blake's case, from 1799 he worked on the long unfinished poem Vala or The Four Zoas, while his period at Felpham led to another major work, Milton, after what he later called disparagingly 'my three years' slumber on the banks of the Ocean' (p. 334). Both present what Blake describes as 'the full history of my Spiritual Sufferings' (Keynes, p. 862), the divisions of self and of society fusing into Blake's extra-ordinary mythic visions of the sick and fractured state of the giant Albion, or England. As with Beethoven, Blake responded even more immediately to Napoleon's self-ennoblement: in The Four Zoas, the child of the revolution, Orc, becomes transformed into a serpent in a

6 Michael Hamburger (ed.), Beethoven: Letters, Journals and Conversations, Thames and Hudson, London 1984, p. 47

passage which, according to David Erdman, was contemporaneous with
Napoleon becoming First Consul in 1799 (Erdman, pp. 316–17).
Blake's work from this time records his having 'fought thro' a Hell of
terrors and horrors (which none could know but myself) in a divided
existence', both personal and social, with the result that he was 'now no
longer divided nor at war with myself' (Keynes, p. 853).

His troubles continued, however, once he and his wife returned to
London. In 1805–6, he was badly treated by a publisher who cheated
him over a commission and stole some of his ideas. In 1809, his only
one-man exhibition was viciously attacked in the influential journal *The
Examiner*, only to be ignored by the general public. This led to some
bitter and sarcastic verses against friends and foes alike in his notebooks,
a declaration of spiritual war which he asserts defiantly in his letters:
' "He who is Not With Me is Against Me." There is no Medium or Middle
state; and if a Man is the Enemy of my Spiritual Life while he pretends to
be the Friend of my Corporeal, he is a Real Enemy' (Keynes, p. 822).

Yet despite all his reversals and difficulties, Blake's vision remained
undiminished. The tragic penury of his later years is offset by the
impression of his continuing joyfulness and radiance. Henry Crabb
Robinson on a visit to Blake in 1825 noticed his 'expression of great
sweetness' and 'air of inspiration'; when asked to comment on the deity
of Jesus, Blake replied, 'He is the only God. But then [. . .] so am I and
so are you' (O'Neill, p. 15). The artist Richmond records that, when
Blake died, 'He burst out in Singing of the things he saw in Heaven'
(Wilson, p. 365).

Blake's Artistic Visions

In a letter of 23 August 1799 to his friend Dr Trusler, Blake writes about
his visionary awareness:

> I know that This World is a World of imagination and Vision. I see
> Every thing I paint In This World, but Every body does not see alike.
> To the Eyes of a Miser a Guinea is more beautiful than the Sun [. . .]
> The tree which moves some to tears of joy is in the Eyes of others
> only a Green thing that stands in the way [. . .] But to the Eyes of the
> Man of Imagination, Nature is Imagination itself. As a man is, So he
> sees. As the Eye is formed, such are its Powers. You certainly
> Mistake when you say that the Visions of Fancy are not to be found
> in This World. To Me This World is One continued Vision of Fancy
> or Imagination.   (Keynes, p. 793)

To enact this imaginative vision, Blake developed his own distinctive blend of visual and verbal art in his illustrated books for which he invented a unique method of engraving which he called 'illuminated printing' (Keynes, p. 207). The luminous energy of these works transforms the printed page into a fully sensory experience so that reading Blake becomes a multi-dimensional activity, an appeal to the whole imagination. In order to capture this, the reader should look at one of the facsimile editions now more widely available or the vivid effects of the reproductions obtainable via the Internet (see Bibliography).

Blake links imagination with energy as the key to visionary and creative liberation. For him, imagination counteracts restricted awareness, the dominance of reason with its 'mind-forg'd manacles' (p. 88) and its authoritarian laws that enforce a restricted view of life. In a poem in one of his letters, Blake gives an example of what he means. The poem which begins 'With Happiness stretch'd across the hills' ('To Thomas Butts', pp. 137–9) describes going for a walk and meeting up with an aged thistle which, Blake imagines, is a threatening spirit condemning him to a miserable state of mind. He is so outraged by this aged man threatening him with melancholy that he gives the thistle a good kick with his boot. Immediately, he sees the spirit of energy and imagination, Los, in the form of the Sun (Los is a reversed anagram for 'Sol' meaning 'sun'), granting him a renewed and enhanced sense of vision. The poem ends with Blake's explanation of his multiple 'fourfold' visionary capacity. What he calls 'single vision, and Newton's sleep' is rationalism, the perception of life as merely material process; double vision involves looking at the world with both the bodily eye and with the eyes of imagination; triple vision adds the bodily awareness of the other senses, sexuality, instinct and so on; while the fourfold vision attains the cosmic level of the prophetic Bard in the opening poem of *Experience*, who 'present, past, and future, sees' (p. 74), and perceives the whole of history as an enactment of the struggle between the energies of Life and the restrictive forces of death.

Now all this might sound eccentric, and led contemporaries of Blake to see him as mad (O'Neill, pp. 12–13). But Blake makes a clear link in his work between the limited mental/spiritual awareness of society and its social oppression. What in fact he is indicating is the psycho-social link between a society and its dominant ideology that functions to support that society's basic structure. An unequal society needs to forge-mind manacles in order to keep its population passively compliant;

and, in dialectical fashion, compliant attitudes perpetrate and perpetuate inequalities, as in the poem 'London' (p. 88).

It is important to remember that Blake presented his work to be read in its original form as an organically whole experience, not just an experience of words on the page, but a complete conception of language, design and vibrant colour, as a means to purge the senses and open the eyes of the imagination. Yet there is a contradiction here. His revolutionary engraving process limited his production of copies to a small number, which were sold to a smaller number of wealthy patrons. During his day his work was not well known, though it reached a wider audience in the late ninetenth century after W. B. Yeats' inaccurate but enthusiastic selected edition. In addition, Blake's work became increasingly visionary and idiosyncratic. When his patron Dr Trusler complained to Blake that he found his work more and more difficult to understand, the poet's reply was uncompromising: 'You say that I want somebody to Elucidate my Ideas. But you ought to know that What is Grand is necessarily obscure to Weak men. That which can be made Explicit to an Idiot is not worth my care. The wisest of the Ancients consider'd what is not too Explicit as the fittest for Instruction, because it rouzes the faculties to act' (Keynes, p. 793). This sounds dangerously arrogant and élitist, though in fact later in this letter Blake goes on to say: 'I am happy to find a Great Majority of Fellow Mortals who can Elucidate My Visions, and Particularly they have been Elucidated by Children, who have taken a greater delight in contemplating my Pictures than I even hoped. Neither Youth nor Childhood is Folly or Incapacity. Some Children are Fools and so are some Old Men. But There is a vast Majority on the side of Imagination or Spiritual Sensation' (Keynes, p. 794). His arrogance is not intellectual – it is visionary: the fools and idiots are quite likely to be the supposedly wise and cultured refined classes, who have a vested interest in maintaining the mind-forged manacles. Blake's visionary writings are uncompromising in their imaginative individualism; but then, as he argues in the Preface to *Jerusalem*, 'Poetry fetter'd fetters the Human Race' (p. 335).

There are some problematic aspects to Blake's increasing use of myth as the vehicle for his prophetic writings. The visionary writings are there from the beginning, but a decisive moment came in 1791, with the poem *The French Revolution* (pp. 209–23). This, the most overtly historical of Blake's prophetic poems, presents a mythic enactment of events in France in almost documentary prophetic fashion, using the actual events and historical characters of the revolution as the figures for a cosmic drama. Blake placed this poem with Joseph Johnson's publishing house, but while Johnson printed the book, he didn't actually publish it. 1792 was the date of the Royal Proclamation against seditious publications, which made it treasonable to print anything encouraging anti-government feeling: it is notable that in the Bastille as described in the poem there is a man 'confin'd for a writing prophetic' (p. 210). The critic David Erdman has argued that it was Blake himself who withdrew *The French Revolution* from fear of prosecution and that the failure to publish this poem was 'decisive' for Blake, for in it he 'came closer than he ever would again to making his interpretation of history comprehensible to the English public of his own day'. Erdman continues: 'Withdrawal of this work was to mean Blake's withdrawal from any audience beyond a few uncritical or even uncomprehending friends, his withdrawal from the essential experience of communication, without which even the most richly significant and creative art cannot attain full stature and true proportions.' Moreover, this encouraged Blake 'to pursue the involuted symbolism and obscure manner he had already made use of in *Tiriel* and *The Marriage*' (Erdman, p. 153). Under pressure from the anti-radical measures of the day, according to this argument, Blake became increasingly obscure in his use of myth.

There is undoubtedly an argument to answer here, and it links with that elevation of the Poet as lone visionary seer which Marilyn Butler notices and which she sees as symptomatic of the retreat of other Romantic poets such as Wordsworth and Coleridge in the face of the reactionary climate of their day and of their attempts to compensate for a sense of alienation from public engagement (Butler, pp. 71–2 and Chapter 3 *passim*). But I myself do not see Blake's mythological approach as the same kind of disengagement as might be seen in the work of Wordsworth or Coleridge. There are important arguments in favour of Blake's decision to develop his own personal mythic system. One corollary to Erdman's view is that, as with creative artists under other repressive or totalitarian systems, Blake used symbolism and myth as a way of evading the censors and government restriction. Even though most of his prophetic work wasn't in fact published until long after the events which produced it, Blake was well aware that, as he puts it in *Jerusalem*, 'deep dissimulation is the only defence an honest man has left' (p. 345). If this is a rather negative rationale, Michael Ferber restates Blake's more positive view quoted above that difficult writing is best because it 'rouzes the faculties to act'; and that both visually and as writing, Blake's work aims to 'radicalise the imagination' and open the eyes of the reader (Ferber, p.

65). Rousing the faculties is how Blake saw the effects of his long poem *Milton* in a letter of 1803: he called it 'a Grand Poem', asserting, 'I may praise it, since I dare not pretend to be any other than the Secretary; the Authors are in Eternity. I consider it as the Grandest Poem that this World Contains. Allegory address'd to the Intellectual powers, while it is altogether hidden from the Corporeal Understanding, is My Definition of the Most Sublime Poetry' (Keynes, p. 825). Obscurity was not a problem for Blake, since the demand for explanation was a criterion of the rational mind: read with visionary imagination, his poems would be transparently clear. He felt that his mythic method was absolutely necessary if he was to be an individual artist: as the representative of imagination, Los, grandly asserts in *Jerusalem*,

> I must Create a System, or be enslav'd by another Man's;
> I will not Reason and Compare: my business is to Create.
>
> (p. 336)

Another equally significant explanation for Blake's mythic narratives is that they were necessary in order that he might fuse together different levels of human experience and show them as interdependent. By moving away from the directly historical into the mythic, Blake does not abandon history. While it might necessitate our decoding the poems to get at the social and historical level, use of myth allowed Blake to demonstrate how the social and historical were linked with the psychological, the ideological and the cosmic. It was only through the imaginatively resonant symbolic narratives that these interrelationships could be shown. In the larger poems like *Vala* and *Jerusalem*, the action takes place within the sick giant Albion, who has fallen into division and whose faculties are at war. Thus the action depicts the warring elements of the individual psyche. But since Albion is also Blake's name for England, this is a war also going on within the body politic. And Albion is also one of the 'Giant forms' (p. 334) who inhabit and animate human history; so that this war is also a historical war for the future welfare of humanity; and at that level, for Blake it is a spiritual war.

Blake's work, then, is undoubtedly demanding, but it is also the most startling, challenging and imaginatively liberating poetry of his time; and its energetic vision still startles, challenges and liberates us today.

DR BRUCE WOODCOCK
University of Hull

CHRONOLOGY

1757   Born London, 28th November

1761   Has vision of God and a tree full of angels

1762   Jean Jacques Rousseau, *Du contrat social*

1768   Begins lyric writing and starts drawing school

1770   Ludwig van Beethoven born

1772   Starts apprenticeship with James Basire (until 1779)

1773   First engravings

1775   Outbreak of American War of Independence

1776   Thomas Paine, *Common Sense* (sells 100,000 copies) and *American Crisis* pamphlets; American *Declaration of Independence*

1779   Admitted to Royal Academy; meets John Flaxman and Joseph Johnson

1780   Gordon Riots and burning of Newgate prison (witnessed by Blake); Blake engraves original 'Glad Day'; first exhibit at Royal Academy

1781   British surrender at Yorktown, virtual end of American War of Independence

1782   Marries Catherine Sophia Boucher (b. 1762) and lives in Leicester Fields; member of artists' circle

1783   *Poetical Sketches* printed but not published

1784   Sets up print-shop with James Parker; writing *An Island in the Moon*

1787   Brother Robert dies

1788   Involved with Swedenborgians; writes *Tiriel*

1789   Fall of the Bastille (July); Versailles stormed and King taken to Paris; *Declaration of the Rights of Man and of Citizens*; Blake, *Songs of Innocence* and *Book of Thel*

1790   Edmund Burke, *Reflections on the Revolution in France*; Blake begins *Marriage of Heaven and Hell* ('Song of Liberty', 1792–3); Mary Wollstonecraft, *Vindication of the Rights of Men* (answer to Burke); formation of London Society for Constitutional Information (SCI)

1791   Flight of French royal family to Varennes leads to their capture
        and imprisonment; Tom Paine, *Rights of Man* Part 1 (answer to
        Burke); Blake, *The French Revolution* (Book 1 printed by Joseph
        Johnson but not published); Blake moves to Lambeth

1792   France and Austria at war; fall of French monarchy after
        storming of Tuilleries; Republic established; London
        Corresponding Society (LCS) formed; SCI prints Tom Paine's
        Rights of Man for sixpence estimated 200,000 copies sold in two
        years; Mary Wollstonecraft, *A Vindication of the Rights of Women*;
        British government repression begins: Royal Proclamation against
        Seditious Publications leading to prosecution of radical
        booksellers and publishers; Paine outlawed from Britain;
        formation of Association for Preserving Liberty and Property
        against Republicans and Levellers; September massacre in Paris
        begins the Terror; death of Joshua Reynolds; Blake completes
        Marriage of Heaven and Hell

1793   Louis XVI executed (January) and Marie Antoinette (October);
        England declares war on France; Blake, *America, A Prophecy* and
        Visions of the Daughters of Albion; Paine arrested and imprisoned
        in France; William Godwin's *Political Justice*; Wordsworth's
        Letter to the Bishop of Llandaff (unpublished)

1794   French victory at Fleurus: French military machine dominates
        Europe for next twenty years; leaders of LCS arrested and tried
        for treason; Habeus Corpus suspended for eight years; fall of
        Robespierre; Blake's *Songs of Innocence and Experience, Europe*
        and *The First Book of Urizen*

1795   George III's coach stoned; Pitt government implements the
        Two Acts; end of popular agitation in Britain; army takes over
        in France; Blake, *Book of Los* and *Book of Ahania*

1796   Collapse of LCS

1797   Blake begins *Vala, or The Four Zoas* (unfinished); mutiny of
        British fleet at Spithead

1798   Joseph Johnson (leading radical publisher of Paine, Blake and
        Wordsworth) jailed; Blake, 'Annotations to Watson's reply to
        Paine'; Wordsworth and Coleridge, *Lyrical Ballads*

1799   Seditious Societies Act; Napoleon becomes First Consul

1800   William Hayley employs Blake; Blake moves to Felpham and
        begins *Milton* (completed 1804)

1802   Peace of Amiens

1803   Renewal of war with France; Blake increasingly irritated with
        Hayley; warrant for Blake's arrest issued after he evicts drunken
        soldier Schofield from his garden; returns to London

1804   Napoleon made Emperor; Blake tried for sedition and acquitted,
        begins *Jerusalem* (completed *circa* 1810–11); Beethoven
        completes Symphony no. 3 in E flat major, op. 55, 'Eroica'

1809   Mocked in *The Examiner*; responds in unpublished Notebook
        Epigrams; his first one-man show is attacked in *The Examiner*;
        Paine dies in obscurity; death of Joseph Johnson

1810   Engraves *Milton*

1812   Luddite movement begins: Lord Percival (Prime Minister)
        assassinated in House of Commons; Byron's speech in the
        House of Lords defending Luddites

1815   End of Napoleonic War; economic depression; Blake very poor

1817   William Cobbett flees to America

1818   Drafts 'The Everlasting Gospel' in notebooks

1819   Cobbett returns from America with bones of Tom Paine (which
        he kept under his bed and which were later lost); Peterloo
        massacre; Shelley's 'The Mask of Anarchy'

1820   Prints *Jerusalem*

1827   Blake dies – according to one report, singing joyfully as he did
        so; death of Beethoven

BIBLIOGRAPHY

Texts

Geoffrey Keynes (ed.), *The Complete Writings of William Blake*, Oxford University Press, London 1966 – for the letters and other prose

W. H. Stevenson (ed.), *Blake – The Complete Poems*, 2nd edition, Longman, London 1989 – the best fully annotated edition

There are a number of readily available and relatively cheap colour reproductions of Blake's original designs, as, for example, *The Marriage of Heaven and Hell,* Oxford University Press, Oxford 1975. There are also Internet sites listed below with full-colour reproductions accompanying the texts.

Critical Works

David Bindman, *William Blake: His Art and Times,* Thames and Hudson, London 1982 – excellent on Blake as visual artist

Jacob Bronowski, *Blake and the Age of Revolution*, Routledge, London 1972 – a very readable introduction and good on the background context

Helen P. Bruder, *William Blake and the Daughters of Albion,* Macmillan, London 1997 – a fascinating feminist approach

Stewart Crehan, *Blake in Context*, Gill and Macmillan, Dublin 1984 – good on Blake as visual artist

David Erdman, *Blake: Prophet Against Empire*, Princeton University Press, Princeton, NJ 1969 – large-scale presentation of Blake's works in their historical contexts; very detailed and indispensable for understanding the prophetic works

David Erdman, *The Illuminated Blake*, Oxford University Press, London 1975 – edition of Blake's designs

Michael Ferber, *The Social Vision of William Blake*, Princeton University Press, Princeton, NJ 1985 – very readable account of Blake in his context

Heather Glen, *Vision and Disenchantment: Blake's Songs and Wordsworth's Lyrical Ballads*, Cambridge University Press, Cambridge 1983 – provides a historically grounded and extremely insightful comparative study

Judith O'Neill (ed.), *Critics on Blake*, George Allen and Unwin, London
    1970
Michael Phillips (ed.), *Interpreting Blake*, Cambridge University Press,
    Cambridge 1978 – good collection of essays, especially those by
    E. P. Thompson and Heather Glen
David Punter (ed.), *William Blake*, Macmillan, Basingstoke 1996 –
    useful collection of recent essays from various social, political and
    theoretical angles, with a good annotated bibliography
Mona Wilson, *The Life of William Blake*, Paladin/Granada, St Albans
    1978

Websites

http://virtual.park.uga.edu/~wblake/home1.html   David Erdman's
    complete version of his latest edition of Blake's poetry and prose,
    with graphics
http://jefferson.village.virginia.edu/blake/   will eventually have three
    thousand images
http://blake.bellevue.com/   a wonderful online Blake compendium
http://members.aa.net/~urizen/blake4.html   complete colour texts
    of a number of works with links to other sites

Background Reading

Marilyn Butler, *Romantics, Rebels and Reactionaries: English Literature and
    its Background, 1760–1830*, Oxford University Press, Oxford 1981
Eric Hobsbawm, *The Age of Revolution: Europe 1789–1848*, Sphere, London
    1977 – an excellent single-volume history
Simon Schama, *Citizens: A Chronicle of the French Revolution*, Viking,
    London 1989 – a remarkably vivid account
E. P.Thompson, *The Making of the English Working Class*, Penguin,
    Harmondsworth 1991 – the classic of historical recovery of this time
Bruce Woodcock and John Coates, *Combative Styles: Romantic Writing and
    Ideology*, University of Hull Press, Hull 1988 – contrasts the varied
    writings of Paine, Burke, Blake and De Quincey

A NOTE ON THE TEXT

This text substantially follows the arrangement done by John Sampson
in his pioneering Clarendon Press edition of 1905, which he rearranged
as *The Poetical Works of William Blake*, Oxford University Press, London
1913. The lyric and other shorter poems take up the first half of the
volume, with the longer prophetic works following on in chronological
order.

ACKNOWLEDGEMENTS

Many thanks to Keith Carabine, Owen Knowles, John Hoyles and Les
Garry for their care in reading my text. My understanding of Blake owes a
particular debt to the work of W. H. Stevenson, David Erdman and Jacob
Bronowski, and to Professor J. R. Watson for his inspiring lectures. This
book is dedicated with love to Les.

CONTENTS

Appendix to

THE ROSSETTI MANUSCRIPT   92

Poems from THE ROSETTI MANUSCRIPT, Part I   94

THE SELECTED POEMS OF WILLIAM BLAKE

POETICAL SKETCHES

Poetical Sketches (1783) In his first apprentice work, Blake is experimenting with poetic forms and genres as various as ballads, songs, verse drama, the gothic and pastoral. Yet for all the conventionalised language and modes of address, there is already an individual vision and voice at work. The song 'How sweet I roam'd' (p. 8) deploys images of freedom and entrapment to which Blake returns, while 'Song by an Old Shepherd' (p. 47) offers a view of 'innocence' as a protective vision and anticipates some of the complexities which develop in *Songs of Innocence and Experience*.

To Spring

O Thou with dewy locks, who lookest down
Thro' the clear windows of the morning, turn
Thine angel eyes upon our western isle,
Which in full choir hails thy approach, O Spring!

The hills tell each other, and the list'ning
Valleys hear; all our longing eyes are turnèd
Up to thy bright pavilions: issue forth,
And let thy holy feet visit our clime.

Come o'er the eastern hills, and let our winds
Kiss thy perfumèd garments; let us taste
Thy morn and evening breath; scatter thy pearls
Upon our love-sick land that mourns for thee.

O deck her forth with thy fair fingers; pour
Thy soft kisses on her bosom; and put
Thy golden crown upon her languish'd head,
Whose modest tresses were bound up for thee.

To Summer

O thou who passest thro' our valleys in
Thy strength, curb thy fierce steeds, allay the heat
That flames from their large nostrils! thou, O Summer,
Oft pitched'st here thy golden tent, and oft
Beneath our oaks hast slept, while we beheld
With joy thy ruddy limbs and flourishing hair.

Beneath our thickest shades we oft have heard
Thy voice, when noon upon his fervid car
Rode o'er the deep of heaven; beside our springs
Sit down, and in our mossy valleys, on

Some bank beside a river clear, throw thy
Silk draperies off, and rush into the stream:
Our valleys love the Summer in his pride.

Our bards are fam'd who strike the silver wire:
Our youth are bolder than the southern swains:
Our maidens fairer in the sprightly dance:
We lack not songs, nor instruments of joy,
Nor echoes sweet, nor waters clear as heaven,
Nor laurel wreaths against the sultry heat.

To Autumn

O Autumn, laden with fruit, and stainèd
With the blood of the grape, pass not, but sit
Beneath my shady roof; there thou may'st rest,
And tune thy jolly voice to my fresh pipe,
And all the daughters of the year shall dance!
Sing now the lusty song of fruits and flowers.

'The narrow bud opens her beauties to
The sun, and love runs in her thrilling veins;
Blossoms hang round the brows of Morning, and
Flourish down the bright cheek of modest Eve,
Till clust'ring Summer breaks forth into singing,
And feather'd clouds strew flowers round her head.

'The spirits of the air live on the smells
Of fruit; and Joy, with pinions light, roves round
The gardens, or sits singing in the trees.'
Thus sang the jolly Autumn as he sat;
Then rose, girded himself, and o'er the bleak
Hills fled from our sight; but left his golden load.

To Winter

'O Winter! bar thine adamantine doors:
The north is thine; there hast thou built thy dark
Deep-founded habitation. Shake not thy roofs,
Nor bend thy pillars with thine iron car.'

He hears me not, but o'er the yawning deep
Rides heavy; his storms are unchain'd, sheathèd
In ribbèd steel; I dare not lift mine eyes,
For he hath rear'd his sceptre o'er the world.

Lo! now the direful monster, whose skin clings
To his strong bones, strides o'er the groaning rocks:
He withers all in silence, and in his hand
Unclothes the earth, and freezes up frail life.

He takes his seat upon the cliffs, – the mariner
Cries in vain. Poor little wretch, that deal'st
With storms! – till heaven smiles, and the monster
Is driv'n yelling to his caves beneath mount Hecla.[1]

To the Evening Star

Thou fair-hair'd angel of the evening,
Now, whilst the sun rests on the mountains, light
Thy bright torch of love; thy radiant crown
Put on, and smile upon our evening bed!
Smile on our loves, and while thou drawest the
Blue curtains of the sky, scatter thy silver dew
On every flower that shuts its sweet eyes
In timely sleep. Let thy west wind sleep on
The lake; speak silence with thy glimmering eyes,
And wash the dusk with silver. Soon, full soon,
Dost thou withdraw; then the wolf rages wide,
And the lion glares thro' the dun forest:
The fleeces of our flocks are cover'd with
Thy sacred dew: protect them with thine influence,

To Morning

O holy virgin! clad in purest white,
Unlock heav'n's golden gates, and issue forth;
Awake the dawn that sleeps in heaven; let light
Rise from the chambers of the east, and bring
The honey'd dew that cometh on waking day.
O radiant morning, salute the sun
Rous'd like a huntsman to the chase, and with
Thy buskin'd feet appear upon our hills.

Fair Elenor

The bell struck one, and shook the silent tower;
The graves give up their dead: fair Elenor
Walk'd by the castle gate, and lookèd in.
A hollow groan ran thro' the dreary vaults.

She shriek'd aloud, and sunk upon the steps,
On the cold stone her pale cheeks. Sickly smells
Of death issue as from a sepulchre,
And all is silent but the sighing vaults.

Chill Death withdraws his hand, and she revives;
Amaz'd, she finds herself upon her feet,
And, like a ghost, thro' narrow passages
Walking, feeling the cold walls with her hands.

Fancy returns, and now she thinks of bones
And grinning skulls, and corruptible death
Wrapp'd in his shroud; and now fancies she hears
Deep sighs, and sees pale sickly ghosts gliding.

At length, no fancy but reality
Distracts her. A rushing sound, and the feet
Of one that fled, approaches – Ellen stood
Like a dumb statue, froze to stone with fear.

The wretch approaches, crying: 'The deed is done;
Take this, and send it by whom thou wilt send;
It is my life – send it to Elenor: –
He's dead, and howling after me for blood!

'Take this,' he cried; and thrust into her arms
A wet napkin, wrapp'd about; then rush'd
Past, howling: she receiv'd into her arms
Pale death, and follow'd on the wings of fear.

They pass'd swift thro' the outer gate; the wretch,
Howling, leap'd o'er the wall into the moat,
Stifling in mud. Fair Ellen pass'd the bridge,
And heard a gloomy voice cry 'Is it done?'

As the deer wounded, Ellen flew over
The pathless plain; as the arrows that fly
By night, destruction flies, and strikes in darkness.
She fled from fear, till at her house arriv'd.

Her maids await her; on her bed she falls,
That bed of joy, where erst her lord hath press'd:
'Ah, woman's fear!' she cried; 'ah, cursèd duke!
Ah, my dear lord! ah, wretched Elenor!

'My lord was like a flower upon the brows
Of lusty May! Ah, life as frail as flower!
O ghastly death! withdraw thy cruel hand,
Seek'st thou that flow'r to deck thy horrid temples?

'My lord was like a star in highest heav'n
Drawn down to earth by spells and wickedness;
My lord was like the opening eyes of day
When western winds creep softly o'er the flowers;

'But he is darken'd; like the summer's noon
Clouded; fall'n like the stately tree, cut down;
The breath of heaven dwelt among his leaves.
O Elenor, weak woman, fill'd with woe!'

Thus having spoke, she raisèd up her head,
And saw the bloody napkin by her side,
Which in her arms she brought; and now, tenfold
More terrifièd, saw it unfold itself.

Her eyes were fix'd; the bloody cloth unfolds,
Disclosing to her sight the murder'd head
Of her dear lord, all ghastly pale, clotted
With gory blood; it groan'd, and thus it spake:

'O Elenor, I am thy husband's head,
Who, sleeping on the stones of yonder tower,
Was 'reft of life by the accursèd duke!
A hirèd villain turn'd my sleep to death!

'O Elenor, beware the cursèd duke;
O give not him thy hand, now I am dead;
He seeks thy love; who, coward, in the night,
Hirèd a villain to bereave my life.'

She sat with dead cold limbs, stiffen'd to stone;
She took the gory head up in her arms;
She kiss'd the pale lips; she had no tears to shed;
She hugg'd it to her breast, and groan'd her last.

Song

How sweet I roam'd from field to field
And tasted all the summer's pride,
Till I the Prince of Love beheld
Who in the sunny beams did glide!

He show'd me lilies for my hair,
And blushing roses for my brow;
He led me through his gardens fair
Where all his golden pleasures grow.

With sweet May dews my wings were wet,
And Phoebus fir'd my vocal rage;

He caught me in his silken net,
And shut me in his golden cage.

He loves to sit and hear me sing,
Then, laughing, sports and plays with me;
Then stretches out my golden wing,
And mocks my loss of liberty.

Song

My silks and fine array,
My smiles and languish'd air,
By love are driv'n away;
And mournful lean Despair
Brings me yew to deck my grave;
Such end true lovers have.

His face is fair as heav'n
When springing buds unfold;
O why to him was't giv'n
Whose heart is wintry cold?
His breast is love's all-worshipp'd tomb,
Where all love's pilgrims come.

Bring me an axe and spade,
Bring me a winding-sheet;
When I my grave have made
Let winds and tempests beat:
Then down I'll lie as cold as clay.
True love doth pass away!

Song

Love and harmony combine,
And around our souls entwine
While thy branches mix with mine,
And our roots together join.

Joys upon our branches sit,
Chirping loud and singing sweet;
Like gentle streams beneath our feet
Innocence and virtue meet.

Thou the golden fruit dost bear,
I am clad in flowers fair;
Thy sweet boughs perfume the air,
And the turtle buildeth there.

There she sits and feeds her young,
Sweet I hear her mournful song;
And thy lovely leaves among,
There is love, I hear his tongue.

There his charming nest doth lay,
There he sleeps the night away;
There he sports along the day,
And doth among our branches play.

Song

I love the jocund dance,
The softly breathing song,
Where innocent eyes do glance,
And where lisps the maiden's tongue.

I love the laughing vale,
I love the echoing hill,
Where mirth does never fail,
And the jolly swain laughs his fill.

I love the pleasant cot,
I love the innocent bow'r,
Where white and brown is our lot,
Or fruit in the mid-day hour.

I love the oaken seat,
Beneath the oaken tree,

Where all the old villagers meet,
And laugh our sports to see.

I love our neighbours all,
But, Kitty, I better love thee;
And love them I ever shall;
But thou art all to me.

Song

Memory, hither come
And tune your merry notes:
And, while upon the wind
Your music floats,
I'll pore upon the stream
Where sighing lovers dream,
And fish for fancies as they pass
Within the watery glass.

I'll drink of the clear stream,
And hear the linnet's song;
And there I'll lie and dream
The day along:
And when night comes, I'll go
To places fit for woe,
Walking along the darken'd valley
With silent Melancholy.

Mad Song

The wild winds weep,
And the night is a-cold;
Come hither, Sleep,
And my griefs unfold:
But lo! the morning peeps
Over the eastern steeps,
And the rustling beds of dawn
The earth do scorn.

Lo! to the vault
Of pavèd heaven,
With sorrow fraught
My notes are driven:
They strike the ear of night,
Make weep the eyes of day;
They make mad the roaring winds,
And with tempests play.

Like a fiend in a cloud,
With howling woe
After night I do crowd,
And with night will go;
I turn my back to the east
From whence comforts have increas'd
For light doth seize my brain
With frantic pain.

Song

Fresh from the dewy hill, the merry year
Smiles on my head and mounts his flaming car;
Round my young brows the laurel wreathes a shade,
And rising glories beam around my head.

My feet are wing'd, while o'er the dewy lawn,
I meet my maiden risen like the morn:
O bless those holy feet, like angels' feet;
O bless those limbs, beaming with heav'nly light.

Like as an angel glitt'ring in the sky
In times of innocence and holy joy;
The joyful shepherd stops his grateful song
To hear the music of an angel's tongue.

So when she speaks, the voice of Heaven I hear;
So when we walk, nothing impure comes near;
Each field seems Eden, and each calm retreat;
Each village seems the haunt of holy feet.

But that sweet village where my black-eyed maid
Closes her eyes in sleep beneath night's shade,
Whene'er I enter, more than mortal fire
Burns in my soul, and does my song inspire.

Song

When early morn walks forth in sober grey,
Then to my black-eyed maid I haste away;
When evening sits beneath her dusky bow'r,
And gently sighs away the silent hour,
The village bell alarms, away I go,
And the vale darkens at my pensive woe.

To that sweet village, where my black-eyed maid
Doth drop a tear beneath the silent shade,
I turn my eyes; and pensive as I go
Curse my black stars and bless my pleasing woe.

Oft when the summer sleeps among the trees,
Whisp'ring faint murmurs to the scanty breeze,
I walk the village round; if at her side
A youth doth walk in stolen joy and pride,
I curse my stars in bitter grief and woe,
That made my love so high and me so low.

O should she e'er prove false, his limbs I'd tear
And throw all pity on the burning air;
I'd curse bright fortune for my mixèd lot,
And then I'd die in peace and be forgot.

To the Muses

Whether on Ida's[2] shady brow,
Or in the chambers of the East,
The chambers of the sun, that now
From ancient melody have ceas'd;

Whether in Heaven ye wander fair,
Or the green corners of the earth,
Or the blue regions of the air
Where the melodious winds have birth;

Whether on crystal rocks ye rove,
Beneath the bosom of the sea
Wand'ring in many a coral grove,
Fair Nine, forsaking Poetry!

How have you left the ancient love
That bards of old enjoy'd in you!
The languid strings do scarcely move!
The sound is forc'd, the notes are few.

Gwin King of Norway

Come, kings, and listen to my song:
When Gwin, the son of Nore,
Over the nations of the North
His cruel sceptre bore;

The nobles of the land did feed
Upon the hungry poor;
They tear the poor man's lamb, and drive
The needy from their door.

'The land is desolate; our wives
And children cry for bread;
Arise, and pull the tyrant down!
Let Gwin be humblèd!'

Gordred the giant rous'd himself
From sleeping in his cave;
He shook the hills, and in the clouds
The troubl'd banners wave.

Beneath them roll'd, like tempests black,
The num'rous sons of blood;
Like lions' whelps, roaring abroad,
Seeking their nightly food.

Down Bleron's hills they dreadful rush,
Their cry ascends the clouds;
The trampling horse and clanging arms
Like rushing mighty floods!

Their wives and children, weeping loud,
Follow in wild array,
Howling like ghosts, furious as wolves
In the bleak wintry day.

'Pull down the tyrant to the dust,
Let Gwin be humblèd,'
They cry, 'and let ten thousand lives
Pay for the tyrant's head.'

From tow'r to tow'r the watchmen cry,
'O Gwin, the son of Nore,
Arouse thyself! the nations, black
Like clouds, come rolling o'er!'

Gwin rear'd his shield, his palace shakes,
His chiefs come rushing round;
Each, like an awful thunder cloud,
With voice of solemn sound:

Like rearèd stones around a grave
They stand around the King;
Then suddenly each seiz'd his spear,
And clashing steel does ring.

The husbandman does leave his plough
To wade thro' fields of gore;
The merchant binds his brows in steel,
And leaves the trading shore;

The shepherd leaves his mellow pipe,
And sounds the trumpet shrill;
The workman throws his hammer down
To heave the bloody bill.

Like the tall ghost of Barraton
Who sports in stormy sky,
Gwin leads his host, as black as night
When pestilence does fly,

With horses and with chariots –
And all his spearmen bold
March to the sound of mournful song,
Like clouds around him roll'd.

Gwin lifts his hand – the nations halt;
'Prepare for war!' he cries –
Gordred appears! – his frowning brow
Troubles our northern skies.

The armies stand, like balances
Held in th' Almighty's hand; –
'Gwin, thou hast fill'd thy measure up:
Thou'rt swept from out the land.'

And now the raging armies rush'd
Like warring mighty seas;
The heav'ns are shook with roaring war,
The dust ascends the skies!

Earth smokes with blood, and groans and shakes
To drink her children's gore,
A sea of blood; nor can the eye
See to the trembling shore!

And on the verge of this wild sea
Famine and death doth cry;
The cries of women and of babes
Over the field doth fly.

The King is seen raging afar,
With all his men of might;
Like blazing comets scattering death
Thro' the red fev'rous night.

Beneath his arm like sheep they die,
And groan upon the plain;
The battle faints, and bloody men
Fight upon hills of slain.

Now death is sick, and riven men
Labour and toil for life;
Steed rolls on steed, and shield on shield,
Sunk in this sea of strife!

The god of war is drunk with blood;
The earth doth faint and fail;
The stench of blood makes sick the heav'ns;
Ghosts glut the throat of hell!

O what have kings to answer for
Before that awful throne;
When thousand deaths for vengeance cry,
And ghosts accusing groan!

Like blazing comets in the sky
That shake the stars of light,
Which drop like fruit unto the earth
Thro' the fierce burning night;

Like these did Gwin and Gordred meet,
And the first blow decides;
Down from the brow unto the breast
Gordred his head divides!

Gwin fell: the sons of Norway fled,
All that remain'd alive;
The rest did fill the vale of death,
For them the eagles strive.

The river Dorman roll'd their blood
Into the northern sea;
Who mourn'd his sons, and overwhelm'd
The pleasant south country.

An Imitation of Spenser

Golden Apollo, that thro' heaven wide
Scatter'st the rays of light, and truth's beams,
In lucent words my darkling verses dight,
And wash my earthy mind in thy clear streams,
That wisdom may descend in fairy dreams,
All while the jocund hours in thy train
Scatter their fancies at thy poet's feet;
And when thou yields to night thy wide domain,
Let rays of truth enlight his sleeping brain.

For brutish Pan in vain might thee assay
With tinkling sounds to dash thy nervous verse,
Sound without sense; yet in his rude affray,
(For ignorance is Folly's leasing nurse
And love of Folly needs none other's curse)
Midas the praise hath gain'd of lengthen'd ears,
For which himself might deem him ne'er the worse
To sit in council with his modern peers,
And judge of tinkling rimes and elegances terse.

And thou, Mercurius, that with wingèd brow
Dost mount aloft into the yielding sky,
And thro' Heav'n's halls thy airy flight dost throw,
Entering with holy feet to where on high
Jove weighs the counsel of futurity;
Then, laden with eternal fate, dost go
Down, like a falling star, from autumn sky,
And o'er the surface of the silent deep dost fly:

If thou arrivest at the sandy shore
Where nought but envious hissing adders dwell,
Thy golden rod, thrown on the dusty floor,

Can charm to harmony with potent spell.
Such is sweet Eloquence, that does dispel
Envy and Hate that thirst for human gore;
And cause in sweet society to dwell
Vile savage minds that lurk in lonely cell.

O Mercury, assist my lab'ring sense
That round the circle of the world would fly,
As the wing'd eagle scorns the tow'ry fence
Of Alpine hills round his high aëry,
And searches thro' the corners of the sky,
Sports in the clouds to hear the thunder's sound,
And see the wingèd lightnings as they fly;
Then, bosom'd in an amber cloud, around
Plumes his wide wings, and seeks Sol's palace high.

And thou, O warrior maid invincible,
Arm'd with the terrors of Almighty Jove,
Pallas, Minerva, maiden terrible,
Lov'st thou to walk the peaceful solemn grove,
In solemn gloom of branches interwove?
Or bear'st thy Ægis o'er the burning field,
Where, like the sea, the waves of battle move?
Or have thy soft piteous eyes beheld
The weary wanderer thro' the desert rove?
Or does th' afflicted man thy heav'nly bosom move?

Blind Man's Buff

When silver snow decks Susan's clothes,
And jewel hangs at th' shepherd's nose,
The blushing bank is all my care,
With hearth so red, and walls so fair;
'Heap the sea-coal, come, heap it higher,
The oaken log lay on the fire.'
The well-wash'd stools, a circling row,
With lad and lass, how fair the show!
The merry can of nut-brown ale,
The laughing jest, the love-sick tale,

Till, tir'd of chat, the game begins.
The lasses prick the lads with pins;
Roger from Dolly twitch'd the stool,
She, falling, kiss'd the ground, poor fool!
She blush'd so red, with sidelong glance
At hob-nail Dick, who griev'd the chance.
But now for Blind man's Buff they call;
Of each encumbrance clear the hall –
Jenny her silken 'kerchief folds,
And blear-eyed Will the black lot holds.
Now laughing stops, with 'Silence! hush!'
And Peggy Pout gives Sam a push.
The Blind man's arms, extended wide,
Sam slips between: – 'O woe betide
Thee, clumsy Will!' – but titt'ring Kate
Is penn'd up in the corner straight!
And now Will's eyes beheld the play;
He thought his face was t'other way.
'Now, Kitty, now! what chance hast thou,
Roger so near thee! – Trips, I vow!'
She catches him – then Roger ties
His own head up – but not his eyes;
For thro' the slender cloth he sees,
And runs at Sam, who slips with ease
His clumsy hold; and, dodging round,
Sukey is tumbled on the ground! –
'See what it is to play unfair!
Where cheating is, there's mischief there.'
But Roger still pursues the chase, –
'He sees! he sees!' cries, softly, Grace;
'O Roger, thou, unskill'd in art,
Must, surer bound, go thro' thy part!'
Now Kitty, pert, repeats the rimes,
And Roger turns him round three times,
Then pauses ere he starts – but Dick
Was mischief bent upon a trick;
Down on his hands and knees he lay
Directly in the Blind man's way,
Then cries out 'Hem!' Hodge heard, and ran
With hood-wink'd chance – sure of his man;

But down he came. – Alas, how frail
Our best of hopes, how soon they fail!
With crimson drops he stains the ground;
Confusion startles all around.
Poor piteous Dick supports his head,
And fain would cure the hurt he made.
But Kitty hasted with a key,
And down his back they straight convey
The cold relief; the blood is stay'd,
And Hodge again holds up his head.
Such are the fortunes of the game,
And those who play should stop the same
By wholesome laws; such as all those
Who on the blinded man impose
Stand in his stead; as, long a-gone,
When men were first a nation grown,
Lawless they liv'd, till wantonness
And liberty began t' increase,
And one man lay in another's way;
Then laws were made to keep fair play.

King Edward the Third

PERSONS

King Edward	The Black Prince	Queen Philippa
Duke of Clarence	Sir John Chandos	Sir Thomas Dagworth
Sir Walter Manny	Lord Audley	Lord Percy
Bishop William,		Peter Blunt,
Dagworth's man		*a common soldier*

Scene: *The Coast of France. King Edward and Nobles before it.
The Army.*

King. O thou, to whose fury the nations are
But as dust, maintain thy servant's right!
Without thine aid, the twisted mail, and spear,
And forgèd helm, and shield of seven-times beaten brass,
Are idle trophies of the vanquisher.
When confusion rages, when the field is in a flame,
When the cries of blood tear horror from heav'n,
And yelling Death runs up and down the ranks,
Let Liberty, the charter'd right of Englishmen,
Won by our fathers in many a glorious field,
Enerve my soldiers; let Liberty
Blaze in each countenance, and fire the battle.
The enemy fight in chains, invisible chains, but heavy;
Their minds are fetter'd, then how can they be free?
While, like the mounting flame,
We spring to battle o'er the floods of death!
And these fair youths, the flow'r of England,
Venturing their lives in my most righteous cause,
O sheathe their hearts with triple steel, that they
May emulate their fathers' virtues.
And thou, my son, be strong; thou fightest for a crown
That death can never ravish from thy brow,
A crown of glory – but from thy very dust
Shall beam a radiance, to fire the breasts
Of youth unborn! Our names are written equal
In fame's wide-trophied hall; 'tis ours to gild
The letters, and to make them shine with gold
That never tarnishes: whether Third Edward,

Or the Prince of Wales, or Montacute, or Mortimer,
Or ev'n the least by birth, shall gain the brightest fame,
Is in His hand to whom all men are equal.
The world of men are like the num'rous stars
That beam and twinkle in the depth of night,
Each clad in glory according to his sphere;
But we, that wander from our native seats
And beam forth lustre on a darkling world,
Grow larger as we advance: and some, perhaps
The most obscure at home, that scarce were seen
To twinkle in their sphere, may so advance
That the astonish'd world, with upturn'd eyes,
Regardless of the moon, and those that once were bright,
Stand only for to gaze upon their splendour.
                    [*He here knights the Prince, and other young Nobles.*
Now let us take a just revenge for those
Brave Lords, who fell beneath the bloody axe
At Paris. Thanks, noble Harcourt, for 'twas
By your advice we landed here in Brittany,
A country not yet sown with destruction,
And where the fiery whirlwind of swift war
Has not yet swept its desolating wing. –
Into three parties we divide by day,
And separate march, but join again at night;
Each knows his rank, and Heav'n marshal all.   [*Exeunt.*

  Scene: *English Court. Lionel, Duke of Clarence; Queen Philippa;
  Lords; Bishop, &c.*

  Clarence. My Lords, I have by the advice of her
Whom I am doubly bound to obey, my Parent
And my Sovereign, call'd you together.
My task is great, my burden heavier than
My unfledg'd years;
Yet, with your kind assistance, Lords, I hope
England shall dwell in peace; that, while my father
Toils in his wars, and turns his eyes on this
His native shore, and sees commerce fly round
With his white wings, and sees his golden London
And her silver Thames, throng'd with shining spires
And corded ships, her merchants buzzing round

Like summer bees, and all the golden cities
In his land overflowing with honey,
Glory may not be dimm'd with clouds of care.
Say, Lords, should not our thoughts be first to commerce?
My Lord Bishop, you would recommend us agriculture?
   Bishop. Sweet Prince, the arts of peace are great,
And no less glorious than those of war,
Perhaps more glorious in the philosophic mind.
When I sit at my home, a private man,
My thoughts are on my gardens and my fields,
How to employ the hand that lacketh bread.
If Industry is in my diocese,
Religion will flourish; each man's heart
Is cultivated and will bring forth fruit:
This is my private duty and my pleasure.
But, as I sit in council with my Prince,
My thoughts take in the gen'ral good of the whole,
And England is the land favour'd by Commerce;
For Commerce, tho' the child of Agriculture,
Fosters his parent, who else must sweat and toil,
And gain but scanty fare. Then, my dear Lord,
Be England's trade our care; and we, as tradesmen,
Looking to the gain of this our native land.
   Clar. O my good Lord, true wisdom drops like honey
From your tongue, as from a worshipp'd oak.
Forgive, my Lords, my talkative youth, that speaks
Not merely what my narrow observation has
Pick'd up, but what I have concluded from your lessons.
Now, by the Queen's advice, I ask your leave
To dine to-morrow with the Mayor of London:
If I obtain your leave, I have another boon
To ask, which is the favour of your company.
I fear Lord Percy will not give me leave.
   Percy. Dear Sir, a prince should always keep his state,
And grant his favours with a sparing hand,
Or they are never rightly valuèd.
These are my thoughts; yet it were best to go
But keep a proper dignity, for now
You represent the sacred person of
Your father; 'tis with princes as 'tis with the sun;

If not sometimes o'er-clouded, we grow weary
Of his officious glory.

    Clar. Then you will give me leave to shine sometimes,
My Lord?

    Lord. Thou hast a gallant spirit, which I fear
Will be imposèd on by the closer sort.   [*Aside*.

    Clar. Well, I'll endeavour to take
Lord Percy's advice; I have been usèd so much
To dignity that I'm sick on 't.

    Queen Phil. Fie, fie, Lord Clarence! you proceed not to business,
But speak of your own pleasures.
I hope their Lordships will excuse your giddiness.

    Clar. My Lords, the French have fitted out many
Small ships of war, that, like to ravening wolves,
Infest our English seas, devouring all
Our burden'd vessels, spoiling our naval flocks.
The merchants do complain and beg our aid.

    Percy. The merchants are rich enough,
Can they not help themselves?

    Bish. They can, and may; but how to gain their will
Requires our countenance and help.

    Percy. When that they find they must, my Lord, they will:
Let them but suffer awhile, and you shall see
They will bestir themselves.

    Bish. Lord Percy cannot mean that we should suffer
This disgrace: if so, we are not sovereigns
Of the sea – our right, that Heaven gave
To England, when at the birth of nature
She was seated in the deep; the Ocean ceas'd
His mighty roar, and fawning play'd around
Her snowy feet, and own'd his awful Queen.
Lord Percy, if the heart is sick, the head
Must be aggriev'd; if but one member suffer,
The heart doth fail. You say, my Lord, the merchants
Can, if they will, defend themselves against
These rovers: this is a noble scheme,
Worthy the brave Lord Percy, and as worthy
His generous aid to put it into practice.

    Percy. Lord Bishop, what was rash in me is wise
In you; I dare not own the plan. 'Tis not

Mine. Yet will I, if you please,
Quickly to the Lord Mayor, and work him onward
To this most glorious voyage; on which cast
I'll set my whole estate,
But we will bring these Gallic rovers under.
   Queen Phil. Thanks, brave Lord Percy; you have the thanks
Of England's Queen, and will, ere long, of England.   [*Exeunt.*

Scene. *At Cressy. Sir Thomas Dagworth and Lord Audley meeting.*

   Audley. Good morrow, brave Sir Thomas; the bright morn
Smiles on our army, and the gallant sun
Springs from the hills like a young hero
Into the battle, shaking his golden locks
Exultingly: this is a promising day.
   Dagworth. Why, my Lord Audley, I don't know.
Give me your hand, and now I'll tell you what
I think you do not know. Edward's afraid of Philip.
   Audley. Ha! Ha! Sir Thomas! you but joke;
Did you e'er see him fear? At Blanchetaque,
When almost singly he drove six thousand
French from the ford, did he fear then?
   Dagw. Yes, fear – that made him fight so.
   Aud. By the same reason I might say tis fear
That makes you fight.
   Dagw. Mayhap you may: look upon Edward's face,
No one can say he fears; but when he turns
His back, then I will say it to his face;
He is afraid: he makes us all afraid.
I cannot bear the enemy at my back.
Now here we are at Cressy; where to-morrow,
To-morrow we shall know. I say, Lord Audley,
That Edward runs away from Philip.
   Aud. Perhaps you think the Prince too is afraid?
   Dagw. No; God forbid! I'm sure he is not.
He is a young lion. O! I have seen him fight
And give command, and lightning has flashèd
From his eyes across the field: I have seen him
Shake hands with death, and strike a bargain for
The enemy; he has danc'd in the field

Of battle, like the youth at morris-play.
I'm sure he's not afraid, nor Warwick, nor none –
None of us but me, and I am very much afraid.

 Aud. Are you afraid too, Sir Thomas?
I believe that as much as I believe
The King's afraid: but what are you afraid of?

 Dagw. Of having my back laid open; we turn
Our backs to the fire, till we shall burn our skirts.

 Aud. And this, Sir Thomas, you call fear? Your fear
Is of a different kind then from the King's;
He fears to turn his face, and you to turn your back.
I do not think, Sir Thomas, you know what fear is.

Enter Sir John Chandos.

 Chand. Good morrow, Generals; I give you joy:
Welcome to the fields of Cressy. Here we stop,
And wait for Philip.

 Dagw. I hope so.

 Aud. There, Sir Thomas, do you call that fear?

 Dagw. I don't know; perhaps he takes it by fits.
Why, noble Chandos, look you here –
One rotten sheep spoils the whole flock;
And if the bell-wether is tainted, I wish
The Prince may not catch the distemper too.

 Chand. Distemper, Sir Thomas! what distemper?
I have not heard.

 Dagw. Why, Chandos, you are a wise man,
I know you understand me; a distemper
The King caught here in France of running away.

 Aud. Sir Thomas, you say you have caught it too.

 Dagw. And so will the whole army; 'tis very catching,
For, when the coward runs, the brave man totters.
Perhaps the air of the country is the cause.
I feel it coming upon me, so I strive against it;
You yet are whole; but, after a few more
Retreats, we all shall know how to retreat
Better than fight. – To be plain, I think retreating
Too often takes away a soldier's courage.

 Chand. Here comes the King himself: tell him your thoughts
Plainly, Sir Thomas.

Dagw. I've told him before, but his disorder
Makes him deaf.

            Enter King Edward and Black Prince.

    King. Good morrow, Generals; when English courage fails
Down goes our right to France.
But we are conquerors everywhere; nothing
Can stand our soldiers; each man is worthy
Of a triumph. Such an army of heroes
Ne'er shouted to the Heav'ns, nor shook the field.
Edward, my son, thou art
Most happy, having such command: the man
Were base who were not fir'd to deeds
Above heroic, having such examples.
    Prince. Sire, with respect and deference I look
Upon such noble souls, and wish myself
Worthy the high command that Heaven and you
Have given me. When I have seen the field glow,
And in each countenance the soul of war
Curb'd by the manliest reason, I have been wing'd
With certain victory; and 'tis my boast,
And shall be still my glory, I was inspir'd
By these brave troops.
    Dagw. Your Grace had better make
Them all generals.
    King. Sir Thomas Dagworth, you must have your joke,
And shall, while you can fight as you did at
The Ford.
    Dagw. I have a small petition to your Majesty.
    King. What can Sir Thomas Dagworth ask that Edward
Can refuse?
    Dagw. I hope your Majesty cannot refuse so great
A trifle; I've gilt your cause with my best blood,
And would again, were I not forbid
By him whom I am bound to obey: my hands
Are tièd up, my courage shrunk and wither'd,
My sinews slacken'd, and my voice scarce heard;
Therefore I beg I may return to England.
    King. I know not what you could have ask'd, Sir Thomas,
That I would not have sooner parted with

Than such a soldier as you have been, and such a friend:
Nay, I will know the most remote particulars
Of this your strange petition: that, if I can,
I still may keep you here.

   Dagw. Here on the fields of Cressy we are settled
Till Philip springs the tim'rous covey again.
The wolf is hunted down by causeless fear;
The lion flees, and fear usurps his heart,
Startled, astonish'd at the clam'rous cock;
The eagle, that doth gaze upon the sun,
Fears the small fire that plays about the fen.
If, at this moment of their idle fear,
The dog doth seize the wolf, the forester the lion,
The negro in the crevice of the rock
Doth seize the soaring eagle; undone by flight,
They tame submit: such the effect flight has
On noble souls. Now hear its opposite:
The tim'rous stag starts from the thicket wild,
The fearful crane springs from the splashy fen,
The shining snake glides o'er the bending grass;
The stag turns head and bays the crying hounds,
The crane o'ertaken fighteth with the hawk,
The snake doth turn, and bite the padding foot.
And if your Majesty's afraid of Philip,
You are more like a lion than a crane:
Therefore I beg I may return to England.

 King. Sir Thomas, now I understand your mirth,
Which often plays with Wisdom for its pastime,
And brings good counsel from the breast of laughter.
I hope you'll stay, and see us fight this battle,
And reap rich harvest in the fields of Cressy;
Then go to England, tell them how we fight,
And set all hearts on fire to be with us.
Philip is plum'd, and thinks we flee from him,
Else he would never dare to attack us. Now,
Now the quarry's set! and Death doth sport
In the bright sunshine of this fatal day.

   Dagw. Now my heart dances, and I am as light
As the young bridegroom going to be marrièd.
Now must I to my soldiers, get them ready,

Furbish our armours bright, new-plume our helms;
And we will sing like the young housewives busièd
In the dairy: my feet are wing'd, but not
For flight, an please your grace.

    King. If all my soldiers are as pleas'd as you,
'Twill be a gallant thing to fight or die;
Then I can never be afraid of Philip.

    Dagw. A raw-bon'd fellow t'other day pass'd by me;
I told him to put off his hungry looks –
He answer'd me, 'I hunger for another battle.'
I saw a little Welshman with a fiery face;
I told him he look'd like a candle half
Burn'd out; he answer'd, he was 'pig enough
To light another pattle.' Last night, beneath
The moon I walk'd abroad, when all had pitch'd
Their tents, and all were still;
I heard a blooming youth singing a song
He had compos'd, and at each pause he wip'd
His dropping eyes. The ditty was 'If he
Return'd victorious, he should wed a maiden
Fairer than snow, and rich as midsummer.'
Another wept, and wish'd health to his father.
I chid them both, but gave them noble hopes
These are the minds that glory in the battle,
And leap and dance to hear the trumpet sound.

    King. Sir Thomas Dagworth, be thou near our person;
Thy heart is richer than the vales of France:
I will not part with such a man as thee.
If Philip came arm'd in the ribs of death,
And shook his mortal dart against my head,
Thou'dst laugh his fury into nerveless shame!
Go now, for thou art suited to the work,
Throughout the camp; inflame the timorous,
Blow up the sluggish into ardour, and
Confirm the strong with strength, the weak inspire,
And wing their brows with hope and expectation:
Then to our tent return, and meet to council.   [*Exit Dagworth.*

    Chand. That man's a hero in his closet, and more
A hero to the servants of his house
Than to the gaping world; he carries windows

In that enlargèd breast of his, that all
May see what's done within.

    Prince. He is a genuine Englishman, my Chandos,
And hath the spirit of Liberty within him.
Forgive my prejudice, Sir John; I think
My Englishmen the bravest people on
The face of the earth.

    Chand. Courage, my Lord, proceeds from self-dependence.
Teach man to think he's a free agent,
Give but a slave his liberty, he'll shake
Off sloth, and build himself a hut, and hedge
A spot of ground; this he'll defend; 'tis his
By right of Nature: thus set in action,
He will still move onward to plan conveniences,
Till glory fires his breast to enlarge his castle;
While the poor slave drudges all day, in hope
To rest at night.

    King. O Liberty, how glorious art thou!
I see thee hov'ring o'er my army, with
Thy wide-stretch'd plumes; I see thee
Lead them on to battle;
I see thee blow thy golden trumpet, while
Thy sons shout the strong shout of victory!
O noble Chandos, think thyself a gardener,
My son a vine, which I commit unto
Thy care: prune all extravagant shoots, and guide
Th' ambitious tendrils in the paths of wisdom;
Water him with thy advice; and Heav'n
Rain fresh'ning dew upon his branches! And,
O Edward, my dear son! learn to think lowly of
Thyself, as we may all each prefer other –
'Tis the best policy, and 'tis our duty.   *[Exit King Edward.*

    Prince. And may our duty, Chandos, be our pleasure.
Now we are alone, Sir John, I will unburden,
And breathe my hopes into the burning air,
Where thousand Deaths are posting up and down,
Commission'd to this fatal field of Cressy.
Methinks I see them arm my gallant soldiers,
And gird the sword upon each thigh, and fit
Each shining helm, and string each stubborn bow,

And dance to the neighing of our steeds.
Methinks the shout begins, the battle burns;
Methinks I see them perch on English crests,
And roar the wild flame of fierce war upon
The throngèd enemy! In truth I am too full
It is my sin to love the noise of war.
Chandos, thou seest my weakness; strong Nature
Will bend or break us: my blood, like a springtide
Does rise so high to overflow all bounds
Of moderation; while Reason, in her
Frail bark, can see no shore or bound for vast
Ambition. Come, take the helm, my Chandos,
That my full-blown sails overset me not
In the wild tempest: condemn my venturous youth,
That plays with danger, as the innocent child
Unthinking plays upon the viper's den:
I am a coward in my reason, Chandos.
   Chand. You are a man, my Prince, and a brave man,
If I can judge of actions; but your heat
Is the effect of youth, and want of use:
Use makes the armèd field and noisy war
Pass over as a summer cloud, unregarded,
Or but expected as a thing of course.
Age is contemplative; each rolling year
Brings forth fruit to the mind's treasure-house:
While vacant youth doth crave and seek about
Within itself, and findeth discontent,
Then, tir'd of thought, impatient takes the wing,
Seizes the fruits of time, attacks experience,
Roams round vast Nature's forest, where no bounds
Are set, the swiftest may have room, the strongest
Find prey; till tired at length, sated and tired
With the changing sameness, old variety,
We sit us down, and view our former joys
With distaste and dislike.
   Prince. Then, if we must tug for experience,
Let us not fear to beat round Nature's wilds,
And rouse the strongest prey: then, if we fall,
We fall with glory. I know the wolf
Is dangerous to fight, not good for food,

Nor is the hide a comely vestment; so
We have our battle for our pains. I know
That youth has need of age to point fit prey,
And oft the stander-by shall steal the fruit
Of th' other's labour. This is philosophy;
These are the tricks of the world; but the pure soul
Shall mount on native wings, disdaining
Little sport, and cut a path into the heaven of glory,
Leaving a track of light for men to wonder at.
I'm glad my father does not hear me talk;
You can find friendly excuses for me, Chandos.
But do you not think, Sir John, that if it please
Th' Almighty to stretch out my span of life,
I shall with pleasure view a glorious action
Which my youth master'd?
    Chand. Considerate age, my Lord, views motives,
And not acts; when neither warbling voice
Nor trilling pipe is heard, nor pleasure sits
With trembling age, the voice of Conscience then,
Sweeter than music in a summer's eve,
Shall warble round the snowy head, and keep
Sweet symphony to feather'd angels, sitting
As guardians round your chair; then shall the pulse
Beat slow, and taste and touch and sight and sound and smell,
That sing and dance round Reason's fine-wrought throne
Shall flee away, and leave them all forlorn;
Yet not forlorn if Conscience is his friend.   [*Exeunt.*

Scene. *In Thomas Dagworth's Tent. Dagworth, and William his Man.*

    Dagw. Bring hither my armour, William.
Ambition is the growth of ev'ry clime.
    Will. Does it grow in England, sir?
    Dagw. Aye, it grows most in lands most cultivated.
    Will. Then it grows most in France; the vines here are finer than any we have in England.
    Dagw. Aye, but the oaks are not.
    Will. What is the tree you mentioned? I don't think I ever saw it.
    Dagw. Ambition.
    Will. Is it a little creeping root that grows in ditches?

Dagw. Thou dost not understand me, William.
It is a root that grows in every breast;
Ambition is the desire or passion that one man
Has to get before another, in any pursuit after glory;
But I don't think you have any of it.

Will. Yes, I have; I have a great ambition to know every thing, Sir.

Dagw. But when our first ideas are wrong, what follows must all be wrong, of course; 'tis best to know a little, and to know that little aright.

Will. Then, Sir, l should be glad to know if it was not ambition that brought over our King to France to fight for his right?

Dagw. Tho' the knowledge of that will not profit thee much, yet I will tell you that it was ambition.

Will. Then, if ambition is a sin, we are all guilty in coming with him, and in fighting for him.

Dagw. Now, William, thou dost thrust the question home; but I must tell you that, guilt being an act of the mind, none are guilty but those whose minds are prompted by that same ambition.

Will. Now, I always thought that a man might be guilty of doing wrong without knowing it was wrong.

Dagw. Thou art a natural philosopher, and knowest truth by instinct, while reason runs aground, as we have run our argument. Only remember, William, all have it in their power to know the motives of their own actions, and 'tis a sin to act without some reason.

Will. And whoever acts without reason may do a great deal of harm without knowing it.

Dagw. Thou art an endless moralist.

Will. Now there's a story come into my head, that I will tell your honour if you'll give me leave.

Dagw. No, William, save it till another time; this is no time for story-telling. But here comes one who is as entertaining as a good story!

Enter Peter Blunt.

Peter. Yonder's a musician going to play before the King; it's a new song about the French and English; and the Prince has made the minstrel a squire, and given him I don't know what, and I can't tell whether he don't mention us all one by one; and he is to write another about all us that are to die, that we may be remembered in Old England, for all our blood and bones are in France; and a great deal more that we shall all hear by and by; and I came to tell your honour, because you love to hear war-songs.

Dagw. And who is this minstrel, Peter, dost know?

Peter. O aye, I forgot to tell that; he has got the same name as Sir John Chandos, that the Prince is always with – the wise man that knows us all as well as your honour, only ain't so good-natured.

Dagw. I thank you, Peter, for your information; but not for your compliment, which is not true. There's as much difference between him and me as between glittering sand and fruitful mould; or shining glass and a wrought diamond, set in rich gold, and fitted to the finger of an Emperor; such is that worthy Chandos.

Peter. I know your honour does not think anything of yourself, but everybody else does.

Dagw. Go, Peter, get you gone; flattery is delicious, even from the lips of a babbler. [*Exit Peter.*

Will. I never flatter your honour.

Dagw. I don't know that.

Will. Why, you know, Sir, when we were in England, at the tournament at Windsor, and the Earl of Warwick was tumbled over, you ask'd me if he did not look well when he fell; and I said no, he look'd very foolish; and you was very angry with me for not flattering you.

Dagw. You mean that I was angry with you for not flattering the Earl of Warwick. [*Exeunt.*

Scene. *Sir Thomas Dagworth's Tent. Sir Thomas Dagworth –
to him enter Sir Walter Manny.*

Sir Walter. Sir Thomas Dagworth, I have been weeping
Over the men that are to die to-day.

Dagw. Why, brave Sir Walter, you or I may fall.

Sir Walter. I know this breathing flesh must lie and rot,
Cover'd with silence and forgetfulness. –
Death wons in cities' smoke, and in still night,
When men sleep in their beds, walketh about!
How many in wallèd cities lie and groan,
Turning themselves upon their beds,
Talking with Death, answering his hard demands!
How many walk in darkness, terrors are round

The curtains of their beds, destruction is
Ready at the door! How many sleep
In earth, cover'd with stones and deathy dust,
Resting in quietness, whose spirits walk
Upon the clouds of heaven, to die no more!
Yet death is terrible, tho' borne on angels' wings.
How terrible then is the field of Death,
Where he doth rend the vault of heaven,
And shake the gates of hell!
O Dagworth, France is sick! the very sky,
Tho' sunshine light it, seems to me as pale
As the pale fainting man on his death-bed,
Whose face is shown by light of sickly taper
It makes me sad and sick at very heart,
Thousands must fall to-day.

    Dagw. Thousands of souls must leave this prison-house,
To be exalted to those heavenly fields,
Where songs of triumph, palms of victory,
Where peace and joy and love and calm content
Sit singing in the azure clouds, and strew
Flowers of heaven's growth over the banquet-table.
Bind ardent Hope upon your feet like shoes,
Put on the robe of preparation,
The table is prepar'd in shining heaven,
The flowers of immortality are blown;
Let those that fight fight in good steadfastness,
And those that fall shall rise in victory.

    Sir Walter. I've often seen the burning field of war,
And often heard the dismal clang of arms;
But never, till this fatal day of Cressy,
Has my soul fainted with these views of death.
I seem to be in one great charnel-house,
And seem to scent the rotten carcases;
I seem to hear the dismal yells of Death,
While the black gore drops from his horrid jaws;
Yet I not fear the monster in his pride –
But O! the souls that are to die to-day!

    Dagw. Stop, brave Sir Walter; let me drop a tear,
Then let the clarion of war begin;
I'll fight and weep, 'tis in my country's cause;

I'll weep and shout for glorious liberty.
Grim War shall laugh and shout, deckèd in tears,
And blood shall flow like streams across the meadows,
That murmur down their pebbly channels, and
Spend their sweet lives to do their country service;
Then shall England's verdure shoot, her fields shall smile,
Her ships shall sing across the foaming sea,
Her mariners shall use the flute and viol,
And rattling guns, and black and dreary war,
Shall be no more.
    Sir Walter. Well, let the trumpet sound, and the drum beat;
Let war stain the blue heavens with bloody banners;
I'll draw my sword, nor ever sheathe it up
Till England blow the trump of victory,
Or I lay stretch'd upon the field of death.   [*Exeunt.*

Scene. *In the Camp. Several of the Warriors meet at the King's Tent*
   with a Minstrel, who sings the following Song:

O sons of Trojan Brutus, cloth'd in war,
Whose voices are the thunder of the field,
Rolling dark clouds o'er France, muffling the sun
In sickly darkness like a dim eclipse,
Threatening as the red brow of storms, as fire
Burning up nations in your wrath and fury!

Your ancestors came from the fires of Troy,
(Like lions rous'd by light'ning from their dens,
Whose eyes do glare against the stormy fires),
Heated with war, fill'd with the blood of Greeks,
With helmets hewn, and shields coverèd with gore,
In navies black, broken with wind and tide:

They landed in firm array upon the rocks
Of Albion; they kiss'd the rocky shore;
'Be thou our mother and our nurse,' they said;
'Our children's mother, and thou shalt be our grave,
The sepulchre of ancient Troy, from whence
Shall rise cities, and thrones, and arms, and awful pow'rs.'

Our fathers swarm from the ships. Giant voices
Are heard from the hills, the enormous sons
Of Ocean run from rocks and caves, wild men,
Naked and roaring like lions, hurling rocks,
And wielding knotty clubs, like oaks entangled
Thick as a forest, ready for the axe.

Our fathers move in firm array to battle;
The savage monsters rush like roaring fire,
Like as a forest roars with crackling flames,
When the red lightning, borne by furious storms,
Lights on some woody shore; the parchèd heavens
Rain fire into the molten raging sea.

The smoking trees are strewn upon the shore,
Spoil'd of their verdure. O how oft have they
Defy'd the storm that howlèd o'er their heads!
Our fathers, sweating, lean on their spears, and view
The mighty dead: giant bodies streaming blood,
Dread visages frowning in silent death.

Then Brutus spoke, inspir'd; our fathers sit
Attentive on the melancholy shore:
Hear ye the voice of Brutus – 'The flowing waves
Of time come rolling o'er my breast,' he said;
'And my heart labours with futurity:
Our sons shall rule the empire of the sea.

'Their mighty wings shall stretch from east to west.
Their nest is in the sea, but they shall roam
Like eagles for the prey; nor shall the young
Crave or be heard; for plenty shall bring forth,
Cities shall sing, and vales in rich array
Shall laugh, whose fruitful laps bend down with fulness.

'Our sons shall rise from thrones in joy,
Each one buckling on his armour; Morning
Shall be prevented by their swords gleaming,
And Evening hear their song of victory:

Their towers shall be built upon the rocks,
Their daughters shall sing, surrounded with shining spears.

'Liberty shall stand upon the cliffs of Albion,
Casting her blue eyes over the green ocean;
Or, tow'ring, stand upon the roaring waves,
Stretching her mighty spear o'er distant lands;
While, with her eagle wings, she covereth
Fair Albion's shore, and all her families.'

Prologue, intended for a Dramatic Piece of King Edward the Fourth

O for a voice like thunder, and a tongue
To drown the throat of war! When the senses
Are shaken, and the soul is driven to madness,
Who can stand? When the souls of the oppressèd
Fight in the troubled air that rages, who can stand?
When the whirlwind of fury comes from the
Throne of God, when the frowns of his countenance
Drive the nations together, who can stand?
When Sin claps his broad wings over the battle,
And sails rejoicing in the flood of Death;
When souls are torn to everlasting fire,
And fiends of Hell rejoice upon the slain,
O who can stand? O who hath causèd this?
O who can answer at the throne of God?
The Kings and Nobles of the Land have done it!
Hear it not, Heaven, thy Ministers have done it!

Prologue to King John

Justice hath heaved a sword to plunge in Albion's breast; for Albion's sins are crimson dy'd, and the red scourge follows her desolate sons. Then Patriot rose; full oft did Patriot rise, when Tyranny hath stain'd fair Albion's breast with her own children's gore. Round his majestic feet deep thunders roll; each heart does tremble, and each knee grows slack. The stars of heaven tremble; the roaring voice of war, the trumpet, calls to battle. Brother in brother's blood must bathe – rivers of death. O land most hapless! O beauteous island, how forsaken! Weep from thy silver fountains, weep from thy gentle rivers! The angel of the island weeps. Thy widowed virgins weep beneath thy shades. Thy aged fathers gird themselves for war. The sucking infant lives to die in battle; the weeping mother feeds him for the slaughter. The husbandman doth leave his bending harvest. Blood cries afar! The land doth sow itself! The glittering youth of courts must gleam in arms. The aged senators their ancient swords assume. The trembling sinews of old age must work the work of death against their progeny; for Tyranny hath stretch'd his purple arm, and 'Blood!' he cries; 'the chariots and the horses, the noise of shout, and dreadful thunder of the battle heard afar!' Beware, O proud! thou shalt be humbled; thy cruel brow, thine iron heart, is smitten, though lingering Fate is slow. O yet may Albion smile again, and stretch her peaceful arms, and raise her golden head exultingly! Her citizens shall throng about her gates, her mariners shall sing upon the sea, and myriads shall to her temples crowd! Her sons shall joy as in the morning! Her daughters sing as to the rising year!

A War Song to Englishmen

Prepare, prepare the iron helm of war,
Bring forth the lots, cast in the spacious orb;
Th' Angel of Fate turns them with mighty hands,
And casts them out upon the darken'd earth!
        Prepare, prepare!

Prepare your hearts for Death's cold hand! prepare
Your souls for flight, your bodies for the earth;
Prepare your arms for glorious victory;
Prepare your eyes to meet a holy God!
        Prepare, prepare!

Whose fatal scroll is that? Methinks 'tis mine!
Why sinks my heart, why faltereth my tongue?
Had I three lives, I'd die in such a cause,
And rise, with ghosts, over the well-fought field.
       Prepare, prepare!

The arrows of Almighty God are drawn!
Angels of Death stand in the louring heavens!
Thousands of souls must seek the realms of light,
And walk together on the clouds of heaven!
       Prepare, prepare!

Soldiers, prepare! Our cause is Heaven's cause;
Soldiers, prepare! Be worthy of our cause:
Prepare to meet our fathers in the sky:
Prepare, O troops, that are to fall to-day!
       Prepare, prepare!

Alfred shall smile, and make his harp rejoice;
The Norman William, and the learnèd Clerk,
And Lion Heart, and black-brow'd Edward, with
His loyal queen, shall rise, and welcome us!
       Prepare, prepare!

The Couch of Death

The veiled Evening walked solitary down the western hills, and Silence reposed in the valley; the birds of day were heard in their nests, rustling in brakes and thickets; and the owl and bat flew round the darkening trees: all is silent when Nature takes her repose. – In former times, on such an evening, when the cold clay breathed with life, and our ancestors, who now sleep in their graves, walked on the steadfast globe, the remains of a family of the tribes of Earth, a mother and a sister, were gathered to the sick bed of a youth. Sorrow linked them together; leaning on one another's necks alternately – like lilies dropping tears in each other's bosom – they stood by the bed like reeds bending over a lake, when the evening drops trickle down. His voice was low as the whisperings of the woods when the wind is asleep, and the visions of Heaven unfold their visitation. 'Parting is hard and death is terrible; I seem to walk through a deep valley, far from

the light of day, alone and comfortless! The damps of death fall thick upon
me! Horrors stare me in the face! I look behind, there is no returning;
Death follows after me; I walk in regions of Death, where no tree is,
without a lantern to direct my steps, without a staff to support me.' Thus
he laments through the still evening, till the curtains of darkness were
drawn. Like the sound of a broken pipe, the aged woman raised her voice.
'O my son, my son, I know but little of the path thou goest! But lo! there is
a God, who made the world; stretch out thy hand to Him.' The youth
replied, like a voice heard from a sepulchre, 'My hand is feeble, how
should I stretch it out? My ways are sinful, how should I raise mine eyes?
My voice hath used deceit, how should I call on Him who is Truth? My
breath is loathsome, how should He not be offended? If I lay my face in the
dust, the grave opens its mouth for me; if I lift up my head, sin covers me
as a cloak. O my dear friends, pray ye for me! Stretch forth your hands that
my Helper may come! Through the void space I walk, between the sinful
world and eternity! Beneath me burns eternal fire! O for a hand to pluck
me forth!' As the voice of an omen heard in the silent valley, when the few
inhabitants cling trembling together; as the voice of the Angel of Death,
when the thin beams of the moon give a faint light, such was this young
man's voice to his friends. Like the bubbling waters of the brook in the
dead of night, the aged woman raised her cry, and said, 'O Voice, that
dwellest in my breast, can I not cry, and lift my eyes to Heaven? Thinking
of this, my spirit is turned within me into confusion! O my child, my child,
is thy breath infected? so is mine. As the deer wounded, by the brooks of
water, so the arrows of sin stick in my flesh; the poison hath entered into
my marrow.' Like rolling waves upon a desert shore, sighs succeeded
sighs; they covered their faces and wept. The youth lay silent, his mother's
arm was under his head; he was like a cloud tossed by the winds, till the
sun shine, and the drops of rain glisten, the yellow harvest breathes, and
the thankful eyes of the villagers are turned up in smiles. The traveller, that
hath taken shelter under an oak, eyes the distant country with joy. Such
smiles were seen upon the face of the youth: a visionary hand wiped away
his tears, and a ray of light beamed around his head. All was still. The
moon hung not out her lamp, and the stars faintly glimmered in the
summer sky; the breath of night slept among the leaves of the forest; the
bosom of the lofty hill drank in the silent dew, while on his majestic brow
the voice of Angels is heard, and stringed sounds ride upon the wings of
night. The sorrowful pair lift up their heads, hovering Angels are around
them, voices of comfort are heard over the Couch of Death, and the youth
breathes out his soul with joy into eternity.

Contemplation

Who is this, that with unerring step dares tempt the wilds, where only Nature's foot hath trod? 'Tis Contemplation, daughter of the grey Morning! Majestical she steppeth, and with her pure quill on every flower writeth Wisdom's name; now lowly bending, whispers in mine ear, 'O man, how great, how little, thou! O man, slave of each moment, lord of eternity! seest thou where Mirth sits on the painted cheek? doth it not seem ashamed of such a place, and grow immoderate to brave it out? O what an humble garb true Joy puts on! Those who want Happiness must stoop to find it; it is a flower that grows in every vale. Vain foolish man, that roams on lofty rocks, where, 'cause his garments are swoln with wind, he fancies he is grown into a giant! Lo, then, Humility, take it, and wear it in thine heart; lord of thyself, thou then art lord of all. Clamour brawls along the streets, and destruction hovers in the city's smoke; but on these plains, and in these silent woods, true joys descend: here build thy nest; here fix thy staff; delights blossom around; numberless beauties blow; the green grass springs in joy, and the nimble air kisses the leaves; the brook stretches its arms along the velvet meadow, its silver inhabitants sport and play; the youthful sun joys like a hunter roused to the chase, he rushes up the sky, and lays hold on the immortal coursers of day; the sky glitters with the jingling trappings. Like a triumph, season follows season, while the airy music fills the world with joyful sounds.' I answered, 'Heavenly goddess! I am wrapped in mortality, my flesh is a prison, my bones the bars of death; Misery builds over our cottage roofs, and Discontent runs like a brook. Even in childhood, Sorrow slept with me in my cradle; he followed me up and down in the house when I grew up; he was my schoolfellow: thus he was in my steps and in my play till he became to me as my brother. I walked through dreary places with him, and in church-yards; and I oft found myself sitting by Sorrow on a tomb-stone.'

Samson

Samson, the strongest of the children of men, I sing; how he was foiled by woman's arts, by a false wife brought to the gates of death! O Truth! that shinest with propitious beams, turning our earthly night to heavenly day, from presence of the Almighty Father, thou visitest our darkling world with blessed feet, bringing good news of Sin and Death destroyed! O white-robed Angel, guide my timorous hand to write as on a lofty rock with iron pen the words of truth, that all who pass may read. – Now Night, noon-tide of damned spirits, over the silent earth spreads her pavilion, while in dark council sat Philista's lords; and, where strength failed, black thoughts in ambush lay. Their helmed youth and aged warriors in dust together lie, and Desolation spreads his wings over the land of Palestine: from side to side the land groans, her prowess lost, and seeks to hide her bruised head under the mists of night, breeding dark plots. For Dalila's fair arts have long been tried in vain; in vain she wept in many a treacherous tear. 'Go on, fair traitress; do thy guileful work; ere once again the changing moon her circuit hath performed, thou shalt overcome, and conquer him by force unconquerable, and wrest his secret from him. Call thine alluring arts and honest-seeming brow, the holy kiss of love, and the transparent tear; put on fair linen that with the lily vies, purple and silver; neglect thy hair, to seem more lovely in thy loose attire; put on thy country's pride, deceit, and eyes of love decked in mild sorrow; and sell thy lord for gold.' For now, upon her sumptuous couch reclined in gorgeous pride, she still entreats, and still she grasps his vigorous knees with her fair arms. 'Thou lov'st me not! thou'rt war, thou art not love! O foolish Dalila! O weak woman! it is death clothed in flesh thou lovest, and thou hast been encircled in his arms! Alas, my lord, what am I calling thee? Thou art my God! To thee I pour my tears for sacrifice morning and evening. My days are covered with sorrow, shut up, darkened! By night I am deceived! Who says that thou wast born of mortal kind? Destruction was thy father, a lioness suckled thee, thy young hands tore human limbs, and gorged human flesh. Come hither, Death; art thou not Samson's servant? 'Tis Dalila that calls, thy master's wife; no, stay, and let thy master do the deed: one blow of that strong arm would ease my pain; then should I lay at quiet and have rest. Pity forsook thee at thy birth! O Dagon furious, and all ye gods of Palestine, withdraw your hand! I am but a weak woman. Alas, I am wedded to your enemy! I will go mad, and tear my crisped hair; I'll run about, and pierce the ears o' th' gods! O Samson, hold me not; thou lovest me not! Look not upon me with those deathful eyes! Thou wouldst my death, and death approaches fast.' Thus, in false tears, she bath'd his feet, and thus she day by day oppressed his soul: he seemed a mountain, his brow among the clouds; she seemed a silver stream, his feet embracing. Dark thoughts rolled to and fro in his mind, like thunder clouds troubling the sky; his visage was troubled; his soul was distressed. 'Though I should tell her all my heart, what can I fear? Though I should tell this secret of my birth, the utmost may be warded off as well when told as now.' She saw him moved, and thus resumes her wiles. 'Samson, I'm thine; do with me what thou wilt: my friends are enemies; my life is death; I am a traitor to my nation, and despised; my joy is given into the hands of him who hates me, using deceit to the wife of his bosom. Thrice hast thou mocked me and grieved my soul. Didst thou not tell me with green withs to bind thy nervous arms; and, after that, when I had found thy falsehood, with new ropes to bind thee fast? I knew thou didst but mock me. Alas, when in thy sleep I bound thee with them to try thy truth, I cried, "The Philistines be upon thee, Samson!" Then did suspicion wake thee; how didst thou rend the feeble ties! Thou fearest nought, what shouldst thou fear? Thy power is more than mortal, none can hurt thee; thy bones are brass, thy sinews are iron. Ten thousand spears are like the summer grass; an army of mighty men are as flocks in the valleys; what canst thou fear? I drink my tears like water; I live upon sorrow! O worse than wolves and tigers, what canst thou give when such a trifle is denied me? But O! at last thou mockest me, to shame my over-fond inquiry. Thou toldest me to weave thee to the beam by thy strong hair; I did even that to try thy truth; but, when I cried "The Philistines be upon thee!" then didst thou leave me to bewail that Samson loved me not.' He sat, and inward griev'd; he saw and lov'd the beauteous suppliant, nor could conceal aught that might appease her; then, leaning on her bosom, thus he spoke: 'Hear, O Dalila! doubt no more of Samson's love; for that fair breast was made the ivory palace of my inmost heart, where it shall lie at rest: for sorrow is the lot of all of woman born: for care was I brought forth, and labour is my lot: nor matchless might, nor wisdom, nor every gift enjoyed, can from the heart of man hide sorrow. Twice was my birth foretold from heaven, and twice a sacred vow enjoined me that I should drink no wine, nor eat of any unclean thing; for holy unto Israel's God I am, a Nazarite even from my mother's womb. Twice was it told, that it might not be broken. "Grant me a son, kind Heaven," Manoa cried; but Heaven refused. Childless he mourned, but thought his God knew best. In solitude, though not obscure, in Israel he lived, till venerable age came on: his flocks increased, and plenty crowned his board, beloved, revered of man. But God hath other joys in store. Is burdened Israel his grief? The son of his old age shall set it free! The venerable sweetener of his life receives the promise first from Heaven. She saw the maidens play, and blessed their innocent mirth; she blessed each new-joined pair; but from her the long-wished deliverer shall spring. Pensive, alone she sat within the house, when busy day was fading, and calm evening, time for contemplation, rose from the forsaken east, and drew the curtains of heaven: pensive she sat, and thought on Israel's grief, and silent prayed to Israel's God; when lo! an angel from the fields of light entered the house. His form was manhood in the prime, and from his spacious brow shot terrors through the evening shade. But mild he hailed her, "Hail, highly favoured!" said he; "for lo! thou shalt conceive, and bear a son, and Israel's strength shall be upon his shoulders, and he shall be called Israel's Deliverer. Now, therefore, drink no wine, and eat not any unclean thing, for he shall be a Nazarite to God." Then, as a neighbour, when his evening tale is told, departs, his blessing leaving, so seemed he to depart: she wondered with exceeding joy, nor knew he was an angel. Manoa left his fields to sit in the house, and take his evening's rest from labour – the sweetest time that God has allotted mortal man. He sat, and heard with joy, and praised God, who Israel still doth keep. The time rolled on, and Israel groaned oppressed. The sword was bright, while the ploughshare rusted, till hope grew feeble, and was ready to give place to doubting. Then prayed Manoa: "O Lord, thy flock is scattered on the hills! The wolf teareth them, Oppression stretches his rod over our land, our country is ploughed with swords, and reaped in blood. The echoes of slaughter reach from hill to hill. Instead of peaceful pipe the shepherd bears a sword, the ox-goad is turned into a spear. O when shall our Deliverer come? The Philistine riots on our flocks, our vintage is gathered by bands of enemies. Stretch forth thy hand, and save!" Thus prayed Manoa. The aged woman walked into the field, and lo! again the angel came, clad as a traveller fresh risen on his journey. She ran and called her husband, who came and talked with him. "O man of God," said he, "thou comest from far! Let us detain thee while I make ready a kid, that thou mayest sit and eat, and tell us of thy name and warfare; that, when thy sayings come to pass, we may honour thee." The Angel answered, "My name is Wonderful; inquire not after it, seeing it is a secret; but, if thou wilt, offer an offering unto the Lord." '

Appendix to POETICAL SKETCHES

Song by a Shepherd

Welcome, stranger, to this place,
Where joy doth sit on every bough,
Paleness flies from every face;
We reap not what we do not sow.

Innocence doth like a rose
Bloom on every maiden's cheek;
Honour twines around her brows,
The jewel health adorns her neck.

Song by an Old Shepherd

When silver snow decks Sylvio's clothes,
And jewel hangs at shepherd's nose,
We can abide life's pelting storm,
That makes our limbs quake, if our hearts be warm.

Whilst Virtue is our walking-staff,
And Truth a lantern to our path,
We can abide life's pelting storm,
That makes our limbs quake, if our hearts be warm.

Blow, boisterous wind, stern winter frown,
Innocence is a winter's gown.
So clad, we'll abide life's pelting storm,
That makes our limbs quake, if our hearts be warm.

AN ISLAND IN THE MOON

Songs from *An Island in the Moon* (1784) *An Island in the Moon* is Blake's affectionate parody of his friends and acquaintances. A cross between Jonathan Swift and Monty Python, it is set on a lunar island with characters such as Steelyard the Lawgiver and Mr Obtuse Angle. The songs display the boisterous, sometimes bawdy humour and satirical bite that characterise Blake's work at times, while they also allow him to explore diverse dramatic voices as ironic masks for social commentary, foreshadowing *Songs of Innocence and Experience*.

I ^{3}

Little Phoebus came strutting in,
With his fat belly and his round chin.
What is it you would please to have?
Ho! Ho!
I won't let it go at only so and so!

II

Honour and Genius is all I ask,
And I ask the Gods no more!
No more! No more!
No more! No more! } *The Three Philosophers bear chorus.*

III

When Old Corruption first begun,
Adorn'd in yellow vest,
He committed on Flesh a whoredom –
O, what a wicked beast!

From then a callow babe did spring,
And Old Corruption smil'd
To think his race should never end,
For now he had a child.

He call'd him Surgery and fed
The babe with his own milk;
For Flesh and he could ne'er agree:
She would not let him suck.

And this he always kept in mind;
And form'd a crooked knife,
And ran about with bloody hands
To seek his mother's life.

And as he ran to seek his mother
He met with a dead woman.
He fell in love and married her –
A deed which is not common!

She soon grew pregnant, and brought forth
Scurvy and Spotted Fever,
The father grinn'd and skipt about,
And said 'I'm made for ever!

'For now I have procur'd these imps
I'll try experiments.'
With that he tied poor Scurvy down,
And stopt up all its vents.

And when the child began to swell
He shouted out aloud –
'I've found the dropsy out, and soon
Shall do the world more good.'

He took up Fever by the neck,
And cut out all its spots;
And, thro' the holes which he had made,
He first discover'd guts.

IV

Hear then the pride and knowledge of a sailor!
His sprit sail, fore sail, main sail, and his mizen.
A poor frail man – God wot! I know none frailer,
I know no greater sinner than John Taylor.

V

The Song of Phoebe and Jellicoe

Phoebe drest like beauty's queen,
Jellicoe in faint pea-green,
Sitting all beneath a grot,
Where the little lambkins trot.

Maidens dancing, loves a-sporting,
All the country folks a-courting,
Susan, Johnny, Bet, and Joe,
Lightly tripping on a row.

Happy people, who can be
In happiness compar'd with ye?
The pilgrim with his crook and hat
Sees your happiness complete.

VI

Lo! the Bat with leathern wing,
Winking and blinking,
Winking and blinking,
Winking and blinking,
Like Dr Johnson.

Quid.   'O ho!' said Dr Johnson
To Scipio Africanus,
'If you don't own me a philosopher,
I'll kick your Roman anus.'

Suction.   'A ha!' to Dr Johnson
Said Scipio Africanus,
'Lift up my Roman petticoat
And kiss my Roman anus.'

And the Cellar goes down with a step.   *(Grand Chorus.)*

VII

Ist Vo.	Want Matches?
2nd Vo.	Yes! Yes! Yes!
Ist Vo.	Want Matches?
2nd Vo.	No!

Ist Vo.	Want Matches?
2nd Vo.	Yes! Yes! Yes!
Ist Vo	Want Matches?
2nd Vo.	No!

VIII

As I walk'd forth one May morning
To see the fields so pleasant and so gay,
O! there did I spy a young maiden sweet,
Among the violets that smell so sweet,
                    smell so sweet,
                    smell so sweet,
Among the violets that smell so sweet.

IX

Hail Matrimony, made of Love!
To thy wide gates how great a drove
On purpose to be yok'd do come;
Widows and Maids and Youths also,
That lightly trip on beauty's toe,
Or sit on beauty's bum.

Hail fingerfooted lovely Creatures!
The females of our human natures,
Formèd to suckle all Mankind.
'Tis you that come in time of need,
Without you we should never breed,
Or any comfort find.

For if a Damsel's blind or lame,
Or Nature's hand has crook'd her frame,
Or if she's deaf, or is wall-eyed;
Yet, if her heart is well inclin'd,
Some tender lover she shall find
That panteth for a Bride.

The universal Poultice this,
To cure whatever is amiss
In Damsel or in Widow gay!
It makes them smile, it makes them skip;
Like birds, just curèd of the pip,
They chirp and hop away.

Then come, ye maidens! come, ye swains!
Come and be cur'd of all your pains
In Matrimony's Golden Cage –

X[4]

To be or not to be
Of great capacity,
Like Sir Isaac Newton,
Or Locke, or Doctor South,
Or Sherlock upon Death –
I'd rather be Sutton!

For he did build a house
For agèd men and youth,
With walls of brick and stone;
He furnish'd it within
With whatever he could win,
And all his own.

He drew out of the Stocks
His money in a box,
And sent his servant
To Green the Bricklayer,
And to the Carpenter;
He was so fervent.

The chimneys were threescore,
The windows many more;
And, for convenience,
He sinks and gutters made,
And all the way he pav'd
To hinder pestilence.

Was not this a good man –
Whose life was but a span,
Whose name was Sutton –
As Locke, or Doctor South,
Or Sherlock upon Death,
Or Sir Isaac Newton?

XI [5]

This city and this country has brought forth many mayors
To sit in state, and give forth laws out' of their old oak chairs,
With face as brown as any nut with drinking of strong ale –
Good English hospitality, O then it did not fail!

With scarlet gowns and broad gold lace, would make a yeoman sweat;
With stockings roll'd above their knees and shoes as black as jet
With eating beef and drinking beer, O they were stout and hale –
Good English hospitality, O then it did not fail!

Thus sitting at the table wide the mayor and aldermen
Were fit to give law to the city; each ate as much as ten:
The hungry poor enter'd the hall to eat good beef and ale –
Good English hospitality, O then it did not fail!

XII

O, I say, you Joe,
Throw us the ball!
I've a good mind to go
And leave you all.
I never saw such a bowler
To bowl the ball in a tansy,
And to clean it with my hankercher
Without saying a word.

That Bill's a foolish fellow;
He has given me a black eye.
He does not know how to handle a bat
Any more than a dog or a cat:
He has knock'd down the wicket,
And broke the stumps,
And runs without shoes to save his pumps.

XIII

Leave, O leave me to my sorrows;
Here I'll sit and fade away,
Till I'm nothing but a spirit,
And I lose this form of clay.

Then if chance along this forest
Any walk in pathless ways,
Thro' the gloom he'll see my shadow
Hear my voice upon the breeze.

XIV

There's Doctor Clash,
And Signor Falalasole,
O they sweep in the cash
Into their purse hole!
Fa me la sol, La me fa sol!

Great A, little A,
Bouncing B!
Play away, play away,
You're out of the key!
Fa me la sol, La me fa sol!

Musicians should have
A pair of very good ears,
And long fingers and thumbs,
And not like clumsy bears.
Fa me la sol, La me fa sol!

Gentlemen! Gentlemen!
Rap! Rap! Rap!
Fiddle! Fiddle! Fiddle!
Clap! Clap! Clap!
Fa me la sol, La me fa sol!

SONGS OF INNOCENCE AND EXPERIENCE
(1789–94)

Songs of Innocence and Experience (1789–94)   *Songs of Innocence* opens with a poem which is childlike, fearless, asserting the need for simple communication 'in a book that all may read' (p.60). This call for democratic speech and writing was also current in the works of the radical Tom Paine and William Wordsworth. When Blake published this set of poems, they were clearly in a tradition: Nonconformist preacher Isaac Watts had published his *Divine Songs for Children* in 1715, containing poems like 'How doth the little busy bee'. Watts's songs enforce an orthodox Christian moral, which Blake subverts: 'The Divine Image', for example, is a direct parody of one of Watts's poems, echoing its language but turning the conventional moral message against itself (see Notes for details). At other times, Blake's songs can leave us guessing. They have an unchallengeable naïvety about them, as in the poem 'Spring' (pp. 64–5), and that naïvety may seem embarrassingly cloying. But this is a crafty reflection on our own lack of innocence: the more we squirm, the more obvious it is how far we are from the innocently optimistic states of mind being expressed. In addition, significant issues are being raised. 'The Echoing Green' (pp. 60–1) presents an image of community and human harmony, but, as with many of these seemingly simple poems, the ending leaves an ambiguous feeling of foreboding, reminding us how many village greens were being overtaken by the devastating effects of the enclosure movement.

This complexity is best epitomised by a poem which Blake printed first in *Innocence*, but later in *Experience*, 'The Schoolboy' (pp. 87–8). There are many poems about children, as one might expect in songs of innocence. In common with other Romantic writers, Blake saw in the child an emblem of unspoilt potential, of the human spirit unfettered. Like Jean Jacques Rousseau in his novel *Emile* (1762), Blake suggests that what creates negative or destructive behaviour in people is not original sin: evil is not inherent in humanity, but created by repression of the human spirit. It is a restrictive, divided society that corrupts the original innocence. But as so often, Blake has a double target: he is attacking social institutions and the states of mind those conditions produce. Oppression and restriction are internalised, becoming the way we see things; and the way we see things *is* what we see. So Blake's aim as a revolutionary artist was not just to challenge a social system; it was also to challenge the thinking which perpetuates that system. As he argues in *The Marriage of Heaven and Hell*: 'If the doors of perception were cleansed everything would appear to man as it is, infinite. For man has closed himself up till he sees all things thro' narrow chinks of his cavern' (p. 201).

This inner limitation is most powerfully captured in the poem 'London' from the *Songs of Experience* (p. 88). Through extraordinary and disturbing imagery, such as the idea of marriage as a hearse, Blake connects together different oppressions: the restrictions of the law and property (the 'charter'd Thames'), the fear in every voice, child exploitation, the oppressive institutional church, death through war and violence instigated by the blood lust of kings and aristocrats, the sexual exploitation of women as prostitutes which is the corollary of the hypocritical purity of marriage. In showing how different forms of oppression are linked, the poem also shows the state of mind that allows them to continue. The speaker in the poem, the 'I', should not be taken as Blake: indeed, none of the *Songs* is to be taken as a direct expression of Blake. The voices they dramatise are to be regarded critically, and endorsed or otherwise. The speaker in 'London' expresses an appalled helplessness at what he sees and hears; but, the poem suggests, by being incapable of resisting such injustices, by being passive and impotent, the speaker actually perpetuates them: 'I [. . .] mark in every face [. . .] marks of weakness'. As Heather Glen has pointed out, there are manifold ambiguities at work in the language here.[1] The word 'mark' means 'notice', but it also suggests 'inscribe', as if the 'I' is inflicting marks by seeing things in this way. The speaker is trapped in 'the mind-forg'd manacles': having nothing to counteract the inequity he sees, he is both its victim and perpetrator. Yet, as the poem states, the manacles are forged, suggesting the blacksmith but also a forgery: they could be seen through and opposed, if only the appalling apathy and hopelessness of this state of mind were overcome.

Opening the manacled 'doors of perception' (p. 201) was part of Blake's purpose in printing *Songs of Innocence* together with *Songs of*

1 Heather Glen, 'The Poet in Society: Blake and Wordsworth on London', *Literature and History*, 3, March 1976, pp. 6–9

Experience. It is as if he is indicating that in an ideal world innocent attitudes and carefree spirits would be fine; but in the real world we need to face what is in front of us, yet never lose hold of our vision that there could be something better. Here Blake's design for the frontispiece to *Experience* is relevant: the Piper who, in the frontispiece to *Innocence*, had been shown wandering freely with an angelic cherub flying at liberty above him, is depicted striding purposefully with a determined look on his face and holding the cherub down firmly on his own head as if hanging on grimly to his vision. Such is the role of the prophetic artist – to provide a critique of the status quo and an inspiration to change it. This aim is presented in the introductory poem to *Experience* (p. 74). Here the prophetic Bard, 'who present, past, and future, sees', looks clear-sightedly at the present injustice and oppressions in order to give a critique of them, but he does so with a vision in mind that suggests a dynamic historical understanding. He is akin to Shelley's view of the poet as the 'unacknowledged legislator' in his essay 'A Defence of Poetry' (1821), asking what conditions have produced this situation, and what might take its place in the future. As Shelley put it in his essay, the poet 'not only beholds intensely the present as it is, and discovers those laws according to which present things ought to be ordered, but he beholds the future in the present, and his thoughts are the germs of the flowers and the fruit of latest time' (Williams, p. 584).

It is not surprising that the change from *Innocence* to *Experience* was expressive of its time. Blake published the *Experience* poems in 1794, after the repression of the radical movements in Britain, the outlawing of Tom Paine, of the revolutionary societies, and the outbreak of the Terror in France. But by publishing the two sets together to show 'the two contrary states of the human soul', as he declares on the title page, Blake was not lapsing into pessimism. Quite the opposite, since the dialectic between innocence and experience is a challenge to pessimism as well as to oppression. Without the visionary hope of *Innocence*, *Experience* would be utterly hopeless and cynical. But equally, by itself *Innocence* is merely escapist; or it is naïve, in danger of exploitation like the little Chimney Sweeper in the *Innocence* poem, who, despite his oppression, believes that all is for the good in the best of all possible worlds (p. 68). As Blake notes in additions to his long prophetic poem, *Vala or The Four Zoas*, 'Unorganis'd Innocence: An Impossibility', since 'Innocence dwells with wisdom, never with ignorance' (Keynes, p. 380). Blake's dialectical thinking between what he calls 'contraries' (p. 196) like innocence and experience is one of the most subversive and challenging aspects of his work, primarily because it constantly undercuts conventional thinking and refuses easy categorisation. As a way of emphasising this dialectic, Blake prints poems in both books to form pairs: 'The Lamb' and 'The Tiger'; 'Infant Joy' and 'Infant Sorrow'; two poems called 'Holy Thursday'; two 'Chimney Sweeper' poems; and there is 'The Divine Image' and 'The Human Abstract'. 'The Divine Image' (p. 69) apparently asserts all the unquestionable virtues. It seems orthodoxly Christian; but Blake sees true Christianity, as opposed to the institutional church forms, as revolutionary. This poem argues that conceptions of God are based on what is divine in humanity; that, in fact, God and the divine are inseparable from humanity. *The Marriage of Heaven and Hell* asserts: 'All Deities reside in the Human breast' (p. 200); 'God only Acts and Is, in existing beings or Men' (p. 202); and 'Jesus was all virtue, and acted from impulse, not from rules' (p.206). But in the world of *Experience*, this image of divine humanity becomes a distorted reflection of the division and oppression of that world, the 'human abstract' (p. 90). The virtues become part of a code of law for binding down human potential, part of a hypocritical system that pretends to offer pity and mercy while inflicting injustice and exploitation. This paradox is summed up in the opening couplet: 'Pity would be no more/If we did not *make* somebody poor' (p. 90 – my emphasis). In other words, social inequality is inflicted by human beings with power and money on others, and pity is merely balm to salve their consciences. Blake's perception of this hypocrisy is not accidental. Heather Glen has argued that it derives from his particular location in London society: as a print-shop keeper he was part of the world of 'plebeian protest'; but as an engraver he was also familiar with 'polite' society, because they were his potential customers. As Glen puts it, by moving daily between two such different social groups, Blake 'stands at a point of clash [. . .] a point from which words like "mercy" and "pity" can very clearly be seen to mean utterly different social realities'.[2] In other words, Blake's dialectical awareness was drawn from, and applied to, the cultural and political contradictions of his society. Hence the biting ironies hidden in these seemingly innocuous little poems, which reveal the true lineaments of society of the time with the force of the concentrated acid with which Blake engraved his metal printing plates.

2 Heather Glen, 'The Poet in Society: Blake and Wordsworth on London', *Literature and History*, 3, March 1976, pp. 22–3

SONGS OF INNOCENCE

Introduction

Piping down the valleys wild,
Piping songs of pleasant glee,
On a cloud I saw a child,
And he laughing said to me:

'Pipe a song about a Lamb!'
So I piped with merry cheer.
'Piper, pipe that song again;'
So I piped: he wept to hear.

'Drop thy pipe, thy happy pipe;
Sing thy songs of happy cheer:'
So I sang the same again,
While he wept with joy to hear.

'Piper, sit thee down and write
In a book, that all may read.'
So he vanish'd from my sight,
And I pluck'd a hollow reed,

And I made a rural pen,
And I stain'd the water clear,
And I wrote my happy songs
Every child may joy to hear.

The Echoing Green

The Sun does arise,
And make happy the skies;
The merry bells ring
To welcome the Spring;
The skylark and thrush,
The birds of the bush,

Sing louder around
To the bells' cheerful sound,
While our sports shall be seen
On the Echoing Green.

Old John, with white hair,
Does laugh away care,
Sitting under the oak,
Among the old folk.
They laugh at our play,
And soon they all say:
'Such, such were the joys
When we all, girls and boys,
In our youth time were seen
On the Echoing Green.'

Till the little ones, weary,
No more can be merry;
The sun does descend,
And our sports have an end.
Round the laps of their mothers
Many sisters and brothers,
Like birds in their nest,
Are ready for rest,
And sport no more seen
On the darkening Green.

The Lamb

Little Lamb, who made thee?
Dost thou know who made thee?
Gave thee life, and bid thee feed,
By the stream and o'er the mead;
Gave thee clothing of delight,
Softest clothing, woolly, bright;
Gave thee such a tender voice,
Making all the vales rejoice?
Little Lamb, who made thee?
Dost thou know who made thee?

Little Lamb, I'll tell thee,
Little Lamb, I'll tell thee:
He is callèd by thy name,
For he calls himself a Lamb.
He is meek, and he is mild;
He became a little child.
I a child, and thou a lamb,
We are callèd by his name.
Little Lamb, God bless thee!
Little Lamb, God bless thee!

The Shepherd

How sweet is the Shepherd's sweet lot!
From the morn to the evening he strays;
He shall follow his sheep all the day,
And his tongue shall be fillèd with praise.

For he hears the lamb's innocent call,
And he hears the ewe's tender reply;
He is watchful while they are in peace,
For they know when their Shepherd is nigh.

Infant Joy

'I have no name:
I am but two days old.'
What shall I call thee?
'I happy am,
Joy is my name.'
Sweet joy befall thee!

Pretty Joy!
Sweet Joy, but two days old.
Sweet Joy I call thee
Thou dost smile,
I sing the while,
Sweet joy befall thee!

The Little Black Boy

My mother bore me in the southern wild,
And I am black, but O! my soul is white;
White as an angel is the English child,
But I am black, as if bereav'd of light.

My mother taught me underneath a tree,
And, sitting down before the heat of day,
She took me on her lap and kissèd me,
And, pointing to the east, began to say:

'Look on the rising sun, – there God does live,
And gives his light, and gives his heat away;
And flowers and trees and beasts and men receive
Comfort in morning, joy in the noonday.

'And we are put on earth a little space,
That we may learn to bear the beams of love;
And these black bodies and this sunburnt face
Is but a cloud, and like a shady grove,

'For when our souls have learn'd the heat to bear,
The cloud will vanish; we shall hear his voice,
Saying: "Come out from the grove, my love and care,
And round my golden tent like lambs rejoice." '

Thus did my mother say, and kissèd me;
And thus I say to little English boy.
When I from black and he from white cloud free,
And round the tent of God like lambs we joy,

I'll shade him from the heat, till he can bear
To lean in joy upon our Father's knee;
And then I'll stand and stroke his silver hair,
And be like him, and he will then love me.

Laughing Song

When the green woods laugh with the voice of joy,
And the dimpling stream runs laughing by;
When the air does laugh with our merry wit,
And the green hill laughs with the noise of it;

When the meadows laugh with lively green,
And the grasshopper laughs in the merry scene,
When Mary and Susan and Emily
With their sweet round mouths sing 'Ha, Ha, He!'

When the painted birds laugh in the shade,
Where our table with cherries and nuts is spread,
Come live, and be merry, and join with me,
To sing the sweet chorus of 'Ha, Ha, He!'

Spring

Sound the flute!
Now it's mute.
Birds delight
Day and night;
Nightingale
In the dale,
Lark in sky,
Merrily,
Merrily, merrily, to welcome in the year.

Little boy,
Full of joy;
Little girl,
Sweet and small;
Cock does crow,
So do you;
Merry voice,
Infant noise,
Merrily, merrily, to welcome in the year.

Little lamb,
Here I am;
Come and lick
My white neck;
Let me pull
Your soft wool;
Let me kiss
Your soft face:
Merrily, merrily, we welcome in the year.

A Cradle Song

Sweet dreams, form a shade
O'er my lovely infant's head;
Sweet dreams of pleasant streams
By happy, silent, moony beams.

Sweet sleep, with soft down
Weave thy brows an infant crown.
Sweet sleep, Angel mild,
Hover o'er my happy child.

Sweet smiles, in the night
Hover over my delight;
Sweet smiles, mother's smiles,
All the livelong night beguiles.

Sweet moans, dovelike sighs,
Chase not slumber from thy eyes.
Sweet moans, sweeter smiles,
All the dovelike moans beguiles.

Sleep, sleep, happy child,
All creation slept and smil'd;
Sleep, sleep, happy sleep,
While o'er thee thy mother weep.

Sweet babe, in thy face
Holy image I can trace.
Sweet babe, once like thee,
Thy Maker lay and wept for me,

Wept for me, for thee, for all,
When he was an infant small.
Thou his image ever see,
Heavenly face that smiles on thee,

Smiles on thee, on me, on all;
Who became an infant small.
Infant smiles are his own smiles;
Heaven and earth to peace beguiles.

Nurse's Song

When the voices of children are heard on the green,
And laughing is heard on the hill,
My heart is at rest within my breast,
And everything else is still.

'Then come home, my children, the sun is gone down,
And the dews of night arise;
Come, come leave off play, and let us away
Till the morning appears in the skies.'

'No, no, let us play, for it is yet day,
And we cannot go to sleep;
Besides, in the sky the little birds fly,
And the hills are all cover'd with sheep.'

'Well, well, go and play till the light fades away,
And then go home to bed.'
The little ones leapèd and shoutèd and laugh'd
And all the hills echoèd.

Holy Thursday [6]

'Twas on a Holy Thursday, their innocent faces clean,
The children walking two and two, in red and blue and green,
Grey-headed beadles walk'd before, with wands as white as snow,
Till into the high dome of Paul's they like Thames' waters flow.

O what a multitude they seem'd, these flowers of London town!
Seated in companies they sit with radiance all their own.
The hum of multitudes was there, but multitudes of lambs,
Thousands of little boys and girls raising their innocent hands.

Now like a mighty wind they raise to Heaven the voice of song,
Or like harmonious thunderings the seats of Heaven among.
Beneath them sit the aged men, wise guardians of the poor;
Then cherish pity, lest you drive an angel from your door.

The Blossom

Merry, merry sparrow!
Under leaves so green,
A happy blossom
Sees you, swift as arrow,
Seek your cradle narrow
Near my bosom.

Pretty, pretty robin!
Under leaves so green,
A happy blossom
Hears you sobbing, sobbing,
Pretty, pretty robin,
Near my bosom.

The Chimney Sweeper [7]

When my mother died I was very young,
And my father sold me while yet my tongue
Could scarcely cry ' 'weep! 'weep! 'weep! 'weep!'
So your chimneys I sweep, and in soot I sleep.

There's little Tom Dacre, who cried when his head,
That curl'd like a lamb's back, was shav'd: so I said
'Hush, Tom! never mind it, for when your head's bare
You know that the soot cannot spoil your white hair.'

And so he was quiet, and that very night,
As Tom was a-sleeping, he had such a sight! –
That thousands of sweepers, Dick, Joe, Ned, and Jack,
Were all of them lock'd up in coffins of black.

And by came an Angel who had a bright key,
And he open'd the coffins and set them all free;
Then down a green plain leaping, laughing, they run,
And wash in a river, and shine in the sun.

Then naked and white, all their bags left behind,
They rise upon clouds and sport in the wind;
And the Angel told Tom, if he'd be a good boy,
He'd have God for his father, and never want joy.

And so Tom awoke; and we rose in the dark,
And got with our bags and our brushes to work.
Tho' the morning was cold, Tom was happy and warm;
So if all do their duty they need not fear harm.

The Divine Image [8]

To Mercy, Pity, Peace, and Love
All pray in their distress;
And to these virtues of delight
Return their thankfulness.

For Mercy, Pity, Peace, and Love
Is God, our Father dear,
And Mercy, Pity, Peace, and Love
Is man, his child and care.

For Mercy has a human heart,
Pity a human face,
And Love, the human form divine,
And Peace, the human dress.

Then every man, of every clime,
That prays in his distress,
Prays to the human form divine,
Love, Mercy, Pity, Peace.

And all must love the human form,
In heathen, Turk, or Jew;
Where Mercy, Love, and Pity dwell
There God is dwelling too.

Night

The sun descending in the west,
The evening star does shine;
The birds are silent in their nest,
And I must seek for mine.
The moon, like a flower,
In heaven's high bower,
With silent delight
Sits and smiles on the night.

Farewell, green fields and happy groves,
Where flocks have took delight.
Where lambs have nibbled, silent moves
The feet of angels bright;
Unseen they pour blessing,
And joy without ceasing,
On each bud and blossom,
And each sleeping bosom.

They look in every thoughtless nest,
Where birds are cover'd warm;
They visit caves of every beast,
To keep them all from harm.
If they see any weeping
That should have been sleeping,
They pour sleep on their head,
And sit down by their bed.

When wolves and tigers howl for prey,
They pitying stand and weep;
Seeking to drive their thirst away,
And keep them from the sheep.
But if they rush dreadful,
The angels, most heedful,
Receive each mild spirit,
New worlds to inherit.

And there the lion's ruddy eyes
Shall flow with tears of gold,
And pitying the tender cries,
And walking round the fold,
Saying 'Wrath, by His meekness,
And, by His health, sickness
Is driven away
From our immortal day.

'And now beside thee, bleating lamb,
I can lie down and sleep;
Or think on Him who bore thy name,
Graze after thee and weep.

For, wash'd in life's river.
My bright mane for ever
Shall shine like the gold
As I guard o'er the fold.'

A Dream

Once a dream did weave a shade
O'er my Angel-guarded bed,
That an emmet lost its way
Where on grass methought I lay.

Troubled, 'wilder'd, and forlorn,
Dark, benighted, travel-worn,
Over many a tangled spray,
All heart-broke I heard her say:

'O, my children! do they cry?
Do they hear their father sigh?
Now they look abroad to see:
Now return and weep for me.'

Pitying, I dropp'd a tear;
But I saw a glow-worm near,
Who replied: 'What wailing wight
Calls the watchman of the night?

'I am set to light the ground,
While the beetle goes his round:
Follow now the beetle's hum;
Little wanderer, hie thee home.'

On Another's Sorrow

Can I see another's woe,
And not be in sorrow too?
Can I see another's grief,
And not seek for kind relief?

Can I see a falling tear,
And not feel my sorrow's share?
Can a father see his child
Weep, nor be with sorrow fill'd?

Can a mother sit and hear
An infant groan, an infant fear?
No, no! never can it be!
Never, never can it be!

And can He who smiles on all
Hear the wren with sorrows small,
Hear the small bird's grief and care,
Hear the woes that infants bear,

And not sit beside the nest,
Pouring pity in their breast;
And not sit the cradle near,
Weeping tear on infant's tear;

And not sit both night and day,
Wiping all our tears away?
O, no! never can it be!
Never, never can it be!

He doth give His joy to all;
He becomes an infant small;
He becomes a man of woe;
He doth feel the sorrow too.

Think not thou canst sigh a sigh,
And thy Maker is not by;
Think not thou canst weep a tear,
And thy Maker is not near.

O! He gives to us His joy
That our grief He may destroy;
Till our grief is fled and gone
He doth sit by us and moan.

The Little Boy Lost

'Father! father! where are you going?
O do not walk so fast.
Speak, father, speak to your little boy,
Or else I shall be lost.'

The night was dark, no father was there;
The child was wet with dew;
The mire was deep, and the child did weep,
And away the vapour flew.

The Little Boy Found

The little boy lost in the lonely fen,
Led by the wand'ring light,
Began to cry; but God, ever nigh,
Appear'd like his father, in white.

He kissèd the child, and by the hand led,
And to his mother brought,
Who in sorrow pale, thro' the lonely dale,
Her little boy weeping sought.

SONGS OF EXPERIENCE

Introduction

Hear the voice of the Bard!
Who present, past, and future, sees;
Whose ears have heard
The Holy Word
That walk'd among the ancient trees,

Calling the lapsèd soul,
And weeping in the evening dew;
That might control
The starry pole,
And fallen, fallen light renew!

'O Earth, O Earth, return!
Arise from out the dewy grass;
Night is worn,
And the morn
Rises from the slumberous mass.

'Turn away no more;
Why wilt thou turn away.
The starry floor,
The wat'ry shore,
Is giv'n thee till the break of day.'

Earth's Answer

Earth rais'd up her head
From the darkness dread and drear.
Her light fled,
Stony dread!
And her locks cover'd with grey despair.

'Prison'd on wat'ry shore,
Starry Jealousy does keep my den:
Cold and hoar,
Weeping o'er,
I hear the Father of the Ancient Men.

'Selfish Father of Men!
Cruel, jealous, selfish Fear!
Can delight,
Chain'd in night,
The virgins of youth and morning bear?

'Does spring hide its joy
When buds and blossoms grow?
Does the sower
Sow by night,
Or the ploughman in darkness plough?

'Break this heavy chain
That does freeze my bones around.
Selfish! vain!
Eternal bane!
That free Love with bondage bound.'

Nurse's Song

When the voices of children are heard on the green
And whisp'rings are in the dale,
The days of my youth rise fresh in my mind,
My face turns green and pale.

Then come home, my children, the sun is gone down,
And the dews of night arise;
Your spring and your day are wasted in play,
And your winter and night in disguise.

The Fly

Little Fly,
Thy summer's play
My thoughtless hand
Has brush'd away.

Am not I
A fly like thee?
Or art not thou
A man like me?

For I dance,
And drink, and sing,
Till some blind hand
Shall brush my wing.

If thought is life
And strength and breath,
And the want
Of thought is death;

Then am I
A happy fly,
If I live
Or if I die.

The Tiger

Tiger! Tiger! burning bright
In the forests of the night,
What immortal hand or eye
Could frame thy fearful symmetry?

In what distant deeps or skies
Burnt the fire of thine eyes?
On what wings dare he aspire?
What the hand dare seize the fire?

And what shoulder, and what art,
Could twist the sinews of thy heart?
And when thy heart began to beat,
What dread hand? and what dread feet?

What the hammer? what the chain?
In what furnace was thy brain?
What the anvil? what dread grasp
Dare its deadly terrors clasp?

When the stars threw down their spears,
And water'd heaven with their tears,
Did he smile his work to see?
Did he who made the Lamb make thee?

Tiger! Tiger! burning bright
In the forests of the night,
What immortal hand or eye,
Dare frame thy fearful symmetry?

The Little Girl Lost

In futurity
I prophetic see
That the earth from sleep
(Grave the sentence deep)

Shall arise and seek
For her Maker meek;
And the desert wild
Become a garden mild.

In the southern clime,
Where the summer's prime
Never fades away,
Lovely Lyca lay.

Seven summers old
Lovely Lyca told;
She had wander'd long
Hearing wild birds' song.

'Sweet sleep, come to me
Underneath this tree.
Do father, mother, weep?
Where can Lyca sleep?

'Lost in desert wild
Is your little child.
How can Lyca sleep
If her mother weep?

'If her heart does ache
Then let Lyca wake;
If my mother sleep,
Lyca shall not weep.

'Frowning, frowning night,
O'er this desert bright,
Let thy moon arise
While I close my eyes.'

Sleeping Lyca lay
While the beasts of prey,
Come from caverns deep,
View'd the maid asleep.

The kingly lion stood,
And the virgin view'd,
Then he gamboll'd round
O'er the hallow'd ground.

Leopards, tigers, play
Round her as she lay,
While the lion old
Bow'd his mane of gold

And her bosom lick,
And upon her neck
From his eyes of flame
Ruby tears there came;

While the lioness
Loos'd her slender dress,
And naked they convey'd
To caves the sleeping maid.

The Little Girl Found

All the night in woe
Lyca's parents go
Over valleys deep,
While the deserts weep.

Tired and woe-begone,
Hoarse with making moan,
Arm in arm seven days
They trac'd the desert ways.

Seven nights they sleep
Among shadows deep,
And dream they see their child
Starv'd in desert wild.

Pale, thro' pathless ways
The fancied image strays
Famish'd, weeping, weak,
With hollow piteous shriek.

Rising from unrest,
The trembling woman prest
With feet of weary woe:
She could no further go.

In his arms he bore
Her, arm'd with sorrow sore;
Till before their way
A couching lion lay.

Turning back was vain:
Soon his heavy mane

Bore them to the ground.
Then he stalk'd around,

Smelling to his prey;
But their fears allay
When he licks their hands,
And silent by them stands.

They look upon his eyes
Fill'd with deep surprise;
And wondering behold
A spirit arm'd in gold.

On his head a crown;
On his shoulders down
Flow'd his golden hair.
Gone was all their care.

'Follow me,' he said;
'Weep not for the maid;
In my palace deep
Lyca lies asleep.'

Then they followèd
Where the vision led,
And saw their sleeping child
Among tigers wild.

To this day they dwell
In a lonely dell;
Nor fear the wolfish howl
Nor the lions' growl.

The Clod and the Pebble

'Love seeketh not itself to please,
Nor for itself hath any care,
But for another gives its ease,
And builds a Heaven in Hell's despair.'

So sang a little Clod of Clay,
Trodden with the cattle's feet,
But a Pebble of the brook
Warbled out these metres meet:

'Love seeketh only Self to please,
To bind another to its delight,
Joys in another's loss of ease,
And builds a Hell in Heaven's despite.'

The Little Vagabond

Dear mother, dear mother, the Church is cold,
But the Ale-house is healthy and pleasant and warm;
Besides I can tell where I am used well,
Such usage in Heaven will never do well.

But if at the Church they would give us some ale,
And a pleasant fire our souls to regale,
We'd sing and we'd pray all the livelong day,
Nor ever once wish from the Church to stray.

Then the Parson might preach, and drink, and sing,
And we'd be as happy as birds in the spring;
And modest Dame Lurch, who is always at church,
Would not have bandy children, nor fasting, nor birch.

And God, like a father, rejoicing to see
His children as pleasant and happy as he,
Would have no more quarrel with the Devil or the barrel,
But kiss him, and give him both drink and apparel.

Holy Thursday

Is this a holy thing to see
In a rich and fruitful land,
Babes reduc'd to misery,
Fed with cold and usurous hand?

Is that trembling cry a song?
Can it be a song of joy?
And so many children poor?
It is a land of poverty!

And their sun does never shine,
And their fields are bleak and bare,
And their ways are fill'd with thorns:
It is eternal winter there.

For where'er the sun does shine,
And where'er the rain does fall,
Babe can never hunger there,
Nor poverty the mind appal.

A Poison Tree

I was angry with my friend:
I told my wrath, my wrath did end.
I was angry with my foe:
I told it not, my wrath did grow.

And I water'd it in fears,
Night and morning with my tears;
And I sunnèd it with smiles,
And with soft deceitful wiles.

And it grew both day and night,
Till it bore an apple bright;
And my foe beheld it shine,
And he knew that it was mine,

And into my garden stole
When the night had veil'd the pole:
In the morning glad I see
My foe outstretch'd beneath the tree.

The Angel

I dreamt a dream! what can it mean?
And that I was a maiden Queen,
Guarded by an Angel mild:
Witless woe was ne'er beguil'd!

And I wept both night and day,
And he wip'd my tears away,
And I wept both day and night,
And hid from him my heart's delight.

So he took his wings and fled;
Then the morn blush'd rosy red;
I dried my tears, and arm'd my fears
With ten thousand shields and spears.

Soon my Angel came again:
I was arm'd, he came in vain;
For the time of youth was fled,
And grey hairs were on my head.

The Sick Rose

O Rose, thou art sick!
The invisible worm,
That flies in the night,
In the howling storm,

Has found out thy bed
Of crimson joy;
And his dark secret love
Does thy life destroy.

To Tirzah

Whate'er is born of mortal birth
Must be consumèd with the earth,
To rise from generation free:
Then what have I to do with thee?

The sexes sprung from shame and pride,
Blow'd in the morn; in evening died;
But Mercy chang'd death into sleep;
The sexes rose to work and weep.

Thou, Mother of my mortal part,
With cruelty didst mould my heart,
And with false self-deceiving tears
Didst bind my nostrils, eyes, and ears;

Didst close my tongue in senseless clay,
And me to mortal life betray:
The death of Jesus set me free:
Then what have I to do with thee?

The Voice of the Ancient Bard

Youth of delight, come hither,
And see the opening morn,
Image of truth new-born.
Doubt is fled, and clouds of reason,
Dark disputes and artful teasing.
Folly is an endless maze,
Tangled roots perplex her ways.
How many have fallen there!
They stumble all night over bones of the dead,
And feel they know not what but care,
And wish to lead others, when they should be led.

My Pretty Rose-Tree

A flower was offer'd to me,
Such a flower as May never bore;
But I said 'I've a pretty Rose-tree,'
And I passed the sweet flower o'er.

Then I went to my pretty Rose-tree,
To tend her by day and by night,
But my Rose turn'd away with jealousy,
And her thorns were my only delight.

Ah! Sun-Flower

Ah, Sun-flower! weary of time,
Who countest the steps of the sun;
Seeking after that sweet golden clime,
Where the traveller's journey is done;

Where the Youth pined away with desire,
And the pale Virgin shrouded in snow,
Arise from their graves, and aspire
Where my Sun-flower wishes to go.

The Lily

The modest Rose puts forth a thorn,
The humble Sheep a threat'ning horn;
While the Lily white shall in love delight,
Nor a thorn, nor a threat, stain her beauty bright.

The Garden of Love

I went to the Garden of Love,
And saw what I never had seen:
A Chapel was built in the midst,
Where I used to play on the green.

And the gates of this Chapel were shut,
And 'Thou shalt not' writ over the door;
So I turn'd to the Garden of Love
That so many sweet flowers bore;

And I saw it was fillèd with graves,
And tomb-stones where flowers should be;
And priests in black gowns were walking their rounds,
And binding with briars my joys and desires.

A Little Boy Lost

'Nought loves another as itself,
Nor venerates another so,
Nor is it possible to Thought
A greater than itself to know:

'And, Father, how can I love you
Or any of my brothers more?
I love you like the little bird
That picks up crumbs around the door.'

The Priest sat by and heard the child,
In trembling zeal he seiz'd his hair:
He led him by his little coat,
And all admir'd the priestly care.

And standing on the altar high,
'Lo! what a fiend is here,' said he,
'One who sets reason up for judge
Of our most holy Mystery.'

The weeping child could not be heard,
The weeping parents wept in vain;
They stripp'd him to his little shirt,
And bound him in an iron chain;

And burn'd him in a holy place,
Where many had been burn'd before:
The weeping parents wept in vain.
Are such things done on Albion's shore?

Infant Sorrow

My mother groan'd, my father wept,
Into the dangerous world I leapt;
Helpless, naked, piping loud,
Like a fiend hid in a cloud.

Struggling in my father's hands,
Striving against my swaddling-bands,
Bound and weary, I thought best
To sulk upon my mother's breast.

The Schoolboy [9]

I love to rise in a summer morn
When the birds sing on every tree;
The distant huntsman winds his horn,
And the skylark sings with me.
O! what sweet company.

But to go to school in a summer morn,
O! it drives all joy away;
Under a cruel eye outworn,
The little ones spend the day
In sighing and dismay.

Ah! then at times I drooping sit,
And spend many an anxious hour,
Nor in my book can I take delight,
Nor sit in learning's bower,
Worn thro' with the dreary shower.

How can the bird that is born for joy
Sit in a cage and sing?
How can a child, when fears annoy,
But droop his tender wing,
And forget his youthful spring?

O! father and mother, if buds are nipp'd
And blossoms blown away,
And if the tender plants are stripp'd
Of their joy in the springing day,
By sorrow and care's dismay,

How shall the summer arise in joy,
Or the summer fruits appear?
Or how shall we gather what griefs destroy,
Or bless the mellowing year,
When the blasts of winter appear?

London

I wander thro' each charter'd street,
Near where the charter'd[10] Thames does flow,
And mark in every face I meet
Marks of weakness, marks of woe.

In every cry of every Man,
In every Infant's cry of fear,
In every voice, in every ban,[11]
The mind-forg'd manacles I hear.

How the chimney-sweeper's cry
Every black'ning church appals;
And the hapless soldier's sigh
Runs in blood down palace walls.

But most thro' midnight streets I hear
How the youthful harlot's curse
Blasts the new-born infant's tear,
And blights with plagues the marriage hearse.

A Little Girl Lost

Children of the future age,
Reading this indignant page,
Know that in a former time,
Love, sweet Love, was thought a crime!

In the Age of Gold,
Free from winter's cold,
Youth and maiden bright
To the holy light,
Naked in the sunny beams delight.

Once a youthful pair,
Fill'd with softest care,
Met in garden bright
Where the holy light
Had just remov'd the curtains of the night.

There, in rising day,
On the grass they play;
Parents were afar,
Strangers came not near,
And the maiden soon forgot her fear.

Tired with kisses sweet,
They agree to meet
When the silent sleep
Waves o'er heaven's deep,
And the weary tired wanderers weep.

To her father white
Came the maiden bright;
But his loving look,
Like the holy book,
All her tender limbs with terror shook.

'Ona! pale and weak!
To thy father speak:
O! the trembling fear.
O! the dismal care,
That shakes the blossoms of my hoary hair!'

The Chimney Sweeper

A little black thing among the snow,
Crying ' 'weep! 'weep!' in notes of woe!
'Where are thy father and mother, say?' –
'They are both gone up to the Church to pray.

'Because I was happy upon the heath,
And smil'd among the winter's snow,
They clothed me in the clothes of death,
And taught me to sing the notes of woe.

'And because I am happy and dance and sing,
They think they have done me no injury,
And are gone to praise God and His Priest and King,
Who make up a Heaven of our misery.'

The Human Abstract

Pity would be no more
If we did not make somebody poor;
And Mercy no more could be
If all were as happy as we.

And mutual fear brings peace,
Till the selfish loves increase;
Then Cruelty knits a snare,
And spreads his baits with care.

He sits down with holy fears,
And waters the ground with tears;
Then Humility takes its root
Underneath his foot.

Soon spreads the dismal shade
Of Mystery over his head;
And the caterpillar and fly
Feed on the Mystery.

And it bears the fruit of Deceit,
Ruddy and sweet to eat;
And the raven his nest has made
In its thickest shade.

The Gods of the earth and sea
Sought thro' Nature to find this tree;
But their search was all in vain:
There grows one in the Human brain.

Appendix to
SONGS OF INNOCENCE AND EXPERIENCE

A Divine Image

Cruelty has a human heart,
And Jealousy a human face;
Terror the human form divine,
And Secrecy the human dress.

The human dress is forgèd iron,
The human form a fiery forge,
The human face a furnace seal'd,
The human heart its hungry gorge.

THE ROSSETTI MANUSCRIPT

Poems from *The Rossetti Manuscript* (1793–1818) Blake's notebook contained sketches for poems that found their way into later works such as *Songs of Innocence and Experience*, but it also contains little gems which Blake never published or printed. Recurrent themes include critiques of possessive love, hypocrisy and the blighting of freedom, all summed up in Nobodaddy (pp. 100, p. 103 and p. 107), a figure resembling the restrictive tyrant Urizen who enforces laws on the free human spirit.

The poems from the later parts of the notebook are some of Blake's most intriguing and powerful. 'I saw a monk of Charlemaine' (pp. 109–10) contains his searing indictment of the cycles of violence he later expands in his prophetic works. 'My spectre round me . . . ' (pp. 105–7) introduces Blake's view of the psyche split by experience between the tyrannous, aggressive male spectre and the willful female emanation. 'Mock on, mock on . . . ' (p. 108) contrasts the limited rationalism Blake associated with Voltaire, Rousseau and Newton against his own visionary faculties. Many of the notebook poems go through various drafts. 'The Everlasting Gospel' (pp. 117–25) is one such, and in some of his most challenging and subversive writing, Blake unfolds a tapestry of variations elaborating his ideas in different directions, all urging the need to see beyond the limits of the material and orthodox moral 'eye' by using the visionary eye of divine humanity:

> This life's five windows of the soul
> Distorts the Heavens from pole to pole,
> And leads you to believe a lie
> When you see with, not thro', the eye.　　　　　(p. 121)

In this poem's 'gnomic clarity', as E. P. Thompson puts it, Blake 'reasserted the values, the almost-Antinomian affirmation of the joy of sexuality, and the affirmation of innocence, which were present in his earlier songs. Almost every line may be seen as a declaration of "mental war" against Methodism and Evangelicalism' (Thompson, p. 411). For Blake, Christ was a rebel and revolutionary, not an enforcer of conventional moral law; and he was a human being, proving that humanity itself is divine:

> Thou art a Man: God is no more:
> Thy own Humanity learn to adore.   (pp. 120–1)

'The naked Human Form Divine' is 'Love's temple that God dwelleth in' (p. 124), and only made shameful by the hypocrisies of deceit, secrecy and moral repression. In supplementary passages to the poem, not printed here, Blake prepares the way for the main theme of his last great long poem, *Jerusalem*: 'Forgiveness of Sins. This alone is the Gospel [. . .] if you Avenge, you Murder the Divine Image' (Keynes, p. 757). The subversiveness of this message of mutual acceptance and forgiveness in contrast to the accusatory orthodox 'Moral Virtues' is made clear in a verse fragment that follows:

> The Christian trumpets loud proclaim
> Thro' all the World in Jesus' name
> Mutual forgiveness of each Vice,
> And oped the Gates of Paradise.
> The Moral Virtues in Great fear
> Formed the Cross and Nails and Spear,
> And the Accuser standing by
> Cried out, 'Crucify! Crucify!
> Our moral Virtues ne'er can be,
> Nor Warlike Pomp and Majesty;
> For Moral Virtues all begin
> In the Accusations of Sin [. . .]'

> (Keynes, pp. 758–9)

As *The Marriage of Heaven and Hell* proposes, 'Prisons are built with stones of Law, Brothels with bricks of Religion.' (p. 198)

Poems from
THE ROSSETTI MANUSCRIPT, Part I
Written *circa* 1793

Never seek to tell thy Love

Never seek to tell thy love,
Love that never told can be;
For the gentle wind does move
Silently, invisibly.

I told my love, I told my love,
I told her all my heart;
Trembling, cold, in ghastly fears,
Ah! she doth depart.

Soon as she was gone from me,
A traveller came by,
Silently, invisibly:
He took her with a sigh.

I laid me down upon a Bank

I laid me down upon a bank,
Where Love lay sleeping;
I heard among the rushes dank
Weeping, weeping.

Then I went to the heath and the wild,
To the thistles and thorns of the waste;
And they told me how they were beguil'd,
Driven out, and compell'd to be chaste.

I saw a Chapel all of Gold

I saw a Chapel all of gold
That none did dare to enter in,
And many weeping stood without,
Weeping, mourning, worshipping.

I saw a Serpent rise between
The white pillars of the door,
And he forc'd and forc'd and forc'd;
Down the golden hinges tore,

And along the pavement sweet,
Set with pearls and rubies bright,
All his slimy length he drew,
Till upon the altar white

Vomiting his poison out
On the Bread and on the Wine.
So I turn'd into a sty,
And laid me down among the swine.

I asked a Thief

I askèd a thief to steal me a peach:
He turnèd up his eyes.
I ask'd a lithe lady to lie her down:
Holy and meek, she cries.

As soon as I went
An Angel came:
He wink'd at the thief,
And smil'd at the dame;

And without one word said
Had a peach from the tree,
And still as a maid
Enjoy'd the lady.

I heard an Angel singing

I heard an Angel singing
When the day was springing:
'Mercy, Pity, Peace
Is the world's release.'

Thus he sang all day
Over the new-mown hay,
Till the sun went down,
And haycocks lookèd brown.

I heard a Devil curse
Over the heath and the furze:
'Mercy could be no more
If there was nobody poor,

'And Pity no more could be,
If all were as happy as we.'
At his curse the sun went down,
And the heavens gave a frown.

Down pour'd the heavy rain
Over the new reap'd grain;
And Misery's increase
Is Mercy, Pity, Peace.

A Cradle Song

Sleep! sleep! beauty bright,
Dreaming o'er the joys of night;
Sleep! sleep! in thy sleep
Little sorrows sit and weep.

Sweet Babe, in thy face
Soft desires I can trace,
Secret joys and secret smiles,
Little pretty infant wiles.

As thy softest limbs I feel,
Smiles as of the morning steal
O'er thy cheek, and o'er thy breast
Where thy little heart does rest.

O! the cunning wiles that creep
In thy little heart asleep.
When thy little heart does wake
Then the dreadful lightnings break,

From thy cheek and from thy eye,
O'er the youthful harvests nigh.
Infant wiles and infant smiles
Heaven and Earth of peace beguiles.

Silent, silent Night

Silent, silent Night,
Quench the holy light
Of thy torches bright;

For possess'd of Day,
Thousand spirits stray
That sweet joys betray.

Why should joys be sweet
Usèd with deceit,
Nor with sorrows meet?

But an honest joy
Does itself destroy
For a harlot coy.

I fear'd the fury of my wind

I fear'd the fury of my wind
Would blight all blossoms fair and true;
And my sun it shin'd and shin'd,
And my wind it never blew.

But a blossom fair or true
Was not found on any tree;
For all blossoms grew and grew
Fruitless, false, tho' fair to see.

Infant Sorrow

i

My mother groan'd, my father wept;
Into the dangerous world I leapt,
Helpless, naked, piping loud,
Like a fiend hid in a cloud.

ii

Struggling in my father's hands,
Striving against my swaddling-bands,
Bound and weary, I thought best
To sulk upon my mother's breast.

iii

When I saw that rage was vain,
And to sulk would nothing gain,
Turning many a trick and wile
I began to soothe and smile.

iv

And I sooth'd day after day,
Till upon the ground I stray;
And I smil'd night after night,
Seeking only for delight.

v

And I saw before me shine
Clusters of the wand'ring vine;
And, beyond, a Myrtle-tree
Stretch'd its blossoms out to me.

vi

But a Priest with holy look,
In his hands a holy book,
Pronouncèd curses on his head
Who the fruits or blossoms shed.

vii

I beheld the Priest by night;
He embrac'd my Myrtle bright:
I beheld the Priest by day,
Where beneath my vines he lay.

viii

Like a serpent in the day
Underneath my vines he lay:
Like a serpent in the night
He embrac'd my Myrtle bright.

ix

So I smote him, and his gore
Stain'd the roots my Myrtle bore;
But the time of youth is fled,
And grey hairs are on my head.

Why should I care for the men of Thames

Why should I care for the men of Thames,
Or the cheating waves of charter'd streams;
Or shrink at the little blasts of fear
That the hireling blows into my ear?

Tho' born on the cheating banks of Thames,
Tho' his waters bathèd my infant limbs,
The Ohio shall wash his stains from me:
I was born a slave, but I go to be free!

Thou has a lap full of seed

Thou hast a lap full of seed,
And this is a fine country.
Why dost thou not cast thy seed,
And live in it merrily.

Shall I cast it on the sand
And turn it into fruitful land?
For on no other ground
Can I sow my seed,
Without tearing up
Some stinking weed.

In a Myrtle Shade

Why should I be bound to thee,
O my lovely Myrtle-tree?
Love, free Love, cannot be bound
To any tree that grows on ground.

O! how sick and weary I
Underneath my Myrtle lie;
Like to dung upon the ground,
Underneath my Myrtle bound.

Oft my Myrtle sigh'd in vain
To behold my heavy chain:
Oft my Father saw us sigh,
And laugh'd at our simplicity.

So I smote him, and his gore
Stain'd the roots my Myrtle bore.
But the time of youth is fled,
And grey hairs are on my head.

To my Myrtle

To a lovely Myrtle bound,
Blossoms show'ring all around,
O how sick and weary I
Underneath my Myrtle lie!
Why should I be bound to thee,
O my lovely Myrtle-tree?

To Nobodaddy [12]

Why art thou silent and invisible,
Father of Jealousy?
Why dost thou hide thyself in clouds
From every searching eye?

Why darkness and obscurity
In all thy words and laws,
That none dare eat the fruit but from
The wily Serpent's jaws?
Or is it because secrecy gains females' loud applause?

Are not the joys of morning sweeter

Are not the joys of morning sweeter
Than the joys of night?
And are the vigorous joys of youth
Ashamèd of the light?

Let age and sickness silent rob
The vineyards in the night;
But those who burn with vigorous youth
Pluck fruits before the light.

The Wild Flower's Song

As I wander'd the forest,
The green leaves among,
I heard a Wild Flower
Singing a song.

'I slept in the earth
In the silent night,
I murmur'd my fears
And I felt delight.

'In the morning I went,
As rosy as morn,
To seek for new joy;
But I met with scorn.'

Day

The sun arises in the East,
Cloth'd in robes of blood and gold;
Swords and spears and wrath increas'd
All around his bosom roll'd,
Crown'd with warlike fires and raging desires.

The Fairy

'Come hither, my Sparrows,
My little arrows.
If a tear or a smile
Will a man beguile,
If an amorous delay
Clouds a sunshiny day,
If the step of a foot
Smites the heart to its root,
'Tis the marriage-ring –
Makes each fairy a king.'

So a Fairy sung.
From the leaves I sprung;
He leap'd from the spray
To flee away;
But in my hat caught,
He soon shall be taught.
Let him laugh, let him cry,
He's my Butterfly;
For I've pull'd out the sting
Of the marriage-ring.

Motto to Songs of Innocence and Experience

The Good are attracted by men's perceptions,
And think not for themselves;
Till Experience teaches them to catch
And to cage the fairies and elves.

And then the Knave begins to snarl,
And the Hypocrite to howl;
And all his good friends show their private ends,
And the eagle is known from the owl.

Lafayette [13]

i

'Let the brothels of Paris be openèd
With many an alluring dance,
To awake the physicians thro' the city!'
Said the beautiful Queen of France.

ii

Then old Nobodaddy aloft
Farted and belched and coughed,
And said, 'I love hanging and drawing and quartering
Every bit as well as war and slaughtering.'

iii

Then he swore a great and solemn oath:
'To kill the people I am loath;
But if they rebel they must go to hell:
They shall have a priest and a passing bell.'

iv

The King awoke on his couch of gold,
As soon as he heard these tidings told:
'Arise and come, both fife and drum,
And the famine shall eat both crust and crumb.'

v

The Queen of France just touch'd this globe,
And the pestilence darted from her robe;
But our good Queen quite grows to the ground,
And a great many suckers grow all around.

vi

Fayette beside King Lewis stood;
He saw him sign his hand;
And soon he saw the famine rage
About the fruitful land.

vii

Fayette beheld the Queen to smile
And wink her lovely eye;
And soon he saw the pestilence
From street to street to fly.

viii

Fayette beheld the King and Queen
In curses and iron bound;
But mute Fayette wept tear for tear,
And guarded them around.

ix

Fayette, Fayette, thou'rt bought and sold
And sold is thy happy morrow;
Thou gavest the tears of pity away
In exchange for the tears of sorrow.

x

Who will exchange his own fireside
For the stone of another's door?
Who will exchange his wheaten loaf
For the links of a dungeon-floor?

xi

O who would smile on the wintry seas
And pity the stormy roar?
Or who will exchange his new-born child
For the dog at the wintry door?

Appendix to the Earlier Poems in
THE ROSSETTI MANUSCRIPT

A Fairy skipp'd upon my knee
Singing and dancing merrily;
I said, 'Thou thing of patches, rings,
Pins, necklaces, and such-like things,
Disguiser of the female form,
Thou paltry, gilded, poisonous worm!'
Weeping, he fell upon my thigh,
And thus in tears did soft reply:
'Knowest thou not, O Fairies' lord!
How much by us contemn'd, abhorr'd,
Whatever hides the female form
That cannot bear the mortal storm?
Therefore in pity still we give
Our lives to make the female live;
And what would turn into disease
We turn to what will joy and please.'

Poems from
THE ROSSETTI MANUSCRIPT, Part II
Written *circa* 1800–10

My Spectre around me night and day [14]

i

My Spectre[15] around me night and day
Like a wild beast guards my way;
My Emanation[16] far within
Weeps incessantly for my sin.

ii

A fathomless and boundless deep,
There we wander, there we weep;
On the hungry craving wind
My Spectre follows thee behind.

iii

He scents thy footsteps in the snow,
Wheresoever thou dost go,
Thro' the wintry hail and rain.
When wilt thou return again?

iv

Dost thou not in pride and scorn
Fill with tempests all my morn,
And with jealousies and fears
Fill my pleasant nights with tears?

v

Seven of my sweet loves thy knife
Has bereavèd of their life.
Their marble tombs I built with tears,
And with cold and shuddering fears.

vi

Seven more loves weep night and day
Round the tombs where my loves lay,
And seven more loves attend each night
Around my couch with torches bright.

vii

And seven more loves in my bed
Crown with wine my mournful head,
Pitying and forgiving all
Thy transgressions great and small.

viii

When wilt thou return and view
My loves, and them to life renew?
When wilt thou return and live?
When wilt thou pity as I forgive?'

a

O'er my sins thou sit and moan:
Hast thou no sins of thy own?
O'er my sins thou sit and weep,
And lull thy own sins fast asleep.

b

What transgressions I commit
Are for thy transgressions fit.
They thy harlots, thou their slave;
And my bed becomes their grave.

ix

Never, never, I return:
Still for victory I burn.
Living, thee alone I'll have;
And when dead I'll be thy grave.

x

Thro' the Heaven and Earth and Hell
Thou shalt never, never quell:
I will fly and thou pursue:
Night and morn the flight renew.

c

Poor, pale, pitiable form
That I follow in a storm;
Iron tears and groans of lead
Bind around my aching head.

xi

Till I turn from Female love
And root up the Infernal Grove,
I shall never worthy be
To step into Eternity.

xii

And, to end thy cruel mocks,
Annihilate thee on the rocks,
And another form create
To be subservient to my fate.

xiii

Let us agree to give up love,
And root up the Infernal Grove;
Then shall we return and see
The worlds of happy Eternity.

xiv

And throughout all Eternity
I forgive you, you forgive me.
As our dear Redeemer said:
'This the Wine, and this the Bread.'

When Klopstock[17] *England defied*

When Klopstock England defied,
Uprose William Blake in his pride;
For old Nobodaddy aloft
Farted and belch'd and cough'd;
Then swore a great oath that made Heaven quake,
And call'd aloud to English Blake.
Blake was giving his body ease,
At Lambeth beneath the poplar trees.
From his seat then started he
And turn'd him round three times three.
The moon at that sight blush'd scarlet red,
The stars threw down their cups and fled,
And all the devils that were in hell,

Answerèd with a ninefold yell.
Klopstock felt the intripled turn,
And all his bowels began to churn,
And his bowels turn'd round three times three,
And lock'd in his soul with a ninefold key,
That from his body it ne'er could be parted
Till to the last trumpet it was farted.
Then again old Nobodaddy swore
He ne'er had seen such a thing before,
Since Noah was shut in the ark,
Since Eve first chose her hellfire spark,
Since 'twas the fashion to go naked,
Since the old Anything was created.
And so feeling he begged him to turn again
And ease poor Klopstock's ninefold pain.
From pity then he reddened round
And the spell removed unwound.

If Blake could do this when he rose up from shite,
What might he not do if he sat down to write?

Mock on, mock on, Voltaire, Rousseau [18]

Mock on, mock on, Voltaire, Rousseau;
Mock on, mock on; 'tis all in vain!
You throw the sand against the wind,
And the wind blows it back again.

And every sand becomes a gem
Reflected in the beams divine;
Blown back they blind the mocking eye,
But still in Israel's paths they shine.

The Atoms of Democritus
And Newton's Particles of Light
Are sands upon the Red Sea shore,
Where Israel's tents do shine so bright.

I saw a Monk of Charlemaine

i

I saw a Monk of Charlemaine
Arise before my sight:
I talk'd to the Grey Monk where he stood
In beams of infernal light.

ii

Gibbon[19] arose with a lash of steel,
And Voltaire with a wracking wheel:
The Schools, in clouds of learning roll'd,
Arose with War in iron and gold.

iii

'Thou lazy Monk,' they said afar,
'In vain condemning glorious War,
And in thy cell thou shall ever dwell.
Rise, War, and bind him in his cell!'

iv

The blood red ran from the Grey Monk's side,
His hands and feet were wounded wide,
His body bent, his arms and knees
Like to the roots of ancient trees.

v

'I see, I see,' the Mother said,
'My children will die for lack of bread.
What more has the merciless tyrant said?'
The Monk sat down on her stony bed.

vi

His eye was dry, no tear could flow;
A hollow groan first spoke his woe.
He trembled and shudder'd upon the bed;
At length with a feeble cry he said:

vii

'When God commanded this hand to write
In the studious hours of deep midnight,
He told me that all I wrote should prove
The bane of all that on Earth I love.

viii

'My brother starv'd between two walls;
Thy children's cry my soul appals:
I mock'd at the wrack and griding chain;
My bent body mocks at their torturing pain.

ix

'Thy father drew his sword in the North;
With his thousands strong he is marchèd forth;
Thy brother has armèd himself in steel
To revenge the wrongs thy children feel.

x

'But vain the sword and vain the bow,
They never can work War's overthrow;
The hermit's prayer and the widow's tear
Alone can free the world from fear.

xi

'The hand of Vengeance sought the bed
To which the purple tyrant fled;
The iron hand crush'd the tyrant's head,
And became a tyrant in his stead.

xii

'Until the tyrant himself relent,
The tyrant who first the black bow bent,
Slaughter shall heap the bloody plain:
Resistance and War is the tyrant's gain.

xiii

'But the tear of love – and forgiveness sweet,
And submission to death beneath his feet –
The tear shall melt the sword of steel,
And every wound it has made shall heal.

xiv

'For the tear is an intellectual thing,
And a sigh is the sword of an Angel King,
And the bitter groan of the martyr's woe
Is an arrow from the Almighty's bow.'

Morning

To find the Western path,
Right thro' the Gates of Wrath
I urge my way;
Sweet Mercy leads me on
With soft repentant moan:
I see the break of day.

The war of swords and spears,
Melted by dewy tears,
Exhales on high;
The Sun is freed from fears,
And with soft grateful tears
Ascends the sky.

The Birds

He. Where thou dwellest, in what grove,
Tell me Fair One, tell me Love;
Where thou thy charming nest dost build,
O thou pride of every field!

She. Yonder stands a lonely tree,
There I live and mourn for thee;
Morning drinks my silent tear,
And evening winds my sorrow bear.

He. O thou summer's harmony,
I have liv'd and mourn'd for thee;
Each day I mourn along the wood,
And night hath heard my sorrows loud.

She. Dost thou truly long for me?
And am I thus sweet to thee?
Sorrow now is at an end,
O my Lover and my Friend!

He. Come, on wings of joy we'll fly
To where my bower hangs on high;
Come, and make thy calm retreat
Among green leaves and blossoms sweet.

You don't believe

You don't believe – I won't attempt to make ye:
You are asleep – I won't attempt to wake ye.
Sleep on! sleep on! while in your pleasant dreams
Of Reason you may drink of Life's clear streams.
Reason and Newton, they are quite two things;
For so the swallow and the sparrow sings.

Reason says 'Miracle': Newton says 'Doubt.'
Aye! that's the way to make all Nature out.
'Doubt, doubt, and don't believe without experiment':
That is the very thing that Jesus meant,
When He said 'Only believe! believe and try!
Try, try, and never mind the reason why!'

If it is true what the Prophets write

If it is true, what the Prophets write,
That the heathen gods are all stocks and stones,
Shall we, for the sake of being polite,
Feed them with the juice of our marrow-bones?

And if Bezaleel and Aholiab[20] drew
What the finger of God pointed to their view,
Shall we suffer the Roman and Grecian rods
To compel us to worship them as gods?

They stole them from the temple of the Lord
And worshipp'd them that they might make inspirèd
      art abhorr'd;

The wood and stone were call'd the holy things,
And their sublime intent given to their kings.
All the atonements of Jehovah spurn'd,
And criminals to sacrifices turn'd.

I will tell you what Joseph of Arimathea

I will tell you what Joseph of Arimathea [21]
Said to my Fairy: was not it very queer?
'Pliny and Trajan! [22] What! are you here?
Come before Joseph of Arimathea.
Listen patient, and when Joseph has done,
'Twill make a fool laugh, and a fairy fun.'

Why was Cupid a boy

Why was Cupid a boy,
And why a boy was he?
He should have been a girl,
For aught that I can see.

For he shoots with his bow,
And the girl shoots with her eye,
And they both are merry and glad,
And laugh when we do cry.

And to make Cupid a boy
Was the Cupid girl's mocking plan;
For a boy can't interpret the thing
Till he is become a man.

And then he's so pierc'd with cares,
And wounded with arrowy smarts,
That the whole business of his life
Is to pick out the heads of the darts.

'Twas the Greeks' love of war
Turn'd Love into a boy,
And woman into a statue of stone –
And away fled every joy.

Now Art has lost its mental charms

'Now Art has lost its mental charms
France shall subdue the world in arms.'
So spoke an Angel at my birth;
Then said 'Descend thou upon earth,
Renew the Arts on Britain's shore,
And France shall fall down and adore.
With works of art their armies meet
And War shall sink beneath thy feet.
But if thy nation Arts refuse,
And if they scorn the immortal Muse,
France shall the arts of peace restore
And save thee from the ungrateful shore.'

Spirit who lov'st Britannia's Isle
Round which the fiends of commerce smile –

Cetera desunt

I rose up at the dawn of day

I rose up at the dawn of day –
'Get thee away! get thee away!
Pray'st thou for riches? Away! away!
This is the Throne of Mammon grey.'

Said I: This, sure, is very odd;
I took it to be the Throne of God.
For everything besides I have:
It is only for riches that I can crave.

I have mental joy, and mental health,
And mental friends, and mental wealth;
I've a wife I love, and that loves me;
I've all but riches bodily.

I am in God's presence night and day,
And He never turns His face away;
The accuser of sins by my side doth stand,
And he holds my money-bag in his hand.

For my worldly things God makes him pay,
And he'd pay for more if to him I would pray;
And so you may do the worst you can do;
Be assur'd, Mr Devil, I won't pray to you.

Then if for riches I must not pray,
God knows, I little of prayers need say;
So, as a church is known by its steeple,
If I pray it must be for other people.

He says, if I do not worship him for a God,
I shall eat coarser food, and go worse shod;
So, as I don't value such things as these,
You must do, Mr Devil, just as God please.

The Caverns of the Grave I've seen [23]

The Caverns of the Grave I've seen,
And these I show'd to England's Queen.
But now the Caves of Hell I view,
Who shall I dare to show them to?
What mighty soul in Beauty's form
Shall dauntless view the infernal storm?
Egremont's Countess can control
The flames of Hell that round me roll;
If she refuse, I still go on
Till the Heavens and Earth are gone,
Still admir'd by noble minds,
Follow'd by Envy on the winds,
Re-engrav'd time after time,
Ever in their youthful prime,
My designs unchang'd remain.
Time may rage, but rage in vain.
For above Time's troubled fountains,
On the great Atlantic Mountains,
In my Golden House on high,
There they shine eternally.

Addendum to the Later Poems in the
THE ROSSETTI MANUSCRIPT

To the Queen [24]

The Door of Death is made of gold,
That mortal eyes cannot behold;
But when the mortal eyes are clos'd,
And cold and pale the limbs repos'd,
The soul awakes; and, wond'ring, sees
In her mild hand the golden Keys:
The Grave is Heaven's Golden Gate,
And rich and poor around it wait;
O Shepherdess of England's fold,
Behold this Gate of Pearl and Gold!

To dedicate to England's Queen
The visions that my soul has seen,
And, by her kind permission, bring
What I have borne on solemn wing,
From the vast regions of the Grave,
Before her throne my wings I wave;
Bowing before my Sov'reign's feet,
'The Grave produc'd these blossoms sweet
In mild repose from earthly strife;
The blossoms of Eternal Life!'

Poem from
THE ROSSETTI MANUSCRIPT, Part III
Written *circa* 1818

The Everlasting Gospel [25]

α

The Vision of Christ that thou dost see
Is my vision's greatest enemy.
Thine has a great hook nose like thine,
Mine has a snub nose like to mine.
Thine is the Friend of all Mankind;
Mine speaks in parables to the blind.
Thine loves the same world that mine hates;
Thy heaven doors are my hell gates.
Socrates taught what Meletus [26]
Loath'd as a nation's bitterest curse,
And Caiaphas [27] was in his own mind
A benefactor to mankind.
Both read the Bible day and night,
But thou read'st black where I read white.

β

Was Jesus gentle, or did He
Give any marks of gentility?
When twelve years old He ran away,
And left His parents in dismay.
When after three days' sorrow found,
Loud as Sinai's [28] trumpet-sound:
'No earthly parents I confess –
My Heavenly Father's business!
Ye understand not what I say,
And, angry, force Me to obey.
Obedience is a duty then,
And favour gains with God and men.
John from the wilderness loud cried;
Satan gloried in his pride.

'Come,' said Satan, 'come away,
I'll soon see if you'll obey!
John for disobedience bled,
But you can turn the stones to bread.
God's high king and God's high priest
Shall plant their glories in your breast,
If Caiaphas you will obey,
If Herod you with bloody prey
Feed with the sacrifice, and be
Obedient, fall down, worship me.'
Thunders and lightnings broke around,
And Jesus' voice in thunders' sound:
'Thus I seize the spiritual prey.
Ye smiters with disease, make way.
I come your King and God to seize,
Is God a smiter with disease?'
The God of this world rag'd in vain:
He bound old Satan in His chain,
And, bursting forth, His furious ire
Became a chariot of fire.
Throughout the land He took His course,
And trac'd diseases to their source.
He curs'd the Scribe and Pharisee,
Trampling down hypocrisy.
Where'er His chariot took its way,
There Gates of Death let in the Day,
Broke down from every chain and bar;
And Satan in His spiritual war
Dragg'd at His chariot-wheels: loud howl'd
The God of this world: louder roll'd
The chariot-wheels, and louder still
His voice was heard from Zion's Hill,
And in His hand the scourge shone bright;
He scourg'd the merchant Canaanite
From out the Temple of His Mind,
And in his body tight does bind
Satan and all his hellish crew;
And thus with wrath He did subdue
The serpent bulk of Nature's dross,
Till He had nail'd it to the Cross.

He took on sin in the Virgin's womb
And put it off on the Cross and tomb
To be worshipp'd by the Church of Rome.

γ

Was Jesus humble? or did He
Give any proofs of humility?
Boast of high things with humble tone,
And give with charity a stone?
When but a child He ran away,
And left His parents in dismay.
When they had wander'd three days long
These were the words upon His tongue:
'No earthly parents I confess:
I am doing My Father's business.'
When the rich learnèd Pharisee
Came to consult Him secretly,
Upon his heart with iron pen
He wrote, 'Ye must be born again.'
He was too proud to take a bribe;
He spoke with authority, not like a Scribe.
He says with most consummate art,
'Follow Me, I am meek and lowly of heart,
As that is the only way to escape
The miser's net and the glutton's trap.'
What can be done with such desperate fools
Who follow after the heathen schools?
I was standing by when Jesus died;
What I call'd humility, they call'd pride.
He who loves his enemies betrays his friends.
This surely is not what Jesus intends;
But the sneaking pride of heroic schools,
And the Scribes' and Pharisees' virtuous rules,
For He acts with honest, triumphant pride,
And this is the cause that Jesus died.
He did not die with Christian ease,
Asking pardon of His enemies:
If He had, Caiaphas would forgive;
Sneaking submission can always live.
He had only to say that God was the Devil,

And the Devil was God, like a Christian civil;
Mild Christian regrets to the Devil confess
For affronting him thrice in the wilderness;
He had soon been bloody Caesar's elf,
And at last he would have been Caesar himself,
Like Dr Priestly and Bacon and Newton [29] –
Poor spiritual knowledge is not worth a button!
For thus the Gospel Sir Isaac confutes:
'God can only be known by His attributes;
And as for the indwelling of the Holy Ghost,
Or of Christ and His Father, it's all a boast
And pride, and vanity of the imagination,
That disdains to follow this world's fashion.'
To teach doubt and experiment
Certainly was not what Christ meant.
What was He doing all that time,
From twelve years old to manly prime?
Was He then idle, or the less
About His Father's business?
Or was His wisdom held in scorn
Before His wrath began to burn
In miracles throughout the land,
That quite unnerv'd the Seraph band?
If He had been Antichrist, Creeping Jesus,
He'd have done anything to please us;
Gone sneaking into synagogues,
And not us'd the Elders and Priests like dogs;
But humble as a lamb or ass
Obey'd Himself to Caiaphas.
God wants not man to humble himself:
That is the trick of the Ancient Elf.
This is the race that Jesus ran:
Humble to God, haughty to man,
Cursing the Rulers before the people
Even to the Temple's highest steeple,
And when He humbled Himself to God
Then descended the cruel rod.
'If Thou humblest Thyself, Thou humblest Me.
Thou also dwell'st in Eternity.
Thou art a Man: God is no more:

Thy own Humanity learn to adore,
For that is My spirit of life.
Awake, arise to spiritual strife,
And Thy revenge abroad display
In terrors at the last Judgement Day.
God's mercy and long suffering
Is but the sinner to judgement to bring.
Thou on the Cross for them shalt pray –
And take revenge at the Last Day.'
Jesus replied, and thunders hurl'd:
'I never will pray for the world.
Once I did so when I pray'd in the Garden;
I wish'd to take with Me a bodily pardon.'
Can that which was of woman born,
In the absence of the morn,
When the Soul fell into sleep,
And Archangels round it weep,
Shooting out against the light
Fibres of a deadly night,
Reasoning upon its own dark fiction,
In doubt which is self-contradiction?
Humility is only doubt,
And does the sun and moon blot out,
Rooting over with thorns and stems
The buried soul and all its gems.
This life's five windows of the soul
Distorts the Heavens from pole to pole,
And leads you to believe a lie
When you see with, not thro', the eye
That was born in a night, to perish in a night,
When the soul slept in the beams of light.

δ

This was spoken by my Spectre to Voltaire, Bacon, &c.
Did Jesus teach doubt? or did He
Give any lessons of philosophy,
Charge Visionaries with deceiving,
Or call men wise for not believing? . . .

ε

Was Jesus born of a Virgin pure
With narrow soul and looks demure?
If He intended to take on sin
The Mother should an harlot been,
Just such a one as Magdalen,
With seven devils in her pen.
Or were Jew virgins still more curs'd,
And more sucking devils nurs'd?
Or what was it which He took on
That He might bring salvation?
A body subject to be tempted,
From neither pain nor grief exempted;
Or such a body as might not feel
The passions that with sinners deal?
Yes, but they say He never fell.
Ask Caiaphas; for he can tell. –
'He mock'd the Sabbath, and He mock'd
The Sabbath's God, and He unlock'd
The evil spirits from their shrines,
And turn'd fishermen to divines;
O'erturn'd the tent of secret sins,
And its golden cords and pins,
In the bloody shrine of war
Pour'd around from star to star, –
Halls of justice, hating vice,
Where the Devil combs his lice.
He turn'd the devils into swine
That He might tempt the Jews to dine;
Since which, a pig has got a look
That for a Jew may be mistook.
"Obey your parents." – What says He?
"Woman, what have I to do with thee?
No earthly parents I confess:
I am doing My Father's business."
He scorn'd Earth's parents, scorn'd Earth's God,
And mock'd the one and the other's rod;
His seventy Disciples sent
Against Religion and Government –
They by the sword of Justice fell,

And Him their cruel murderer tell.
He left His father's trade to roam,
A wand'ring vagrant without home;
And thus He others' labour stole,
That He might live above control.
The publicans and harlots He
Selected for His company,
And from the adulteress turn'd away
God's righteous law, that lost its prey.'

ζ

Was Jesus chaste? or did He
Give any lessons of chastity?
The Morning blushèd fiery red:
Mary was found in adulterous bed;
Earth groan'd beneath, and Heaven above
Trembled at discovery of Love
Jesus was sitting in Moses' chair.
They brought the trembling woman there.
Moses commands she be ston'd to death.
What was the sound of Jesus' breath?
He laid His hand on Moses' law;
The ancient Heavens, in silent awe,
Writ with curses from pole to pole,
All away began to roll.
The Earth trembling and naked lay
In secret bed of mortal clay;
On Sinai felt the Hand Divine
Pulling back the bloody shrine;
And she heard the breath of God,
As she heard by Eden's flood:
'Good and Evil are no more!
Sinai's trumpets cease to roar!
Cease, finger of God, to write!
The Heavens are not clean in Thy sight.
Thou art good, and Thou alone;
Nor may the sinner cast one stone.
To be good only, is to be
A God or else a Pharisee.
Thou Angel of the Presence Divine,

That didst create this Body of Mine,
Wherefore hast thou writ these laws
And created Hell's dark jaws?
My Presence I will take from thee:
A cold leper thou shalt be.
Tho' thou wast so pure and bright
That Heaven was impure in thy sight,
Tho' thy oath turn'd Heaven pale,
Tho' thy covenant built Hell's jail,
Tho' thou didst all to chaos roll
With the Serpent for its soul,
Still the breath Divine does move,
And the breath Divine is Love.
Mary, fear not! Let me see
The seven devils that torment thee.
Hide not from My sight thy sin,
That forgiveness thou may'st win.
Has no man condemnèd thee?'
'No man, Lord.' 'Then what is he
Who shall accuse thee? Come ye forth,
Fallen fiends of heavenly birth,
That have forgot your ancient love,
And driven away my trembling Dove.
You shall bow before her feet;
You shall lick the dust for meat;
And tho' you cannot love, but hate,
Shall be beggars at Love's gate.
What was thy love? Let Me see it;
Was it love or dark deceit?'
'Love too long from me has fled;
'Twas dark deceit, to earn my bread;
'Twas covet, or 'twas custom, or
Some trifle not worth caring for;
That they may call a shame and sin
Love's temple that God dwelleth in,
And bide in secret hidden shrine
The naked Human Form Divine,
And render that a lawless thing
On which the Soul expands its wing.
But this, O Lord, this was my sin,

When first I let these devils in,
In dark pretence to chastity
Blaspheming Love, blaspheming Thee,
Thence rose secret adulteries,
And thence did covet also rise.
My sin Thou hast forgiven me;
Canst Thou forgive my blasphemy?
Canst Thou return to this dark hell,
And in my burning bosom dwell?
And canst Thou die that I may live?
And canst Thou pity and forgive?'
Then roll'd the shadowy Man away
From the limbs of Jesus, to make them His prey,
An ever devouring appetite,
Glittering with festering venoms bright;
Crying, 'Crucify this cause of distress,
Who don't keep the secrets of holiness!
The mental powers by diseases we bind;
But He heals the deaf, the dumb, and the blind.
Whom God has afflicted for secret ends,
He comforts and heals and calls them friends.'
But, when Jesus was crucified,
Then was perfected His galling pride.
In three nights He devour'd His prey,
And still He devours the body of clay;
For dust and clay is the Serpent's meat,
Which never was made for Man to eat.

η

Seeing this False Christ, in fury and passion
I made my voice heard all over the nation.
What are those . . .

θ

Epilogue
I am sure this Jesus will not do,
Either for Englishman or Jew.

THE PICKERING MANUSCRIPT

Poems from *The Pickering Manuscript* (*c.*1801–3) This notebook contains one of Blake's most famous lines, 'To see a World in a grain of sand', an idea that, in miniature, contains the whole of his work. But the rest of 'Auguries of Innocence' (pp. 135–9) from which the line comes is an equally startling catalogue of Blakean contraries and devilish proverbs. Many of these have a sharp satirical awareness of the social inequalities in an increasingly commercialised society and intensifying market economy:

> The whore and gambler, by the state
> Licensed, build that nation's fate.
> The harlot's cry from street to street
> Shall weave Old England's winding-sheet.
> The winner's shout, the loser's curse,
> Dance before dead England's hearse. (p. 138)

These energetic couplets culminate in a dazzling climax as Blake strips away the layers of religious obfuscation to reveal his clear vision of human divinity:

> God appears, and God is Light,
> To those poor souls who dwell in Night;
> But does a Human Form display
> To those who dwell in realms of Day. (p. 139)

Other poems such as 'The Mental Traveller' (pp. 128–31) present visionary parables of gender warfare and the consequent cycles of violence between the sexes. These poems offer some of Blake's most elusive and disturbing images. In 'The Grey Monk', the possibility of redemption from the cycles of violence through the monk's vision is undercut by the view of the monk himself as ineffectual in the face of the mother's opening cries, while the ending reinstates the cycles of tyranny in terms which recur in Blake's prophetic books as the spirit of revolution becomes distorted into violent oppression:

> 'The hand of Vengeance found the bed
> To which the purple tyrant fled;
> The iron hand crush'd the tyrant's head,
> And became a tyrant in his stead.' (p. 135)

The Smile

There is a smile of love,
And there is a smile of deceit,
And there is a smile of smiles
In which these two smiles meet.

And there is a frown of hate,
And there is a frown of disdain,
And there is a frown of frowns
Which you strive to forget in vain,

For it sticks in the heart's deep core
And it sticks in the deep backbone –
And no smile that ever was smil'd,
But only one smile alone,

That betwixt the cradle and grave
It only once smil'd can be;
And, when it once is smil'd,
There's an end to all misery.

The Golden Net

Three Virgins at the break of day:
'Whither, young man, whither away
Alas for woe! alas for woe!'
They cry, and tears for ever flow.
The one was cloth'd in flames of fire,
The other cloth'd in iron wire,
The other cloth'd in tears and sighs
Dazzling bright before my eyes.
They bore a Net of golden twine
To hang upon the branches fine.
Pitying I wept to see the woe

That Love and Beauty undergo,
To be consum'd in burning fires
And in ungratified desires,
And in tears cloth'd night and day
Melted all my soul away.
When they saw my tears, a smile
That did Heaven itself beguile,
Bore the Golden Net aloft
As on downy pinions soft,
Over the Morning of my day.
Underneath the net I stray,
Now entreating Burning Fire
Now entreating Iron Wire,
Now entreating Tears and Sighs –
O! when will the morning rise?

The Mental Traveller

I travell'd thro' a land of men,
A land of men and women too;
And heard and saw such dreadful things
As cold earth-wanderers never knew.

For there the Babe is born in joy
That was begotten in dire woe;
Just as we reap in joy the fruit
Which we in bitter tears did sow.

And if the Babe is born a boy
He's given to a Woman Old,
Who nails him down upon a rock,
Catches his shrieks in cups of gold.

She binds iron thorns around his head,
She pierces both his hands and feet,
She cuts his heart out at his side,
To make it feel both cold and heat.

Her fingers number every nerve,
Just as a miser counts his gold;
She lives upon his shrieks and cries,
And she grows young as he grows old.

Till he becomes a bleeding Youth,
And she becomes a Virgin bright;
Then he rends up his manacles,
And binds her down for his delight.

He plants himself in all her nerves,
Just as a husbandman his mould;
And she becomes his dwelling-place
And garden fruitful seventyfold.

An agèd Shadow, soon he fades,
Wandering round an earthly cot,
Full fillèd all with gems and gold
Which he by industry had got.

And these are the gems of the human soul,
The rubies and pearls of a love-sick eye,
The countless gold of the aching heart,
The martyr's groan and the lover's sigh.

They are his meat, they are his drink,
He feeds the beggar and the poor
And the wayfaring traveller:
For ever open is his door.

His grief is their eternal joy;
They make the roofs and walls to ring;
Till from the fire on the hearth
A little Female Babe does spring

And she is all of solid fire
And gems and gold, that none his hand
Dares stretch to touch her baby form,
Or wrap her in his swaddling-band.

But she comes to the man she loves,
If young or old, or rich or poor;
They soon drive out the Agèd Host,
A beggar at another's door.

He wanders weeping far away,
Until some other take him in;
Oft blind and age-bent, sore distrest,
Until he can a Maiden win.

And to allay his freezing age,
The poor man takes her in his arms;
The cottage fades before his sight,
The garden and its lovely charms.

The guests are scatter'd thro' the land,
For the eye altering alters all;
The senses roll themselves in fear,
And the flat earth becomes a ball;

The stars, sun, moon, all shrink away,
A desert vast without a bound,
And nothing left to eat or drink,
And a dark desert all around.

The honey of her infant lips,
The bread and wine of her sweet smile,
The wild game of her roving eye,
Does him to infancy beguile;

For as he eats and drinks he grows
Younger and younger every day;
And on the desert wild they both
Wander in terror and dismay.

Like the wild stag she flees away,
Her fear plants many a thicket wild;
While he pursues her night and day,
By various arts of love beguil'd;

By various arts of love and hate,
Till the wide desert planted o'er
With labyrinths of wayward love,
Where roam the lion, wolf, and boar.

Till he becomes a wayward Babe,
And she a weeping Woman Old.
Then many a lover wanders here;
The sun and stars are nearer roll'd;

The trees bring forth sweet ecstasy
To all who in the desert roam;
Till many a city there is built,
And many a pleasant shepherd's home.

But when they find the Frowning Babe,
Terror strikes thro' the region wide:
They cry, 'The Babe! the Babe is born!'
And flee away on every side.

For who dare touch the Frowning Form,
His arm is wither'd to its root;
Lions, boars, wolves, all howling flee,
And every tree does shed its fruit.

And none can touch that Frowning Form,
Except it be a Woman Old;
She nails him down upon the rock,
And all is done as I have told.

The Land of Dreams

Awake, awake, my little boy!
Thou wast thy mother's only joy;
Why dost thou weep in thy gentle sleep?
Awake! thy father does thee keep.

'O, what land is the Land of Dreams?
What are its mountains, and what are its streams?
O father! I saw my mother there,
Among the lilies by waters fair.

'Among the lambs, clothèd in white,
She walk'd with her Thomas in sweet delight.
I wept for joy, like a dove I mourn;
O! when shall I again return?'

Dear child, I also by pleasant streams
Have wander'd all night in the Land of Dreams;
But tho' calm and warm the waters wide,
I could not get to the other side.

'Father, O father! what do we here
In this land of unbelief and fear?
The Land of Dreams is better far,
Above the light of the morning star.'

Mary

Sweet Mary, the first time she ever was there,
Came into the ballroom among the fair;
The young men and maidens around her throng,
And these are the words upon every tongue:

'An Angel is here from the heavenly climes,
Or again does return the golden times;
Her eyes outshine every brilliant ray,
She opens her lips – 'tis the Month of May.'

Mary moves in soft beauty and conscious delight,
To augment with sweet smiles all the joys of the night,
Nor once blushes to own to the rest of the fair
That sweet Love and Beauty are worthy our care.

In the morning the villagers rose with delight,
And repeated with pleasure the joys of the night,
And Mary arose among friends to be free,
But no friend from henceforward thou, Mary, shalt see.

Some said she was proud, some call'd her a whore,
And some, when she passèd by, shut to the door;
A damp cold came o'er her, her blushes all fled;
Her lilies and roses are blighted and shed.

'O, why was I born with a different face?
Why was I not born like this envious race?
Why did Heaven adorn me with bountiful hand,
And then set me down in an envious land?

'To be weak as a lamb and smooth as a dove,
And not to raise envy, is call'd Christian love;
But if you raise envy your merit's to blame
For planting such spite in the weak and the tame.

'I will humble my beauty, I will not dress fine,
I will keep from the ball, and my eyes shall not shine;
And if any girl's lover forsakes her for me
I'll refuse him my hand, and from envy be free.'

She went out in morning attir'd plain and neat;
'Proud Mary's gone mad,' said the child in the street;
She went out in morning in plain neat attire,
And came home in evening bespatter'd with mire.

She trembled and wept, sitting on the bedside,
She forgot it was night, and she trembled and cried;
She forgot it was night, she forgot it was morn,
Her soft memory imprinted with faces of scorn;

With faces of scorn and with eyes of disdain,
Like foul fiends inhabiting Mary's mild brain;
She remembers no face like the Human Divine,
All faces have envy, sweet Mary, but thine;

And thine is a face of sweet love in despair,
And thine is a face of mild sorrow and care,
And thine is a face of wild terror and fear
That shall never be quiet till laid on its bier.

The Crystal Cabinet

The Maiden caught me in the wild,
Where I was dancing merrily;
She put me into her Cabinet,
And lock'd me up with a golden key.

This Cabinet is form'd of gold
And pearl and crystal shining bright,
And within it opens into a world
And a little lovely moony night.

Another England there I saw,
Another London with its Tower,
Another Thames and other hills,
And another pleasant Surrey bower,

Another Maiden like herself,
Translucent, lovely, shining clear,
Threefold each in the other clos'd –
O, what a pleasant trembling fear!

O, what a smile! a threefold smile
Fill'd me, that like a flame I burn'd;
I bent to kiss the lovely Maid,
And found a threefold kiss return'd.

I strove to seize the inmost form
With ardour fierce and hands of flame,
But burst the Crystal Cabinet,
And like a weeping Babe became –

A weeping Babe upon the wild,
And weeping Woman pale reclin'd,
And in the outward air again
I fill'd with woes the passing wind.

The Grey Monk

'I die, I die!' the Mother said,
'My children die for lack of bread.
What more has the merciless tyrant said?'
The Monk sat down on the stony bed.

The blood red ran from the Grey Monk's side,
His hands and feet were wounded wide,
His body bent, his arms and knees
Like to the roots of ancient trees.

His eye was dry; no tear could flow:
A hollow groan first spoke his woe.
He trembled and shudder'd upon the bed;
At length with a feeble cry he said:

'When God commanded this hand to write
In the studious hours of deep midnight,
He told me the writing I wrote should prove
The bane of all that on Earth I love.

'My brother starv'd between two walls,
His children's cry my soul appalls;
I mock'd at the wrack and griding chain,
My bent body mocks their torturing pain.

'Thy father drew his sword in the North,
With his thousands strong he marchèd forth;
Thy brother has arm'd himself in steel,
To avenge the wrongs thy children feel.

'But vain the sword and vain the bow,
They never can work War's overthrow.
The hermit's prayer and the widow's tear
Alone can free the world from fear.

'For a tear is an intellectual thing,
And a sigh is the sword of an Angel King,
And the bitter groan of the martyr's woe
Is an arrow from the Almighty's bow.

'The hand of Vengeance found the bed
To which the purple tyrant fled;
The iron hand crush'd the tyrant's head,
And became a tyrant in his stead.'

Auguries of Innocence [30]

To see a World in a grain of sand,
And a Heaven in a wild flower,
Hold Infinity in the palm of your hand,
And Eternity in an hour.
A robin redbreast in a cage
Puts all Heaven in a rage.
A dove-house fill'd with doves and pigeons

Shudders Hell thro' all its regions.
A dog starv'd at his master's gate
Predicts the ruin of the State.
A horse misus'd upon the road
Calls to Heaven for human blood.
Each outcry of the hunted hare
A fibre from the brain does tear.
A skylark wounded in the wing,
A cherubim does cease to sing.
The game-cock clipt and arm'd for fight
Does the rising sun affright.
Every wolf's and lion's howl
Raises from Hell a Human soul.
The wild deer, wandering here and there,
Keeps the Human soul from care.
The lamb misus'd breeds public strife,
And yet forgives the butcher's knife.
The bat that flits at close of eve
Has left the brain that won't believe.
The owl that calls upon the night
Speaks the unbeliever's fright.
He who shall hurt the little wren
Shall never be belov'd by men.
He who the ox to wrath has mov'd
Shall never be by woman lov'd.
The wanton boy that kills the fly
Shall feel the spider's enmity.
He who torments the chafer's sprite
Weaves a bower in endless night.
The caterpillar on the leaf
Repeats to thee thy mother's grief.
Kill not the moth nor butterfly,
For the Last Judgement draweth nigh.
He who shall train the horse to war
Shall never pass the polar bar.
The beggar's dog and widow's cat,
Feed them, and thou wilt grow fat.
The gnat that sings his summer's song
Poison gets from Slander's tongue.
The poison of the snake and newt

Is the sweat of Envy's foot.
The poison of the honey-bee
Is the artist's jealousy.
The prince's robes and beggar's rags
Are toadstools on the miser's bags.
A truth that's told with bad intent
Beats all the lies you can invent.
It is right it should be so;
Man was made for joy and woe;
And when this we rightly know,
Thro' the world we safely go.
Joy and woe are woven fine,
A clothing for the soul divine;
Under every grief and pine
Runs a joy with silken twine.
The babe is more than swaddling-bands;
Throughout all these human lands
Tools were made, and born were hands,
Every farmer understands.
Every tear from every eye
Becomes a babe in Eternity;
This is caught by Females bright,
And return'd to its own delight.
The bleat, the bark, bellow, and roar
Are waves that beat on Heaven's shore.
The babe that weeps the rod beneath
Writes revenge in realms of death.
The beggar's rags, fluttering in air,
Does to rags the heavens tear.
The soldier, arm'd with sword and gun,
Palsied strikes the summer's sun.
The poor man's farthing is worth more
Than all the gold on Afric's shore.
One mite wrung from the labourer's hands
Shall buy and sell the miser's lands
Or, if protected from on high,
Does that whole nation sell and buy.
He who mocks the infant's faith
Shall be mock'd in Age and Death.
He who shall teach the child to doubt

The rotting grave shall ne'er get out.
He who respects the infant's faith
Triumphs over Hell and Death.
The child's toys and the old man's reasons
Are the fruits of the two seasons.
The questioner, who sits so sly,
Shall never know how to reply.
He who replies to words of Doubt
Doth put the light of knowledge out.
The strongest poison ever known
Came from Caesar's laurel crown.
Nought can deform the human race
Like to the armour's iron brace.
When gold and gems adorn the plough
To peaceful arts shall Envy bow.
A riddle, or the cricket's cry,
Is to Doubt a fit reply.
The emmet's inch and eagle's mile
Make lame Philosophy to smile.
He who doubts from what he sees
Will ne'er believe, do what you please.
If the Sun and Moon should doubt,
They'd immediately go out.
To be in a passion you good may do,
But no good if a passion is in you.
The whore and gambler, by the state
Licensed, build that nation's fate.
The harlot's cry from street to street
Shall weave Old England's winding-sheet.
The winner's shout, the loser's curse,
Dance before dead England's hearse.
Every night and every morn
Some to misery are born.
Every morn and every night
Some are born to sweet delight.
Some are born to sweet delight,
Some are born to endless night.
We are led to believe a lie
When we see not thro' the eye,
Which was born in a night, to perish in a night,

When the Soul slept in beams of light.
God appears, and God is Light,
To those poor souls who dwell in Night;
But does a Human Form display
To those who dwell in realms of Day.

Long John Brown and Little Mary Bell

Little Mary Bell had a Fairy in a nut,
Long John Brown had the Devil in his gut;
Long John Brown lov'd little Mary Bell,
And the Fairy drew the Devil into the nutshell.

Her Fairy skipp'd out and her Fairy skipp'd in;
He laugh'd at the Devil, saying 'Love is a sin.'
The Devil he raged, and the Devil he was wroth,
And the Devil enter'd into the young man's broth.

He was soon in the gut of the loving young swain,
For John ate and drank to drive away love's pain;
But all he could do he grew thinner and thinner,
Tho' he ate and drank as much as ten men for his dinner.

Some said he had a wolf in his stomach day and night,
Some said he had the Devil, and they guess'd right;
The Fairy skipp'd about in his glory, joy and pride,
And he laugh'd at the Devil till poor John Brown died.

Then the Fairy skipp'd out of the old nutshell,
And woe and alack for pretty Mary Bell!
For the Devil crept in when the Fairy skipp'd out,
And there goes Miss Bell with her fusty old nut.

William Bond

I wonder whether the girls are mad,
And I wonder whether they mean to kill,
And I wonder if William Bond will die,
For assuredly he is very ill.

He went to church in a May morning,
Attended by Fairies, one, two, and three;
But the Angels of Providence drove them away,
And he return'd home in misery.

He went not out to the field nor fold,
He went not out to the village nor town,
But he came home in a black, black cloud,
And took to his bed, and there lay down.

And an Angel of Providence at his feet,
And an Angel of Providence at his head,
And in the midst a black, black cloud,
And in the midst the sick man on his bed.

And on his right hand was Mary Green,
And on his left hand was his sister Jane,
And their tears fell thro' the black, black cloud
To drive away the sick man's pain.

'O William, if thou dost another love,
Dost another love better than poor Mary,
Go and take that other to be thy wife,
And Mary Green shall her servant be.'

'Yes, Mary, I do another love,
Another I love far better than thee,
And another I will have for my wife;
Then what have I to do with thee?

'For thou art melancholy pale,
And on thy head is the cold moon's shine,
But she is ruddy and bright as day,
And the sunbeams dazzle from her eyne.'

Mary trembled and Mary chill'd,
And Mary fell down on the right-hand floor,
That William Bond and his sister Jane
Scarce could recover Mary more.

When Mary woke and found her laid
On the right hand of her William dear,
On the right hand of his loved bed,
And saw her William Bond so near,

The Fairies that fled from William Bond
Dancèd around her shining head;
They dancèd over the pillow white,
And the Angels of Providence left the bed.

I thought Love lived in the hot sunshine,
But O, he lives in the moony light!
I thought to find Love in the heat of day,
But sweet Love is the comforter of night.

Seek Love in the pity of others' woe,
In the gentle relief of another's care,
In the darkness of night and the winter's snow,
In the naked and outcast, seek Love there!

POEMS FROM LETTERS

Poems from *Letters* (1800–3)   As we saw in the general introduction, Blake's letters contain some of the most vivid expressions of his visionary capacities. The poems he included in some letters give a further insight, particularly 'With Happiness stretch'd across the hills' ('To Thomas Butts', pp. 146–8). Here Blake undergoes a characteristic Romantic journey from a state of mind in which he is beset by negative thoughts, through a meeting with the spirit of the imagination, to a renewed vision. The 'double vision' to which Blake refers early in the poem (p. 147) is the outer bodily eye and the 'inward eye' of the imagination. By the end this has been enhanced to a 'fourfold vision' (p. 148), embracing all levels of experience, including the cosmic and the sexual (often associated in Blake's work with 'Beulah'). The final prayer is to fend off 'single vision, and Newton's sleep', by which Blake means the purely material vision of the bodily eye with its associations of scientific rationalism and limited perception.

To my dearest Friend, John Flaxman,[31] these lines:

I bless thee, O Father of Heaven and Earth! that ever I saw
                                   Flaxman's face:
Angels stand round my spirit in Heaven; the blessèd of Heaven
                            are my friends upon Earth
When Flaxman was taken to Italy, Fuseli[32] was given to me for a season;
And now Flaxman hath given me Hayley, his friend, to be
                         mine – such my lot upon Earth!
Now my lot in the Heavens is this: Milton lov'd me in childhood
                         and show'd me his face;
Ezra[33] came with Isaiah the Prophet, but Shakespeare in riper
                         years gave me his hand;
Paracelsus and Behmen[34] appear'd to me; terrors appear'd in
                         the Heavens above;
The American War began; all its dark horrors pass'd before my face
Across the Atlantic to France; then the French Revolution
                         commenc'd in thick clouds;
And my Angels have told me that, seeing such visions, I could
                         not subsist on the Earth,
But by my conjunction with Flaxman, who knows to forgive
                         nervous fear.
                         12 September 1800

To my dear Friend, Mrs Anna Flaxman[35]

This song to the flower of Flaxman's joy,
To the blossom of hope for a sweet decoy;
Do all that you can, or all that you may,
To entice him to Felpham and far away.

Away to sweet Felpham, for Heaven is there;
The Ladder of Angels descends thro' the air;
On the turret its spiral does softly descend,
Thro' the village then winds, at my cot it does end.

You stand in the village and look up to Heaven;
The precious stones glitter on flights seventy-seven;
And my brother is there, and my friend and thine
Descend and ascend with the bread and the wine.

The bread of sweet thought and the wine of delight
Feed the village of Felpham by day and by night,
And at his own door the bless'd Hermit[36] does stand,
Dispensing unceasing to all the wide land.

To Thomas Butts [37]

To my friend Butts I write
My first vision of light,
On the yellow sands sitting.
The sun was emitting
His glorious beams
From Heaven's high streams.
Over sea, over land,
My eyes did expand
Into regions of air,
Away from all care;
Into regions of fire,
Remote from desire;
The light of the morning
Heaven's mountains adorning:
In particles bright,
The jewels of light
Distinct shone and clear.
Amaz'd and in fear
I each particle gazèd,
Astonish'd, amazèd;
For each was a Man
Human-form'd. Swift I ran,
For they beckon'd to me,
Remote by the sea,
Saying: 'Each grain of sand,
Every stone on the land,
Each rock and each hill,

Each fountain and rill,
Each herb and each tree,
Mountain, hill, earth, and sea,
Cloud, meteor, and star,
Are men seen afar.'
I stood in the streams
Of Heaven's bright beams,
And saw Felpham sweet
Beneath my bright feet,
In soft Female charms;
And in her fair arms
My Shadow I knew,
And my wife's Shadow too,
And my sister, and friend.
We like infants descend
In our Shadows on earth,
Like a weak mortal birth.
My eyes, more and more,
Like a sea without shore,
Continue expanding,
The Heavens commanding;
Till the jewels of light,
Heavenly men beaming bright,
Appear'd as One Man,
Who complacent began
My limbs to enfold
In His beams of bright gold;
Like dross purg'd away
All my mire and my clay
Soft consum'd in delight,
In His bosom sun-bright
I remain'd. Soft He smil'd,
And I heard His voice mild,
Saying: 'This is My fold,
O thou ram horn'd with gold,
Who awakest from sleep
On the sides of the deep.
On the mountains around
The roarings resound
Of the lion and wolf,

The loud sea, and deep gulf.
These are guards of My fold,
O thou ram horn'd with gold!'
And the voice faded mild:
I remain'd as a child;
All I ever had known
Before me bright shone:
I saw you and your wife
By the fountains of life.
Such the vision to me
Appear'd on the sea.

To Mrs Butts

Wife of the friend of those I most revere,
Receive this tribute from a harp sincere;
Go on in virtuous seed-sowing on mould
Of human vegetation, and behold
Your harvest springing to eternal life,
Parent of youthful minds, and happy wife!

To Thomas Butts [38]

With Happiness stretch'd across the hills
In a cloud that dewy sweetness distils;
With a blue sky spread over with wings,
And a mild sun that mounts and sings;
With trees and fields full of fairy elves,
And little devils who fight for themselves –
Rememb'ring the verses that Hayley sung
When my heart knock'd against the root of my tongue –
With angels planted in hawthorn bowers,
And God Himself in the passing hours;
With silver angels across my way,
And golden demons that none can stay;
With my father hovering upon the wind,
And my brother Robert [39] just behind,
And my brother John, [40] the evil one,
In a black cloud making his moan, –

Tho' dead, they appear upon my path,
Notwithstanding my terrible wrath;
They beg, they entreat, they drop their tears,
Fill'd full of hopes, fill'd full of fears –
With a thousand angels upon the wind
Pouring disconsolate from behind
To drive them off, and before my way
A frowning thistle implores my stay.
What to others a trifle appears
Fills me full of smiles or tears;
For double the vision my eyes do see,
And a double vision is always with me.
With my inward eye, 'tis an Old Man grey,
With my outward, a Thistle across my way.
'If thou goest back,' the Thistle said,
'Thou art to endless woe betray'd;
For here does Theotormon[41] lour,
And here is Enitharmon's[42] bower;
And Los the Terrible thus hath sworn,
Because thou backward dost return,
Poverty, envy, old age, and fear,
Shall bring thy wife upon a bier;
And Butts shall give what Fuseli gave,
A dark black rock and a gloomy cave.'

I struck the Thistle with my foot,
And broke him up from his delving root.
'Must the duties of life each other cross?
Must every joy be dung and dross?
Must my dear Butts feel cold neglect
Because I give Hayley his due respect?
Must Flaxman look upon me as wild,
And all my friends be with doubts beguil'd?
Must my wife live in my sister's bane,
Or my sister survive on my love's pain?
The curses of Los,[43] the terrible Shade,
And his dismal terrors make me afraid.'
So I spoke, and struck in my wrath
The Old Man weltering upon my path.
Then Los appear'd in all his power:

In the sun he appear'd, descending before
My face in fierce flames; in my double sight
'Twas outward a sun, inward Los in his might.
'My hands are labour'd day and night,
And ease comes never in my sight.
My wife has no indulgence given
Except what comes to her from Heaven.
We eat little, we drink less,
This Earth breeds not our happiness.
Another sun feeds our life's streams,
We are not warmèd with thy beams;
Thou measurest not the time to me,
Nor yet the space that I do see;
My mind is not with thy light array'd,
Thy terrors shall not make me afraid.'

When I had my defiance given,
The sun stood trembling in heaven;
The moon, that glow'd remote below,
Became leprous and white as snow;
And every soul of men on the earth
Felt affliction, and sorrow, and sickness, and dearth.
Los flam'd in my path, and the sun was hot
With the bows of my mind and the arrows of thought.
My bowstring fierce with ardour breathes;
My arrows glow in their golden sheaves;
My brothers and father march before;
The heavens drop with human gore.

Now I a fourfold vision see,
And a fourfold vision is given to me;
'Tis fourfold in my supreme delight,
And threefold in soft Beulah's[44] night,
And twofold always. – May God us keep
From single vision, and Newton's sleep!

To Thomas Butts[45]

O! why was I born with a different face?
Why was I not born like the rest of my race?
When I look, each one starts; when I speak, I offend;
Then I'm silent and passive, and lose every friend.

Then my verse I dishonour, my pictures despise,
My person degrade, and my temper chastise;
And the pen is my terror, the pencil my shame;
All my talents I bury, and dead is my fame.

I am either too low, or too highly priz'd;
When elate I'm envied; when meek I'm despis'd.

GNOMIC VERSES, EPIGRAMS AND
SHORT SATIRICAL PIECES

Gnomic Verses, On Art and Artists, On Friends and Foes, Miscellaneous Epigrams   Often pithy and provocative, some of these pieces are as incisive and memorable as anything to be found in the more famous *Songs*: 'Love to faults' (p. 151), for example, is a dialectical view of love and deceit akin to 'The Clod and the Pebble'. The sarcastic verses on art and artists display Blake's savage disdain for the hypocrisy and tastes of the artistic establishment epitomised by Sir Joshua Reynolds; while the epigrams on friends and foes reveal Blake's response to the criticisms of his contemporaries, some of whom had proclaimed themselves his supporters. Blake became alienated from some of his friends after being treated badly by the publisher Cromek (who had betrayed him by cheating him over a design commission as well as stealing some of Blake's ideas), being attacked by Leigh Hunt in the journal *The Examiner*, and the failure of his 1809 exhibition, his only one-man show – *The Examiner* review of this described Blake as 'an unfortunate lunatic' (O'Neill, pp. 12–13). The biting effect of these pieces, along with the predominant form of the couplet, reminds us that Blake emerges from the eighteenth-century tradition of satire, though the generally octosyllabic line-length looks back to Andrew Marvell rather than the heroic couplet of Pope. One epigram, indeed, acknowledges Pope as its model, only to present a sarcastically repetitive imitation (p. 171), while another humorously suggests just how far Blake felt himself to be from such eighteenth-century decorum, and from the 'false friends' who were still its champions:

> Flaxman and Stothard, smelling a sweet savour,
> Cry: 'Blakified drawing spoils painter and engraver';
> While I, looking up to my umbrella,
> Resolv'd to be a very contrary fellow,
> Cry, looking quite from skumference to centre:
> 'No one can finish so high as the original Inventor.'

(p. 169)

GNOMIC VERSES⁴⁶

i

Great things are done when men and mountains meet;
This is not done by jostling in the street.

ii
To God
If you have form'd a circle to go into,
Go into it yourself, and see how you would do.

iii

They said this mystery never shall cease:
The priest promotes war, and the soldier peace.

iv
An Answer to the Parson
Why of the sheep do you not learn peace?
Because I don't want you to shear my fleece.

v
Lacedaemonian Instruction
Come hither, my boy, tell me what thou seest there.
A fool tangled in a religious snare.

vi

Nail his neck to the cross: nail it with a nail.
Nail his neck to the cross: ye all have power over his tail.

vii

Love to faults is always blind;
Always is to joy inclin'd,
Lawless, wing'd and unconfin'd,
And breaks all chains from every mind.

Deceit to secrecy confin'd,
Lawful, cautious and refin'd;
To anything but interest blind,
And forges fetters for the mind.

viii

There souls of men are bought and sold,
And milk-fed Infancy for gold;
And Youth to slaughter-houses led,
And Beauty, for a bit of bread.

ix
Soft Snow

I walkèd abroad on a snowy day:
I ask'd the soft Snow with me to play:
She play'd and she melted in all her prime;
And the Winter call'd it a dreadful crime.

x

Abstinence sows sand all over
The ruddy limbs and flaming hair,
But Desire gratified
Plants fruits of life and beauty there.

xi
Merlin's Prophecy

The harvest shall flourish in wintry weather
When two Virginities meet together:
The king and the priest must be tied in a tether
Before two Virgins can meet together.

xii

If you trap the moment before it's ripe,
The tears of repentance you'll certainly wipe;
But if once you let the ripe moment go,
You can never wipe off the tears of woe.

xiii

An Old Maid early ere I knew
Aught but the love that on me grew;
And now I'm cover'd o'er and o'er,
And wish that I had been a whore.

O! I cannot, cannot find
The undaunted courage of a virgin mind;
For early I in love was crost,
Before my flower of love was lost.

xiv

The sword sung on the barren heath,
The sickle in the fruitful field:
The sword he sung a song of death,
But could not make the sickle yield.

xv

O lapwing! thou fliest around the heath,
Nor seest the net that is spread beneath.
Why dost thou not fly among the corn fields?
They cannot spread nets where a harvest yields.

xvi

Terror in the house does roar;
But Pity stands before the door.

xvii

Several Questions Answered

1

Eternity

He who binds to himself a Joy
Does the wingèd life destroy;
But he who kisses the Joy as it flies
Lives in Eternity's sunrise.

2

The look of love alarms,
Because it's fill'd with fire;
But the look of soft deceit
Shall win the lover's hire.

3

Soft deceit and idleness,
These are Beauty's sweetest dress.

4

The Question answered

What is it men in women do require?
The lineaments of gratified desire.
What is it women do in men require?
The lineaments of gratified desire.

5

An ancient Proverb
Remove away that black'ning church,
Remove away that marriage hearse,
Remove away that man of blood –
You'll quite remove the ancient curse.

xviii

If I e'er grow to man's estate,
O! give to me a woman's fate.
May I govern all, both great and small,
Have the last word, and take the wall.

xix

Since all the riches of this world
May be gifts from the Devil and earthly kings,
I should suspect that I worshipp'd the Devil
If I thank'd my God for worldly things.

xx

Riches
The countless gold of a merry heart,
The rubies and pearls of a loving eye,
The indolent never can bring to the mart,
Nor the secret hoard up in his treasury.

xxi

The Angel that presided o'er my birth
Said, 'Little creature, form'd of joy and mirth,
Go, love without the help of anything on earth.'

xxii

Grown old in love from seven till seven times seven,
I oft have wish'd for Hell, for ease from Heaven.

xxiii

Do what you will this life's a fiction,
And is made up of contradiction.

ON ART AND ARTISTS[47]

i

Advice of the Popes who succeeded the Age of Raphael
Degrade first the Arts if you'd mankind degrade,
Hire idiots to paint with cold light and hot shade,
Give high price for the worst, leave the best in disgrace,
And with labours of ignorance fill every place.

ii

On the great encouragement given by English nobility and
gentry to Correggio, Rubens, Reynolds, Gainsborough,
Catalani, Du Crow, and Dilbury Doodle[18]
As the ignorant savage will sell his own wife
For a sword, or a cutlass, a dagger, or knife;
So the taught, savage Englishman, spends his whole fortune
On a smear, or a squall, to destroy picture or tune;
And I call upon Colonel Wardle[49]
To give these rascals a dose of caudle!

iii

I askèd my dear friend Orator Prig:
'What's the first part of oratory?' He said: 'A great wig.'
'And what is the second?' Then, dancing a jig
And bowing profoundly, he said: 'A great wig.'
'And what is the third?' Then he snored like a pig,
And, puffing his cheeks out, replied: 'A great wig.'
So if a great painter with questions you push,
'What's the first part of painting?' he'll say: 'A paint-brush.'
'And what is the second?' with most modest blush,
He'll smile like a cherub, and say: 'A paint-brush.'
'And what is the third?' he'll bow like a rush,
With a leer in his eye, he'll reply: 'A paint-brush.'
Perhaps this is all a painter can want:
But, look yonder – that house is the house of Rembrandt!

iv

'O dear Mother Outline! of wisdom most sage,
What's the first part of painting?' She said: 'Patronage.'
'And what is the second, to please and engage?'
She frowned like a fury, and said: 'Patronage.'
'And what is the third? She put off old age,
And smil'd like a siren, and said: 'Patronage.'

v

On the Foundation of the Royal Academy
When nations grow old, the Arts grow cold,
And Commerce settles on every tree;
And the poor and the old can live upon gold,
For all are born poor, aged sixty-three.

vi

These are the idiots' chiefest arts:
To blend and not define the parts
The swallow sings, in courts of kings,
That fools have their high finishings.

And this the princes' golden rule,
The laborious stumble of a fool.
To make out the parts is the wise man's aim,
But to loose them the fool makes his foolish game.

vii

The cripple every step drudges and labours,
And says: 'Come, learn to walk of me, good neighbours.'
Sir Joshua in astonishment cries out:
'See, what great labour! pain in modest doubt!

'He walks and stumbles as if he crep,
And how high labour'd is every step!'
Newton and Bacon cry 'Being badly nurst,
He is all experiments from last to first.'

viii

You say their pictures well painted be,
And yet they are blockheads you all agree:
Thank God! I never was sent to school

To be flogg'd into following the style of a fool.
The errors of a wise man make your rule,
Rather than the perfections of a fool.

ix

When you look at a picture, you always can see
If a man of sense has painted he.
Then never flinch, but keep up a jaw
About freedom, and 'Jenny sink awa'.'
As when it smells of the lamp, we can
Say all was owing to the skilful man;
For the smell of water is but small:
So e'en let ignorance do it all.

x

The Washerwoman's Song
I wash'd them out and wash'd them in,
And they told me it was a great sin.

xi

English Encouragement of Art:[50]
Cromek's opinions put into rhyme
If you mean to please everybody you will
Set to work both ignorance and skill.
For a great multitude are ignorant,
And skill to them seems raving and rant.
Like putting oil and water in a lamp,
'Twill make a great splutter with smoke and damp.
For there is no use as it seems to me
Of lighting a lamp, when you don't wish to see.

xii

When I see a Rubens, Rembrandt, Correggio,
I think of the crippled Harry and slobbering Joe;
And then I question thus: Are artists' rules
To be drawn from the works of two manifest fools?
Then God defend us from the Arts I say!
Send battle, murder, sudden death, O pray!
Rather than be such a blind human fool
I'd be an ass, a hog, a worm, a chair, a stool!

xiii

Give pensions to the learned pig,
Or the hare playing on a tabor;
Anglus can never see perfection
But in the journeyman's labour.

xiv

On Sir Joshua Reynolds's disappointment at
his first impressions of Raphael[51]
Some look to see the sweet outlines,
And beauteous forms that Love does wear;
Some look to find out patches, paint,
Bracelets and stays and powder'd hair.

xv

Sir Joshua praisèd Rubens with a smile,
By calling his the ornamental style;
And yet his praise of Flaxman was the smartest,
When he called him the ornamental artist.
But sure such ornaments we well may spare
As crooked limbs and lousy heads of hair.

xvi

Sir Joshua praises Michael Angelo.
'Tis Christian mildness when knaves praise a foe;
But 'twould be madness, all the world would say,
Should Michael Angelo praise Sir Joshua –
Christ us'd the Pharisees in a rougher way.

xvii

Can there be anything more mean,
More malice in disguise,
Than praise a man for doing what
That man does most despise?
Reynolds lectures exactly so
When he praises Michael Angelo.

xviii
To the Royal Academy
A strange erratum in all the editions
Of Sir Joshua Reynolds' lectures
Should be corrected by the young gentlemen
And the Royal Academy's directors.

Instead of 'Michael Angelo,'
Read 'Rembrandt'; for it is fit
To make mere common honesty
In all that he has writ.

xix
Florentine Ingratitude
Sir Joshua sent his own portrait to
The birthplace of Michael Angelo,
And in the hand of the simpering fool
He put a dirty paper scroll,
And on the paper, to be polite,
Did 'Sketches by Michael Angelo' write.
The Florentines said ' 'Tis a Dutch-English bore,
Michael Angelo's name writ on Rembrandt's door.'
The Florentines call it an English fetch,
For Michael Angelo never did sketch;
Every line of his has meaning,
And needs neither suckling nor weaning.
'Tis the trading English-Venetian cant
To speak Michael Angelo, and act Rembrandt:
It will set his Dutch friends all in a roar
To write 'Mich. Ang.' on Rembrandt's door;
But you must not bring in your hand a lie
If you mean that the Florentines should buy.
Giotto's circle or Apelles' line
Were not the work of sketchers drunk with wine;
Nor of the city clock's running . . . fashion;
Nor of Sir Isaac Newton's calculation.

xx

No real style of colouring ever appears,
But advertising in the newspapers.
Look there – you'll see Sir Joshua's colouring:
Look at his pictures – all has taken wing!

xxi

When Sir Joshua Reynolds died,
All Nature was degraded;
The King dropp'd a tear into the Queen's ear,
And all his pictures faded.

xxii
A Pitiful Case

The villain at the gallows tree,
When he is doom'd to die,
To assuage his misery
In virtue's praise does cry.

So Reynolds when he came to die,
To assuage his bitter woe,
Thus aloud did howl and cry:
'Michael Angelo! Michael Angelo!'

xxiii
On Sir Joshua Reynolds

O Reader, behold the Philosopher's grave!
He was born quite a Fool, but he died quite a Knave.

xxiv

I, Rubens, am a statesman and a saint.
Deceptions both – and so I'll learn to paint.

xxv
On the school of Rubens

Swelled limbs, with no outline that you can descry,
That stink in the nose of a stander-by,
But all the pulp-wash'd, painted, finish'd with labour,
Of an hundred journeymen's – how-d'ye do neighbour?

xxvi
To English Connoisseurs
You must agree that Rubens was a fool,
And yet you make him master of your School,
And give more money for his slobberings
Than you will give for Raphael's finest things.
I understood Christ was a carpenter
And not a brewer's servant, my good Sir.

xxvii
A Pretty Epigram for the encouragement of those
who have paid great sums in the Venetian and Flemish ooze
Nature and Art in this together suit:
What is most grand is always most minute.
Rubens thinks tables, chairs and stools are grand,
But Raphael thinks a head, a foot, a hand.

xxviii
Raphael, sublime, majestic, graceful, wise –
His executive power must I despise?
Rubens, low, vulgar, stupid, ignorant –
His power of execution I must grant,
Learn the laborious stumble of a fool!
And from an idiot's action form my rule? –
Go, send your Children to the Slobbering School!

xxix
On the Venetian Painter
He makes the lame to walk, we all agree,
But then he strives to blind all who can see.

xxx
A pair of stays to mend the shape
Of crookèd humpy woman,
Put on, O Venus; now thou art
Quite a Venetian Roman.

xxxi

Venetian! all thy colouring is no more
Than bolster'd plasters on a crooked whore.

xxxii
To Venetian Artists

That God is colouring Newton does show,
And the Devil is a black outline, all of us know.
Perhaps this little fable may make us merry:
A dog went over the water without a wherry;
A bone which he had stolen he had in his mouth;
He cared not whether the wind was north or south.
As he swam he saw the reflection of the bone.
'This is quite perfection – one generalising tone!
Outline! There's no outline, there's no such thing:
All is chiaroscuro, poco-pen – it's all colouring!'
Snap, snap! He has lost shadow and substance too.
He had them both before. 'Now how do ye do?'
'A great deal better than I was before:
Those who taste colouring love it more and more.'

xxxiii

All pictures that's painted with sense and with thought
Are painted by madmen, as sure as a groat;
For the greater the fool is the pencil more blest,
As when they are drunk they always paint best.
They never can Raphael it, Fuseli it, nor Blake it;
If they can't see an outline, pray how can they make it?
When men will draw outlines begin you to jaw them;
Madmen see outlines and therefore they draw them.

xxxiv

Call that the public voice which is their error!
Like as a monkey, peeping in a mirror,
Admires all his colours brown and warm,
And never once perceives his ugly form.

ON FRIENDS AND FOES[52]

i

I am no Homer's hero you all know;
I profess not generosity to a foe.
My generosity is to my friends,
That for their friendship I may make amends.
The generous to enemies promotes their ends,
And becomes the enemy and betrayer of his friends.

ii

Anger and wrath my bosom rends:
I thought them the errors of friends.
But all my limbs with warmth glow:
I find them the errors of the foe.

iii

If you play a game of chance, know, before you begin,
If you are benevolent you will never win.

iv

Of Hayley's birth

Of H—'s birth this was the happy lot:
His mother on his father him begot.

v

On Hayley

To forgive enemies H— does pretend,
Who never in his life forgave a friend,
And when he could not act upon my wife
Hired a villain to bereave my life.

vi

To Hayley

Thy friendship oft has made my heart to ache:
Do be my enemy – for friendship's sake.

vii
On Hayley's Friendship
When H—y finds out what you cannot do,
That is the very thing he'll set you to;
If you break not your neck, 'tis not his fault;
But pecks of poison are not pecks of salt.

viii
On Hayley the Pickthank
I write the rascal thanks, till he and I
With thanks and compliments are quite drawn dry.

ix
My title as a genius thus is prov'd:
Not prais'd by Hayley, nor by Flaxman lov'd.

x
To Flaxman
You call me mad, 'tis folly to do so,
To seek to turn a madman to a foe.
If you think as you speak, you are an ass;
If you do not, you are but what you was.

xi
To Flaxman
I mock thee not, though I by thee am mockèd;
Thou call'st me madman, but I call thee blockhead.

xii
To Nancy Flaxman
How can I help thy husband's copying me?
Should that make difference 'twixt me and thee?

xiii
To Flaxman and Stothard
I found them blind: I taught them how to see;
And now they know neither themselves nor me.
'Tis excellent to turn a thorn to a pin,
A fool to a bolt, a knave to a glass of gin.

xiv
To Stothard

You all your youth observ'd the golden rule,
Till you're at last become the golden fool:
I sport with fortune, merry, blithe and gay,
Like to the lion sporting with his prey.
Take you the hide and horns which you may wear,
Mine is the flesh – the bones may be your share.

xv
Cromek speaks

I always take my judgement from a fool
Because his judgement is so very cool;
Not prejudiced by feelings great or small,
Amiable state! he cannot feel at all.

xvi
On Stothard

You say reserve and modesty he has,
Whose heart is iron, his head wood, and his face brass.
The fox, the owl, the beetle, and the bat
By sweet reserve and modesty get fat.

xvii
On Stothard

S—, in childhood, on the nursery floor,
Was extreme old and most extremely poor;
He has grown old, and rich, and what he will;
He is extreme old, and extreme poor still.

xviii
Mr Stothard to Mr Cromek

For Fortune's favours you your riches bring,
But Fortune says she gave you no such thing
Why should you be ungrateful to your friends, –
Sneaking and backbiting, and odds and ends?

xix
Mr Cromek to Mr Stothard

Fortune favours the brave, old proverbs say;
But not with money; that is not the way.
Turn back! turn back! you travel all in vain;
Turn through the iron gate down Sneaking Lane.

xx

xx
On Cromek

Cr— loves artists as he loves his meat:
He loves the Art; but 'tis the art to cheat.

xxi
On Cromek

A petty sneaking knave I knew –
O! Mr Cr—, how do ye do?

xxii
On P—

P— lovèd me not as he lov'd his friends;
For he lov'd them for gain, to serve his ends:
He lovèd me, and for no gain at all,
But to rejoice and triumph in my fall.

xxiii
On William Haines

The Sussex men are noted fools,
And weak is their brain pan –
I wonder if H— the painter
Is not a Sussex man.

xxiv
On Fuseli

The only man that e'er I knew
Who did not make me almost spew
Was Fuseli: he was both Turk and Jew –
And so, dear Christian friends, how do you do?

xxv
To Hunt

'Madman' I have been call'd: 'Fool' they call thee.
I wonder which they envy – thee or me?

xxvi
To Hunt

You think Fuseli is not a great painter. I'm glad.
This is one of the best compliments he ever had.

xxvii

On certain Mystics

Cosway, Frazer, and Baldwin of Egypt's lake
Fear to associate with Blake.
This life is a warfare against evils;
They heal the sick: he casts out devils.

Hayley, Flaxman, and Stothard are also in doubt
Lest their virtue should be put to the rout.
One grins, t'other spits, and in corners hides,
And all the virtuous have shown their backsides.

xxviii [53]

– And his legs carried it like a long fork,
Reached all the way from Chichester to York,
From York all across Scotland to the sea;
This was a man of men, as seems to me.
Not only in his mouth his own soul lay,
But my soul also would he bear away.
Like as a pedlar bears his weary pack,
He would hear my soul buckled to his back.
But once, alas! committing a mistake,
He bore the wretched soul of William Blake
That he might turn it into eggs of gold;
But neither back nor mouth those eggs could hold.
His under jaw dropp'd as those eggs he laid,
And all my eggs are addled and decay'd.
The Examiner, whose very name is Hunt,
Call'd Death a madman, trembling for the affront;
Like trembling hare sits on his weakly paper
On which he used to dance and sport and caper.
Yorkshire Jack Hemp and Quibble, blushing daw,
Clapp'd Death into the corner of their jaw,
And Felpham Billy rode out every morn,
Horseback with Death, over the fields of corn;
Who with iron hand cuff'd, in the afternoon,
The ears of Billy's Lawyer and Dragoon.
And Cur my lawyer, and Daddy, Jack Hemp's parson,
Both went to law with Death to keep our ears on.
For how to starve Death we had laid a plot

Against his price – but Death was in the pot.
He made them pay his price, alackaday!
He knew both Law and Gospel better than they.
O that I ne'er had seen that William Blake,
Or could from Death Assassinette wake!
We thought – Alas, that such a thought could be! –
That Blake would etch for him and draw for me.
For 'twas a kind of bargain Screwmuch made
That Blake's designs should be by us display'd,
Because he makes designs so very cheap.
Then Screwmuch at Blake's soul took a long leap.
'Twas not a mouse. 'Twas Death in a disguise.
And I, alas! live to weep out my eyes.
And Death sits laughing on their monuments
On which he's written 'Receivèd the contents.'
But I have writ – so sorrowful my thought is –
His epitaph; for my tears are aquafortis.
'Come, Artists, knock your head against this stone,
For sorrow that our friend Bob Screwmuch's gone.'
And now the Muses upon me smile and laugh
I'll also write my own dear epitaph,
And I'll be buried near a dyke
That my friends may weep as much as they like:
'Here lies Stewhard the Friend of all mankind;
He has not left one enemy behind.'

xxix

– For this is being a friend just in the nick,
Not when he's well, but waiting till he's sick;
He calls you to his help; be you not mov'd
Until, by being sick, his wants are prov'd.

You see him spend his soul in prophecy:
Do you believe it a confounded lie,
Till some bookseller, and the public fame,
Prove there is truth in his extravagant claim.

For 'tis atrocious in a friend you love
To tell you anything that he can't prove,
And 'tis most wicked in a Christian nation
For any man to pretend to inspiration.

xxx

Was I angry with Hayley who us'd me so ill
Or can I be angry with Felpham's old mill?
Or angry with Flaxman, or Cromek, or Stothard,
Or poor Schiavonetti, whom they to death bother'd?
Or angry with Macklin, or Boydell, or Bowyer,[54]
Because they did not say 'O what a beau ye are'?
At a friend's errors anger show,
Mirth at the errors of a foe.

xxxi

Having given great offence by writing in prose,
I'll write in verse as soft as Bartoloze.[55]
Some blush at what others can see no crime in;
But nobody sees any harm in riming.
Dryden, in rime, cries 'Milton only plann'd':
Every fool shook his bells throughout the land.
Tom Cooke cut Hogarth down with his clean graving:
Thousands of connoisseurs with joy ran raving.
Thus, Hayley on his toilette seeing the soap,
Cries, 'Homer is very much improv'd by Pope.'
Some say I've given great provision to my foes,
And that now I lead my false friends by the nose.
Flaxman and Stothard, smelling a sweet savour,
Cry: 'Blakified drawing spoils painter and engraver';
While I, looking up to my umbrella,
Resolv'd to be a very contrary fellow,
Cry, looking quite from skumference to centre:
'No one can finish so high as the original Inventor.'
Thus poor Schiavonetti died of the Cromek –
A thing that's tied around the Examiner's neck!
This is my sweet apology to my friends,
That I may put them in mind of their latter ends.
If men will act like a maid smiling over a churn,
They ought not, when it comes to another's turn,
To grow sour at what a friend may utter,
Knowing and feeling that we all have need of butter.
False friends, fie! fie! Our friendship you shan't sever;
In spite we will be greater friends than ever.

MISCELLANEOUS EPIGRAMS[56]

i

His whole life is an epigram smart, smooth and neatly penn'd,
Plaited quite neat to catch applause, with a hang-noose at the end.

ii

He has observ'd the golden rule,
Till he's become the golden fool.

iii

– And in melodious accents I
Will sit me down, and cry 'I! I!'

iv

Some people admire the work of a fool,
For it's sure to keep your judgement cool;
It does not reproach you with want of wit;
It is not like a lawyer serving a writ.

v

He's a blockhead who wants a proof of what he can't perceive;
And he's a fool who tries to make such a blockhead believe.

vi

Great men and fools do often me inspire;
But the greater fool, the greater liar.

vii

Some men, created for destruction, come
Into the world, and make the world their home.
Be they as vile and base as e'er they can,
They'll still be callèd 'The World's Honest Man.'

viii

An Epitaph

Come knock your heads against this stone.
For sorrow that poor John Thompson's gone.

ix
Another

I was buried near this dyke,
That my friends may weep as much as they like.

x
Another

Here lies John Trot, the friend of all mankind:
He has not left one enemy behind.
Friends were quite hard to find, old authors say;
But now they stand in everybody's way.

xi

When France got free, Europe, 'twixt fools and knaves,
Were savage first to France, and after – slaves.

xii
On the virginity of the Virgin Mary
and Johanna Southcott [57]

Whate'er is done to her she cannot know,
And if you'll ask her she will swear it so.
Whether 'tis good or evil none's to blame:
No one can take the pride, no one the shame.

xiii
Imitation of Pope:
a compliment to the Ladies

Wondrous the gods, more wondrous are the men,
More wondrous, wondrous still, the cock and hen,
More wondrous still the table, stool and chair;
But ah! more wondrous still the charming fair.

xiv

When a man has married a wife, he finds out whether
Her knees and elbows are only glued together.

xv

To Chloe's breast young Cupid slyly stole,
But he crept in at Myra's pocket-hole.

TIRIEL
Manuscript *circa* 1788–9

Tiriel (*circa* 1789) This is Blake's earliest attempt at a long semi-mythological poem in the mode of the 'prophetic' books. The tragic themes of tyrannical power and the jealous conflicts of youth and age recall *King Lear* as well as anticipating later elements of Blake's own mythology. Tiriel, King of the West, is a tyrant who, alienated by his own power, curses and is cursed by the remaining members of his family – Zazel, the brother he has enslaved; Ijim, his other alienated brother; his parents Har and Heva; his daughter Hela. He dies cursing. As well as some characters and names that recur elsewhere later, this gloomy gothic story contains the beginnings of the strange and thought-provoking quality of Blake's longer works. When Tiriel berates his father, Har, for passing on the doom-laden patriarchal legacy of alienated power, we have a glimpse of Blake's own voice emerging from this cloudy narrative:

> O weak mistaken father of a lawless race,
> Thy laws, O Har, and Tiriel's wisdom, end together in a curse.
> Why is one law given to the lion and the patient ox? [. . .]
> The father forms a whip to rouse the sluggish senses to act,
> And scourges off all youthful fancies from the new-born man.

(pp. 172–3)

I

And agèd Tiriel stood before the gates of his beautiful palace
With Myratana, once the Queen of all the western plains;
But now his eyes were darkenèd, and his wife fading in death.
They stood before their once delightful palace; and thus the voice
Of agèd Tiriel arose, that his sons might hear in their gates: –

'Accursèd race of Tiriel! behold your father;
Come forth and look on her that bore you! Come, you accursèd sons!
In my weak arms I here have borne your dying mother.
Come forth, sons of the Curse, come forth! see the death of Myratana!'

His sons ran from their gates, and saw their agèd parents stand;
And thus the eldest son of Tiriel rais'd his mighty voice: –

'Old man! unworthy to be call'd the father of Tiriel's race!
For every one of those thy wrinkles, each of those grey hairs
Are cruel as death, and as obdurate as the devouring pit!
Why should thy sons care for thy curses, thou accursèd man?
Were we not slaves till we rebell'd? Who cares for Tiriel's curse?
His blessing was a cruel curse; his curse may be a blessing.'

He ceas'd: the agèd man rais'd up his right hand to the heavens.
His left supported Myratana, shrinking in pangs of death:
The orbs of his large eyes he open'd, and thus his voice went forth: –

'Serpents, not sons, wreathing around the bones of Tiriel!
Ye worms of death, feasting upon your agèd parent's flesh!
Listen! and hear your mother's groans! No more accursèd sons
She bears; she groans not at the birth of Heuxos or Yuva.
These are the groans of death, ye serpents! these are the groans of death!
Nourish'd with milk, ye serpents, nourish'd with mother's tears and cares!
Look at my eyes, blind as the orbless skull among the stones!
Look at my bald head! Hark! listen, ye serpents, listen! . . .
What, Myratana! What, my wife! O Soul! O Spirit! O Fire!

What, Myratana! art thou dead? Look here, ye serpents, look!
The serpents sprung from her own bowels have drain'd her dry as this.
Curse on your ruthless heads, for I will bury her even here!'

So saying, he began to dig a grave with his agèd hands;
But Heuxos call'd a son of Zazel to dig their mother a grave.

'Old Cruelty, desist! and let us dig a grave for thee.
Thou hast refus'd our charity, thou hast refus'd our food,
Thou hast refus'd our clothes, our beds, our houses for thy dwelling,
Choosing to wander like a son of Zazel in the rocks.
Why dost thou curse? Is not the curse now come upon your head?
Was it not you enslav'd the sons of Zazel? And they have curs'd,
And now you feel it. Dig a grave, and let us bury our mother.'

'There, take the body, cursed sons! and may the heavens rain wrath
As thick as northern fogs, around your gates, to choke you up!
That you may lie as now your mother lies, like dogs cast out,
The stink of your dead carcases annoying man and beast,
Till your white bones are bleached with age for a memorial.
No! your remembrance shall perish; for, when your carcases
Lie stinking on the earth, the buriers shall arise from the East,
And not a bone of all the sons of Tiriel remain.
Bury your mother! but you cannot bury the curse of Tiriel.'

He ceas'd, and darkling o'er the mountains sought his pathless way.

ii

He wander'd day and night: to him both day and night were dark.
The sun he felt, but the bright moon was now a useless globe:
O'er mountains and thro' vales of woe the blind and agèd man
Wander'd, till he that leadeth all led him to the vales of Har.

And Har and Heva, like two children, sat beneath the oak:
Mnetha, now agèd, waited on them, and brought them food and
          clothing;
But they were as the shadow of Har, and as the years forgotten.
Playing with flowers and running after birds they spent the day,
And in the night like infants slept, delighted with infant dreams.

Soon as the blind wanderer enter'd the pleasant gardens of Har,
They ran weeping, like frighted infants, for refuge in Mnetha's arms.
The blind man felt his way, and cried: 'Peace to these open doors!
Let no one fear, for poor blind Tiriel hurts none but himself.
Tell me, O friends, where am I now, and in what pleasant place?'

'This is the valley of Har,' said Mnetha, 'and this the tent of Har.
Who art thou, poor blind man, that takest the name of Tiriel on thee?
Tiriel is King of all the West. Who art thou? I am Mnetha;
And this is Har and Heva, trembling like infants by my side.'
'I know Tiriel is King of the West, and there he lives in joy.
No matter who I am, O Mnetha! If thou hast any food,
Give it me; for I cannot stay; my journey is far from hence.'

Then Har said: 'O my mother Mnetha, venture not so near him;
For he is the king of rotten wood, and of the bones of death;
He wanders without eyes, and passes thro' thick walls and doors.
Thou shalt not smite my mother Mnetha, O thou eyeless man!'

'A wanderer, I beg for food: you see I cannot weep:
I cast away my staff, the kind companion of my travel,
And I kneel down that you may see I am a harmless man.'

He kneelèd down. And Mnetha said: 'Come, Har and Heva, rise!
He is an innocent old man, and hungry with his travel.'

Then Har arose, and laid his hand upon old Tiriel's head.

'God bless thy poor bald pate! God bless thy hollow winking eyes!
God bless thy shrivell'd beard! God bless thy many-wrinkled forehead!
Thou hast no teeth, old man! and thus I kiss thy sleek bald head.
Heva, come kiss his bald head, for he will not hurt us, Heva.'

Then Heva came, and took old Tiriel in her mother's arms.

'Bless thy poor eyes, old man, and bless the old father of Tiriel!
Thou art my Tiriel's old father; I know thee thro' thy wrinkles,
Because thou smellest like the fig-tree, thou smellest like ripe figs.
How didst thou lose thy eyes, old Tiriel? Bless thy wrinkled face!'

Mnetha said: 'Come in, aged wanderer! tell us of thy name.
Why shouldest thou conceal thyself from those of thine own flesh?'

'I am not of this region,' said Tiriel dissemblingly.
'I am an agèd wanderer, once father of a race
Far in the North; but they were wicked, and were all destroy'd,
And I their father sent an outcast. I have told you all.
Ask me no more, I pray, for grief hath seal'd my precious sight.'

'O Lord!' said Mnetha, 'how I tremble! Are there then more people,
More human creatures on this earth, beside the sons of Har?'

'No more,' said Tiriel, 'but I, remain on all this globe;
And I remain an outcast. Hast thou anything to drink?'

Then Mnetha gave him milk and fruits, and they sat down together.

iii

They sat and ate, and Har and Heva smil'd on Tiriel.

'Thou art a very old old man, but I am older than thou.
How came thine hair to leave thy forehead? how came thy face so
    brown?
My hair is very long, my beard doth cover all my breast.
God bless thy piteous face! To count the wrinkles in thy face
Would puzzle Mnetha. Bless thy face! for thou art Tiriel.'

'Tiriel I never saw but once: I sat with him and ate;
He was as cheerful as a prince, and gave me entertainment;
But long I stay'd not at his palace, for I am forc'd to wander.'

'What! wilt thou leave us too?' said Heva: 'thou shalt not leave us too,
For we have many sports to show thee, and many songs to sing;
And after dinner we will walk into the cage of Har,
And thou shalt help us to catch birds, and gather them ripe cherries.
Then let thy name be Tiriel, and never leave us more.'

'If thou dost go,' said Har, 'I wish thine eyes may see thy folly.
My sons have left me; did thine leave thee? O, 'twas very cruel!'

'No! venerable man,' said Tiriel, 'ask me not such things,
For thou dost make my heart to bleed: my sons were not like thine,
But worse. O never ask me more, or I must flee away!'

'Thou shalt not go,' said Heva, 'till thou hast seen our singing-birds,
And heard Har sing in the great cage, and slept upon our fleeces.
Go not! for thou art so like Tiriel that I love thine head,
Tho' it is wrinkled like the earth parch'd with the summer heat.'

Then Tiriel rose up from the seat, and said: 'God bless these tents!
My journey is o'er rocks and mountains, not in pleasant vales:
I must not sleep nor rest, because of madness and dismay.'

And Mnetha said: 'Thou must not go to wander dark, alone;
But dwell with us, and let us be to thee instead of eyes,
And I will bring thee food, old man, till death shall call thee hence.'

Then Tiriel frown'd, and answer'd: 'Did I not command you, saying,
"Madness and deep dismay possess the heart of the blind man,
The wanderer who seeks the woods, leaning upon his staff"?'

Then Mnetha, trembling at his frowns, led him to the tent door,
And gave to him his staff, and bless'd him. He went on his way.

But Har and Heva stood and watch'd him till he enter'd the wood;
And then they went and wept to Mnetha: but they soon forgot their tears.

iv
Over the weary hills the blind man took his lonely way;
To him the day and night alike was dark and desolate;

But far he had not gone when Ijim from his woods came down,
Met him at entrance of the forest, in a dark and lonely way.

'Who art thou, eyeless wretch, that thus obstruct'st the lion's path?
Ijim shall rend thy feeble joints, thou tempter of dark Ijim!
Thou hast the form of Tiriel, but I know thee well enough.
Stand from my path, foul fiend! Is this the last of thy deceits,
To be a hypocrite, and stand in shape of a blind beggar?'

The blind man heard his brother's voice, and kneel'd down on his knee.

'O brother Ijim, if it is thy voice that speaks to me,
Smite not thy brother Tiriel, tho' weary of his life.
My sons have smitten me already; and, if thou smitest me,
The curse that rolls over their heads will rest itself on thine.
'Tis now seven years since in my palace I beheld thy face.'

Come, thou dark fiend, I dare thy cunning! know that Ijim scorns
To smite thee in the form of helpless age and eyeless policy.
Rise up! for I discern thee, and I dare thy eloquent tongue.
Come! I will lead thee on thy way, and use thee as a scoff.'

'O brother Ijim, thou beholdest wretched Tiriel:
Kiss me, my brother, and then leave me to wander desolate!'

'No! artful fiend, but I will lead thee; dost thou want to go?
Reply not, lest I bind thee with the green flags of the brook.
Aye! now thou art discover'd, I will use thee like a slave.'

When Tiriel heard the words of Ijim, he sought not to reply:
He knew 'twas vain, for Ijim's words were as the voice of Fate.

And they went on together, over hills, thro' woody dales,
Blind to the pleasures of the sight, and deaf to warbling birds:
All day they walk'd, and all the night beneath the pleasant moon,
Westwardly journeying, till Tiriel grew weary with his travel.

'O Ijim, I am faint and weary, for my knees forbid
To bear me further: urge me not, lest I should die with travel.
A little rest I crave, a little water from a brook,
Or I shall soon discover that I am a mortal man,
And you will lose your once-lov'd Tiriel. Alas! how faint I am!'

'Impudent fiend!' said Ijim, 'hold thy glib and eloquent tongue!
Tiriel is a king, and thou the tempter of dark Ijim.
Drink of this running brook, and I will bear thee on my shoulders.'

He drank; and Ijim rais'd him up, and bore him on his shoulders:

All day he bore him; and, when evening drew her solemn curtain,
Enter'd the gates of Tiriel's palace, and stood and call'd aloud: –

'Heuxos, come forth! I here have brought the fiend that troubles Ijim.
Look! knowst thou aught of this grey beard, or of these blinded eyes?'

Heuxos and Lotho ran forth at the sound of Ijim's voice,
And saw their agèd father borne upon his mighty shoulders.
Their eloquent tongues were dumb, and sweat stood on their
                                            trembling limbs:
They knew 'twas vain to strive with Ijim. They bow'd and silent stood.

'What, Heuxos! call thy father, for I mean to sport to-night.
This is the hypocrite that sometimes roars a dreadful lion;
Then I have rent his limbs, and left him rotting in the forest
For birds to eat. But I have scarce departed from the place,
But like a tiger he would come: and so I rent him too.
When like a river he would seek to drown me in his waves;
But soon I buffeted the torrent: anon like to a cloud
Fraught with the swords of lightning; but I brav'd the vengeance too.
Then he would creep like a bright serpent; till around my neck,
While I was sleeping, he would twine: I squeez'd his poisonous soul.
Then like a toad, or like a newt, would whisper in my ears;
Or like a rock stood in my way, or like a poisonous shrub.
At last I caught him in the form of Tiriel, blind and old,
And so I'll keep him! Fetch your father, fetch forth Myratana!'

They stood confounded, and thus Tiriel rais'd his silver voice: –

'Serpents, not sons, why do you stand? Fetch hither Tiriel!
Fetch hither Myratana! and delight yourselves with scoffs;
For poor blind Tiriel is return'd, and this much-injur'd head
Is ready for your bitter taunts. Come forth, sons of the Curse!'

Meantime the other sons of Tiriel ran around their father,
Confounded at the terrible strength of Ijim: they knew 'twas vain.
Both spear and shield were useless, and the coat of iron mail,
When Ijim stretch'd his mighty arm; the arrow from his limbs
Rebounded, and the piercing sword broke on his naked flesh.

'Then is it true, Heuxos, that thou hast turn'd thy agèd parent
To be the sport of wintry winds?' said Ijim, 'is this true?
It is a lie, and I am like the tree torn by the wind,
Thou eyeless fiend, and you dissemblers! Is this Tiriel's house?
It is as false as Matha, and as dark as vacant Orcus.
Escape, ye fiends! for Ijim will not lift his hand against ye.'

So saying, Ijim gloomy turn'd his back, and silent sought
The secret forests, and all night wander'd in desolate ways.

v

And agèd Tiriel stood and said: 'Where does the thunder sleep?
Where doth he hide his terrible head? And his swift and fiery daughters,
Where do they shroud their fiery wings, and the terrors of their hair?
Earth, thus I stamp thy bosom! Rouse the earthquake from his den,
To raise his dark and burning visage thro' the cleaving ground,
To thrust these towers with his shoulders! Let his fiery dogs
Rise from the centre, belching flames and roarings, dark smoke!
Where art thou, Pestilence, that bathest in fogs and standing lakes?
Rise up thy sluggish limbs, and let the loathsomest of poisons
Drop from thy garments as thou walkest, wrapp'd in yellow clouds!
Here take thy seat in this wide court; let it be strewn with dead;
And sit and smile upon these cursèd sons of Tiriel!
Thunder, and fire, and pestilence, hear you not Tiriel's curse?'
He ceas'd. The heavy clouds confus'd roll'd round the lofty towers,
Discharging their enormous voices at the father's curse.
The earth tremblèd; fires belchèd from the yawning clefts;
And when the shaking ceas'd, a fog possess'd the accursèd clime.

The cry was great in Tiriel's palace: his five daughters ran,
And caught him by the garments, weeping with cries of bitter woe.

'Aye, now you feel the curse, you cry! but may all ears be deaf
 As Tiriel's, and all eyes as blind as Tiriel's to your woes!
May never stars shine on your roofs! may never sun nor moon
Visit you, but eternal fogs hover around your walls!
Hela, my youngest daughter, you shall lead me from this place;
And let the curse fall on the rest, and wrap them up together!'

He ceas'd: and Hela led her father from the noisome place.

In haste they fled; while all the sons and daughters of Tiriel,
Chain'd in thick darkness, utterèd cries of mourning all the night.
And in the morning, lo! an hundred men in ghastly death!
The four daughters, stretch'd on the marble pavement, silent all,
Fall'n by the pestilence! – the rest mop'd round in guilty fears;
And all the children in their beds were cut off in one night.
Thirty of Tiriel's sons remain'd, to wither in the palace,
Desolate, loathèd, dumb, astonish'd – waiting for black death.

vi

And Hela led her father thro' the silence of the night,
Astonish'd, silent, till the morning beams began to spring.

'Now, Hela, I can go with pleasure, and dwell with Har and Heva,
Now that the curse shall clean devour all those guilty sons.
This is the right and ready way; I know it by the sound
That our feet make. Remember, Hela, I have savèd thee from death;
Then be obedient to thy father, for the curse is taken off thee.
I dwelt with Myratana five years in the desolate rock;
And all that time we waited for the fire to fall from heaven,
Or for the torrents of the sea to overwhelm you all.
But now my wife is dead, and all the time of grace is past:
You see the parent's curse. Now lead me where I have commanded.'

'O leaguèd with evil spirits, thou accursèd man of sin!
True, I was born thy slave! Who ask'd thee to save me from death?
'Twas for thyself, thou cruel man, because thou wantest eyes.'

'True, Hela, this is the desert of all those cruel ones.
Is Tiriel cruel? Look! his daughter, and his youngest daughter,
Laughs at affection, glories in rebellion, scoffs at love.
I have not ate these two days. Lead me to Har and Heva's tent,
Or I will wrap thee up in such a terrible father's curse
That thou shalt feel worms in thy marrow creeping thro' thy bones.
Yet thou shalt lead me! Lead me, I command, to Har and Heva!'

'O cruel! O destroyer! O consumer! O avenger!
To Har and Heva I will lead thee: then would that they would curse!
Then would they curse as thou hast cursèd! But they are not like thee!
O! they are holy and forgiving, fill'd with loving mercy,

Forgetting the offences of their most rebellious children,
Or else thou wouldest not have liv'd to curse thy helpless children.'

'Look on my eyes, Hela, and see, for thou hast eyes to see,
The tears swell from my stony fountains. Wherefore do I weep?
Wherefore from my blind orbs art thou not seiz'd with poisonous stings?
Laugh, serpent, youngest venomous reptile of the flesh of Tiriel!
Laugh! for thy father Tiriel shall give thee cause to laugh,
Unless thou lead me to the tent of Har, child of the Curse!'

'Silence thy evil tongue, thou murderer of thy helpless children!
I lead thee to the tent of Har; not that I mind thy curse,
But that I feel they will curse thee, and hang upon thy bones
Fell shaking agonies, and in each wrinkle of that face
Plant worms of death to feast upon the tongue of terrible curses.'

'Hela, my daughter, listen! thou art the daughter of Tiriel.
Thy father calls. Thy father lifts his hand unto the heavens,
For thou hast laughèd at my tears, and curs'd thy agèd father.
Let snakes rise from thy bedded locks, and laugh among thy curls!'

He ceas'd. Her dark hair upright stood, while snakes infolded round
Her madding brows: her shrieks appall'd the soul of Tiriel.

'What have I done, Hela, my daughter? Fear'st thou now the curse,
Or wherefore dost thou cry? Ah, wretch, to curse thy agèd father!
Lead me to Har and Heva, and the curse of Tiriel
Shall fail. If thou refuse, howl in the desolate mountains!'

                              vii
She, howling, led him over mountains and thro' frighted vales,
Till to the caves of Zazel they approach'd at eventide.
Forth from their caves old Zazel and his sons ran, when they saw
Their tyrant prince blind, and his daughter howling and leading him.

They laugh'd and mocked; some threw dirt and stones as they pass'd by;
But when Tiriel turn'd around and rais'd his awful voice,
Some fled away; but Zazel stood still, and thus begun: –

'Bald tyrant, wrinkled cunning, listen to Zazel's chains!
'Twas thou that chainèd thy brother Zazel! Where are now thine eyes?
Shout, beautiful daughter of Tiriel! thou singest a sweet song!
Where are you going? Come and eat some roots, and drink some water.
Thy crown is bald, old man; the sun will dry thy brains away,
And thou wilt be as foolish as thy foolish brother Zazel.'

The blind man heard, and smote his breast, and trembling passèd on.
They threw dirt after them, till to the covert of a wood
The howling maiden led her father, where wild beasts resort,
Hoping to end her woes; but from her cries the tigers fled.
All night they wander'd thro' the wood; and when the sun arose,
They enter'd on the mountains of Har: at noon the happy tents
Were frighted by the dismal cries of Hela on the mountains.

But Har and Heva slept fearless as babes on loving breasts.
Mnetha awoke: she ran and stood at the tent door, and saw
The agèd wanderer led towards the tents; she took her bow,
And chose her arrows, then advanc'd to meet the terrible pair.

viii

And Mnetha hasted, and met them at the gate of the lower garden.
'Stand still, or from my bow receive a sharp and wingèd death!'
Then Tiriel stood, saying: 'What soft voice threatens such bitter things?
Lead me to Har and Heva; I am Tiriel, King of the West.'

And Mnetha led them to the tent of Har; and Har and Heva
Ran to the door. When Tiriel felt the ankles of agèd Har,
He said: 'O weak mistaken father of a lawless race,
Thy laws, O Har, and Tiriel's wisdom, end together in a curse.

Why is one law given to the lion and the patient ox?
And why men bound beneath the heavens in a reptile form,
A worm of sixty winters creeping on the dusky ground?
The child springs from the womb; the father ready stands to form
The infant head, while the mother idle plays with her dog on her couch:
The young bosom is cold for lack of mother's nourishment, and milk
Is cut off from the weeping mouth with difficulty and pain:
The little lids are lifted, and the little nostrils open'd:
The father forms a whip to rouse the sluggish senses to act,

And scourges off all youthful fancies from the new-born man.
Then walks the weak infant in sorrow, compell'd to number footsteps
Upon the sand. And when the drone has reach'd his crawling length,
Black berries appear that poison all round him. Such was Tiriel,
Compell'd to pray repugnant, and to humble the immortal spirit;
Till I am subtil as a serpent in a paradise,
Consuming all, both flowers and fruits, insects and warbling birds.
And now my paradise is fall'n, and a drear sandy plain
Returns my thirsty hissings in a curse on thee, O Har,
Mistaken father of a lawless race! – My voice is past.'

He ceas'd, outstretch'd at Har and Heva's feet in awful death.

THE BOOK OF THEL
Engraved 1789

The Book of Thel (1789)   Written during the same period as *Songs of Innocence*, this poem takes a dialectical approach to the dangers of innocence. Thel is a girl whose fearfulness prevents her from engaging with life. Blakean emblems in the forms of a lily, a cloud, a worm and a clod of clay all encourage her to leave her pastoral idyll in the vales of Har and to commit herself to living. But Thel is too self-engrossed in her anxieties, unable to see that the individual life is part of a wider process. In the final section she accepts the clay's invitation to see what that involves, glimpsing the land of experience. The perplexing questions she hears rising from her own grave-plot articulate in Blake's most powerful manner the sensory limits of material experience which restrict perception and awareness:

> Why an Ear, a whirlpool fierce to draw creations in?
> Why a Nostril wide inhaling terror, trembling, and affright?
> Why a tender curb upon the youthful, burning boy?
> Why a little curtain of flesh on the bed of our desire?

(p. 190)

This revelation of the limits of experience is too much for Thel, and she flies back to her pastoral retreat, shrieking.

With *Thel*, Blake achieves his first vivid embodiment of the distinctive prophetic mode of writing, with all its strange names, weird and wonderful stories, obscurities and terrific verses, that goes into the making of his most challenging work.

Thel's Motto

Does the Eagle know what is in the pit;
Or wilt thou go ask the Mole?
Can Wisdom be put in a silver rod,
Or Love in a golden bowl?

i

The daughters of the Seraphim led round their sunny flocks –
All but the youngest: she in paleness sought the secret air,
To fade away like morning beauty from her mortal day:
Down by the river of Adona her soft voice is heard,
And thus her gentle lamentation falls like morning dew: –

'O life of this our spring! why fades the lotus of the water?
Why fade these children of the spring, born but to smile and fall?
Ah! Thel is like a wat'ry bow, and like a parting cloud;
Like a reflection in a glass; like shadows in the water;
Like dreams of infants, like a smile upon an infant's face;
Like the dove's voice; like transient day; like music in the air
Ah! gentle may I lay me down, and gentle rest my head,
And gentle sleep the sleep of death, and gentle hear the voice
Of Him that walketh in the garden in the evening time.'

The Lily of the Valley, breathing in the humble grass,
Answerèd the lovely maid and said: 'I am a wat'ry weed,
And I am very small, and love to dwell in lowly vales;
So weak, the gilded butterfly scarce perches on my head.
Yet I am visited from heaven, and He that smiles on all
Walks in the valley, and each morn over me spreads His hand,
Saying, "Rejoice, thou humble grass, thou new-born lily-flower,
Thou gentle maid of silent valleys and of modest brooks;
For thou shalt be clothèd in light, and fed with morning manna,
Till summer's heat melts thee beside the fountains and the springs,
To flourish in eternal vales." Then why should Thel complain?
Why should the mistress of the vales of Har utter a sigh?'

She ceas'd, and smil'd in tears, then sat down in her silver shrine.

Thel answer'd: 'O thou little Virgin of the peaceful valley,
Giving to those that cannot crave, the voiceless, the o'ertired;
Thy breath doth nourish the innocent lamb, he smells thy
milky garments,
He crops thy flowers while thou sittest smiling in his face,
Wiping his mild and meeking mouth from all contagious taints.
Thy wine doth purify the golden honey; thy perfume,
Which thou dost scatter on every little blade of grass that springs,
Revives the milkèd cow, and tames the fire-breathing steed.
But Thel is like a faint cloud kindled at the rising sun:
I vanish from my pearly throne, and who shall find my place?'

'Queen of the vales,' the Lily answer'd, 'ask the tender Cloud,
And it shall tell thee why it glitters in the morning sky,
And why it scatters its bright beauty thro' the humid air.
Descend, O little Cloud, and hover before the eyes of Thel.'

The Cloud descended, and the Lily bowèd her modest head,
And went to mind her numerous charge among the verdant grass.

ii
'O little Cloud,' the Virgin said, 'I charge thee tell to me
Why thou complainest not, when in one hour thou fade away:
Then we shall seek thee, but not find. Ah! Thel is like to thee:
I pass away yet I complain, and no one hears my voice.'
The Cloud then show'd his golden head and his bright form emerg'd,
Hovering and glittering on the air before the face of Thel.

'O Virgin, know'st thou not our steeds drink of the golden springs
Where Luvah doth renew his horses? Look'st thou on my youth,
And fearest thou, because I vanish and am seen no more,
Nothing remains? O Maid, I tell thee, when I pass away,
It is to tenfold life, to love, to peace, and raptures holy:
Unseen descending, weigh my light wings upon balmy flowers,
And court the fair-eyed dew, to take me to her shining tent:
The weeping virgin, trembling, kneels before the risen sun,
Till we arise link'd in a golden band and never part,
But walk united, bearing food to all our tender flowers.'

'Dost thou, O little Cloud? I fear that I am not like thee,
For I walk thro' the vales of Har, and smell the sweetest flowers,
But I feed not the little flowers; I hear the warbling birds,
But I feed not the warbling birds; they fly and seek their food:
But Thel delights in these no more, because I fade away;
And all shall say, "Without a use this shining woman liv'd,
Or did she only live to be at death the food of worms?" '

The Cloud reclin'd upon his airy throne, and answer'd thus: –

'Then if thou art the food of worms, O Virgin of the skies,
How great thy use, how great thy blessing! Everything that lives
Lives not alone nor for itself. Fear not, and I will call
The weak Worm from its lowly bed, and thou shalt hear its voice
Come forth, Worm of the silent valley, to thy pensive Queen.'

The helpless Worm arose, and sat upon the Lily's leaf,
And the bright Cloud sail'd on, to find his partner in the vale.

iii

Then Thel astonish'd view'd the Worm upon its dewy bed.

'Art thou a Worm? Image of weakness, art thou but a Worm?
I see thee like an infant wrappèd in the Lily's leaf.
Ah! weep not, little voice, thou canst not speak, but thou canst weep.
Is this a Worm? I see thee lay helpless and naked, weeping,
And none to answer, none to cherish thee with mother's smiles.'

The Clod of Clay heard the Worm's voice and rais'd her pitying head:
She bow'd over the weeping infant, and her life exhal'd
In milky fondness: then on Thel she fix'd her humble eyes.

'O Beauty of the vales of Har! we live not for ourselves.
Thou seest me, the meanest thing, and so I am indeed.
My bosom of itself is cold, and of itself is dark;
But He, that loves the lowly, pours His oil upon my head,
And kisses me, and binds His nuptial bands around my breast,
And says: "Thou mother of my children, I have lovèd thee,
And I have given thee a crown that none can take away."
But how this is, sweet Maid, I know not, and I cannot know;
I ponder, and I cannot ponder; yet I live and love.'

The Daughter of Beauty wip'd her pitying tears with her white veil,
And said: 'Alas! I knew not this, and therefore did I weep.
That God would love a worm I knew, and punish the evil foot
That wilful bruis'd its helpless form; but that He cherish'd it
With milk and oil I never knew, and therefore did I weep;
And I complain'd in the mild air, because I fade away,
And lay me down in thy cold bed, and leave my shining lot.'

'Queen of the vales,' the matron Clay answer'd, 'I heard thy sighs,
And all thy moans flew o'er my roof, but I have call'd them down.
Wilt thou, O Queen, enter my house? 'Tis given thee to enter
And to return: fear nothing, enter with thy virgin feet.'

iv

The eternal gates' terrific Porter lifted the northern bar:
Thel enter'd in and saw the secrets of the land unknown.
She saw the couches of the dead, and where the fibrous roots
Of every heart on earth infixes deep its restless twists:
A land of sorrows and of tears where never smile was seen.

She wander'd in the land of clouds thro' valleys dark, list'ning
Dolours and lamentations; waiting oft beside a dewy grave
She stood in silence, list'ning to the voices of the ground,
Till to her own grave-plot she came, and there she sat down,
And heard this voice of sorrow breathèd from the hollow pit.

'Why cannot the Ear be closèd to its own destruction?
Or the glist'ning Eye to the poison of a smile?
Why are Eyelids stor'd with arrows ready drawn,
Where a thousand fighting men in ambush lie,
Or an Eye of gifts and graces show'ring fruits and coinèd gold?
Why a Tongue impress'd with honey from every wind?
Why an Ear, a whirlpool fierce to draw creations in?
Why a Nostril wide inhaling terror, trembling, and affright?
Why a tender curb upon the youthful, burning boy?
Why a little curtain of flesh on the bed of our desire?'

The Virgin started from her seat, and with a shriek
Fled back unhinder'd till she came into the vales of Har.

THE MARRIAGE OF HEAVEN AND HELL
Engraved *circa* 1790

The Marriage of Heaven and Hell, 1790–3 *The Marriage of Heaven and Hell* subverts orthodox moral categories in an anarchic visionary imagining which is in part a virtual manifesto for Blake's writings. Formally, it is experimental: part poem, satire, prose fable, book of proverbs – a unique text. This utterly individual vision does have antecedents in the anarchic satires of the eighteenth century and the dialectical epic of the great Republican poet John Milton. *The Marriage* is almost an answer to Milton whom Blake berates for allowing his poetic imagination to become enslaved by orthodox morality: 'The reason Milton wrote in fetters when he wrote of Angels and God, and at liberty when of Devils and Hell, is because he was a true Poet, and of the Devil's party without knowing it' (p. 197).

The Marriage also draws critically on the visionary writings of a little-known Swedish mystic, Emanuel Swedenborg (1688–1772). Swedenborg, an engineer, claimed to have had divine revelations: his crucial ideas were that humanity was divine; that the spiritual world was real; and that human beings could enter the spiritual world at will if only they could enlarge their vision. These ideas chimed with Blake's own, but Swedenborg was otherwise rather conventional in his moral outlook and theological principles: his notion of divine humanity, for example, was limited to Christ as being simultaneously human and divine; whereas for Blake all human beings were divine. One impetus for *The Marriage*, then, was to parody Swedenborg, adopting some of his writing strategies, like the 'Memorable Fancies' or the arguments between angels and devils, but giving them a more radical edge. As a sarcastic dig at Swedenborg, Blake portrays him as the angel sitting in Christ's tomb with the empty linen cloths, waiting for the resurrection, when in fact it has already taken place (p. 195). Blake dates this new heaven as starting thirty-three years earlier, which, given that the book was begun in 1790, happily coincided with the birth of William Blake.

As elsewhere, Blake's subversive intelligence works here through the exploration of opposites and contradictions, turning conventional moral thinking upside down. By its very title, *The Marriage of Heaven and Hell* suggests an impossible contradiction. Its dialectical world is offered with little or no explanation to the reader: we are faced with the immediate and often apparently bewildering anarchy of Blake's imagination. The opening verses of 'The Argument' portray the shadowy character, Rintrah (p. 195). There is no obvious indication in the text or elsewhere in Blake's work as to who Rintrah is, or what he stands for. But if we follow through the argument, his significance is actually quite clear: the paths of truth have been invaded by villains and hypocrites, while the just have been forced out into the wilds, to rage alienated and ignored. By the time Blake printed *The Marriage*, the just had been alienated by the government repression of radical sympathisers with the French Revolution. Rintrah's ranting in the wilds is perhaps Blake's mocking parody of himself, delivering his counter-attack on conventional thinking from the margins.

Never usually one for imposing laws, in *The Marriage* Blake does exactly that with his laws of 'contraries' (p. 196); but they are entirely the opposite of the orthodox ten commandments. The laws of contraries are partly expounded by the voice of the devil. Are we then to take them as deliberately evil? Well, yes, in a sense, but for Blake that is all to the good, because it is abstract goodness itself that has created the distorting moral strictures which repress and divide the human psyche. By attributing his laws to the voice of the Devil, Blake deliberately confuses the reader's sense of whom to trust in this text. Yet the 'contraries' are in many ways clearly Blakean principles. Human life is seen as being made up of contraries 'necessary to human existence'. The problems come when people split up those organic contraries and insist on the primacy of one side and reject or repress the other. Thus orthodox religion splits the human psyche in half, labelling one side 'good', the other side 'evil'. But what is termed 'evil' is, for Blake, the very energy of life, which manifests itself indiscriminately in the material body and cannot be separated from it. For Blake, there is no abstract good or evil, as such; there are simply those aspects of the human psyche which orthodox religion has labelled evil – the body, desire, individual energies – whereas in Blake's devilish eyes, these are themselves the creative force in human beings. His stress is upon the whole person. Dividing the psyche leads to repression, which in turn leads to distortion, law, inequality, the 'mind-forg'd manacles' of Urizen; whereas accepting the energy of human contradictions leads to wholeness. Blake invites us not simply to turn conventional morality on its head, as a way of liberating ourselves; he is challenging us to see human existence as made up of dialectical opposites, of differences, of individualities, and these are not to be reconciled in some false harmony or liberal synthesis. As he says later in the text: 'One Law for the Lion and Ox is Oppression' (p. 206).

This acceptance of difference and individuality is a crucial idea in *The Marriage*. Some of the 'Proverbs' insist upon it: 'No bird soars too high, if he soars with his own wings' (p. 198). One of the 'Memorable Fancies' is a comic episode that asserts the same idea (pp. 203–5). An angel confronts the devilish Blakean narrator and threatens him with hell-fire and damnation for his irreligious views. He shows him a horrible scene which he tells the narrator will be his punishment for his irreligious ideas; but once the angel disappears, the horrible scene is replaced by an idyllic one. Blake's narrator explains this to the angel and then shows the angel *his* conception of the angel's eternal lot. The implication is clear: individuality is what matters, if you're a clod, be a clod; if a pebble, be a pebble; but don't let someone else's system or view impose on you and squash your individuality. *The Marriage* doesn't seek to reconcile opposites in a marriage of merging; rather, it recognises that a true relationship can only obtain between different entities which remain themselves.

As well as engaging in dialectical thinking, Blake offers devilish provocations with an implicit or explicit socio-political edge to them. 'The Proverbs of Hell' (pp. 198–200) contain some startling satirical critiques of hypocrisy. Their subversive effects can be measured by one of the most powerful of them: 'Prisons are built with stones of Law, Brothels with bricks of Religion' (p. 198). This assertion argues that social law and institutional morality themselves create crime and immorality. Law creates crime, the opposite of the orthodox way of looking at things. It does so by imposing prohibitive strictures: morality denies desire, and as a result creates a divided and destructive human psyche. Remember the poem 'The Schoolboy': 'How can the bird that is born for joy / Sit in a cage and sing?' (p. 87). This is Blake at his most anarchistic, in the true sense of the term – that is, being against institutional forms and for the positive belief in the creative potential of free humanity. This anti-repressive strand can be linked with Blake's contemporary fellow radical, Tom Paine, who proposed similarly utopian arguments against the insistence on law, order and government which, as we saw in the general introduction, was being put forward by Edmund Burke. In *The Rights of Man*, Paine maintained: 'Man, were he not corrupted by governments, is naturally the friend of man, and [. . .] human nature is not of itself vicious.'[3]

Blake argues for human freedom partly because of his belief that humans are divine. In *The Marriage*, he asserts decisively that 'All Deities reside in the Human breast' (p. 200) and that 'Priesthood' is merely an abstraction of that divine capacity, masking the desire of one group to have power over another. A generation later, Shelley was to argue with energetic sarcasm: 'It seems less credible that the God whose immensity is uncircumscribed by space, should have committed adultery with a carpenter's wife, than that some bold knaves or insane dupes had deceived the credulous multitude.'[4] Similarly, Blake proposes that organised religion was formed into a system by an élite which 'enslav'd the vulgar' (p. 200). For Blake, 'God only Acts and Is, in existing beings or Men' (p. 202), all of whom are endowed with the potential for what he calls 'Poetic Genius' (p. 200), the capacity to see the eternal cosmic spiritual world in action within the material world. Not surprisingly the existing engraved copies of *The Marriage* end with a poem composed some two years later, 'A Song of Liberty', printed here in a separate section (pp. 225–6), but perhaps best read as a climax to this text.

3 Michael Foot and Isaac Kramnick (eds), *Thomas Paine Reader*, Penguin, Harmondsworth 1987, p. 306
4 Paul Foot, *Red Shelley*, Sidgwick and Jackson, London 1980, p.64

THE MARRIAGE OF HEAVEN AND HELL
Engraved *circa* 1790

The Argument

Rintrah roars, and shakes his fires in the burden'd air;
Hungry clouds swag on the deep.

Once meek, and in a perilous path,
The just man kept his course along
The vale of death.
Roses are planted where thorns grow,
And on the barren heath
Sing the honey bees.

Then the perilous path was planted,
And a river and a spring
On every cliff and tomb,
And on the bleachèd bones
Red clay brought forth;

Till the villain left the paths of ease,
To walk in perilous paths, and drive
The just man into barren climes.

Now the sneaking serpent walks
In mild humility,
And the just man rages in the wilds
Where lions roam.

Rintrah roars, and shakes his fires in the burden'd air;
Hungry clouds swag on the deep.

As a new heaven is begun, and it is now thirty-three years since its advent, the Eternal Hell revives. And lo! Swedenborg is the Angel sitting at the tomb: his writings are the linen clothes folded up. Now is the dominion of Edom, and the return of Adam into Paradise. See Isaiah xxxiv and xxxv chap.

Without Contraries is no progression. Attraction and Repulsion, Reason and Energy, Love and Hate, are necessary to Human existence.

From these contraries spring what the religious call Good and Evil. Good is the passive that obeys Reason. Evil is the active springing from Energy.

Good is Heaven. Evil is Hell.

The Voice of the Devil

All Bibles or sacred codes have been the causes of the following Errors: –

1. That Man has two real existing principles, viz. a Body and a Soul.
2. That Energy, call'd Evil, is alone from the Body; and that Reason, call'd Good, is alone from the Soul.
3. That God will torment Man in Eternity for following his Energies.

But the following Contraries to these are True: –

1. Man has no Body distinct from his Soul; for that call'd Body is a portion of Soul discern'd by the five Senses, the chief inlets of Soul in this age.
2. Energy is the only life, and is from the Body; and Reason is the bound or outward circumference of Energy.
3. Energy is Eternal Delight.

Those who restrain Desire, do so because theirs is weak enough to be restrained; and the restrainer or Reason usurps its place and governs the unwilling.

And being restrained, it by degrees becomes passive, till it is only the shadow of Desire.

The history of this is written in *Paradise Lost*, and the Governor or Reason is call'd Messiah.

And the original Archangel, or possessor of the command of the Heavenly Host, is call'd the Devil or Satan, and his children are call'd Sin and Death.

But in the Book of Job, Milton's Messiah is called Satan.

For this history has been adopted by both parties.

It indeed appear'd to Reason as if Desire was cast out; but the

Devil's account is, that the Messiah fell, and formed a Heaven of what he stole from the Abyss.

This is shown in the Gospel, where he prays to the Father to send the Comforter, or Desire, that Reason may have Ideas to build on; the Jehovah of the Bible being no other than he who dwells in flaming fire.

Know that after Christ's death, he became Jehovah.

But in Milton, the Father is Destiny, the Son a Ratio of the five senses, and the Holy-ghost Vacuum!

Note. The reason Milton wrote in fetters when he wrote of Angels and God, and at liberty when of Devils and Hell, is because he was a true Poet, and of the Devil's party without knowing it.

A Memorable Fancy

As I was walking among the fires of Hell, delighted with the enjoyments of Genius, which to Angels look like torment and insanity, I collected some of their Proverbs; thinking that as the sayings used in a nation mark its character, so the Proverbs of Hell show the nature of Infernal wisdom better than any description of buildings or garments.

When I came home, on the abyss of the five senses, where a flat-sided steep frowns over the present world, I saw a mighty Devil, folded in black clouds, hovering on the sides of the rock; with corroding fires he wrote the following sentence now perceived by the minds of men, and read by them on earth: –

> How do you know but ev'ry Bird that cuts the airy way,
> Is an immense World of Delight, clos'd by your senses five?

Proverbs of Hell

In seed time learn, in harvest teach, in winter enjoy.
Drive your cart and your plough over the bones of the dead.
The road of excess leads to the palace of wisdom.
Prudence is a rich, ugly old maid courted by Incapacity.
He who desires but acts not, breeds pestilence.
The cut worm forgives the plough.
Dip him in the river who loves water.
A fool sees not the same tree that a wise man sees.
He whose face gives no light, shall never become a star.
Eternity is in love with the productions of time.
The busy bee has no time for sorrow.
The hours of folly are measur'd by the clock; but of wisdom, no clock can
     measure.
All wholesome food is caught without a net or a trap.
Bring out number, weight, and measure in a year of dearth.
No bird soars too high, if he soars with his own wings.
A dead body revenges not injuries.
The most sublime act is to set another before you.
If the fool would persist in its folly he would become wise.
Folly is the cloak of knavery.
Shame is Pride's cloak.
Prisons are built with stones of Law, Brothels with bricks of Religion.
The pride of the peacock is the glory of God
The lust of the goat is the bounty of God.
The wrath of the lion is the wisdom of God.
The nakedness of woman is the work of God.
Excess of sorrow laughs. Excess of joy weeps.
The roaring of lions, the howling of wolves, the raging of the stormy sea,
     and the destructive sword are portions of eternity too great for the
     eye of man.
The fox condemns the trap, not himself.
Joys impregnate. Sorrows bring forth.
Let man wear the fell of the lion, woman the fleece of the sheep.
The bird a nest, the spider a web, man friendship.
The selfish, smiling fool, and the sullen, frowning fool shall be both
     thought wise, that they may be a rod.
What is now proved was once only imagin'd.

*The rat, the mouse, the fox, the rabbit watch the roots; the lion, the
    tiger, the horse, the elephant watch the fruits.*

The cistern contains: the fountain overflows.

One thought fills immensity.

Always be ready to speak your mind, and a base man will avoid you.

Everything possible to be believ'd is an image of truth.

*The eagle never lost so much time as when he submitted to learn of the
    crow.*

The fox provides for himself; but God provides for the lion.

*Think in the morning. Act in the noon. Eat in the evening. Sleep in the
    night.*

He who has suffer'd you to impose on him, knows you.

As the plough follows words, so God rewards prayers.

The tigers of wrath are wiser than the horses of instruction.

Expect poison from the standing water.

You never know what is enough unless you know what is more than enough.

Listen to the fools reproach! it is a kingly title!

The eyes of fire, the nostrils of air, the mouth of water, the beard of earth.

The weak in courage is strong in cunning.

*The apple tree never asks the beech how he shall grow; nor the lion, the
    horse, how he shall take his prey.*

The thankful receiver bears a plentiful harvest.

If others had not been foolish, we should be so.

The soul of sweet delight can never be defil'd.

When thou seest an eagle, thou seest a portion of Genius; lift up thy head!

*As the caterpillar chooses the fairest leaves to lay her eggs on, so the
    priest lays his curse on the fairest joys.*

To create a little flower is the labour of ages.

Damn braces. Bless relaxes.

The best wine is the oldest, the best water the newest.

Prayers plough not! Praises reap not!

Joys laugh not! Sorrows weep not!

*The head Sublime, the heart Pathos, the genitals Beauty, the hands and
    feet Proportion.*

As the air to a bird or the sea to a fish, so is contempt to the contemptible.

The crow wish'd everything was black, the owl that everything was white.

Exuberance is Beauty.

If the lion was advised by the fox, he would be cunning.

*Improvement makes straight roads; but the crooked roads without
    improvement are roads of Genius.*

Sooner murder an infant in its cradle than nurse unacted desires.
Where man's not, nature is barren.
Truth can never be told so as to be understood, and not be believ'd.
Enough! or Too much.

The ancient Poets animated all sensible objects with Gods or Geniuses, calling them by the names and adorning them with the properties of woods, rivers, mountains, lakes, cities, nations, and whatever their enlarged and numerous senses could perceive.

And particularly they studied the Genius of each city and country, placing it under its Mental Deity;

Till a System was formed, which some took advantage of, and enslav'd the vulgar by attempting to realise or abstract the Mental Deities from their objects – thus began Priesthood;

Choosing forms of worship from poetic tales.

And at length they pronounc'd that the Gods had order'd such things.

Thus men forgot that All Deities reside in the Human breast.

A Memorable Fancy

The Prophets Isaiah and Ezekiel dined with me, and I asked them how they dared so roundly to assert that God spoke to them; and whether they did not think at the time that they would be misunderstood, and so be the cause of imposition.

Isaiah answer'd: 'I saw no God, nor heard any, in a finite organical perception; but my senses discover'd the infinite in everything, and as I was then persuaded, and remain confirm'd, that the voice of honest indignation is the voice of God, I cared not for consequences, but wrote.'

Then I asked: 'Does a firm persuasion that a thing is so, make it so?'

He replied: 'All Poets believe that it does, and in ages of imagination this firm persuasion removed mountains; but many are not capable of a firm persuasion of anything.'

Then Ezekiel said: 'The philosophy of the East taught the first principles of human perception. Some nations held one principle for the origin, and some another: we of Israel taught that the Poetic Genius (as you now call it) was the first principle and all the others merely derivative, which was the cause of our despising the Priests and Philosophers of other countries, and prophesying that all Gods would at last be proved to originate in ours and to be the tributaries of the Poetic

Genius. It was this that our great poet, King David, desired so fervently and invokes so pathetically, saying by this he conquers enemies and governs kingdoms; and we so loved our God, that we cursed in his name all the Deities of surrounding nations, and asserted that they had rebelled. From these opinions the vulgar came to think that all nations would at last be subject to the Jews.'

'This,' said he, 'like all firm persuasions, is come to pass; for all nations believe the Jews' code and worship the Jews' god, and what greater subjection can be?'

I heard this with some wonder, and must confess my own conviction. After dinner I ask'd Isaiah to favour the world with his lost works; he said none of equal value was lost. Ezekiel said the same of his.

I also asked Isaiah what made him go naked and barefoot three years. He answer'd: 'The same that made our friend Diogenes, the Grecian.'

I then asked Ezekiel why he ate dung, and lay so long on his right and left side. He answer'd, 'The desire of raising other men into a perception of the infinite: this the North American tribes practise, and is he honest who resists his genius or conscience only for the sake of present ease or gratification?'

The ancient tradition that the world will be consumed in fire at the end of six thousand years is true, as I have heard from Hell.

For the cherub with his flaming sword is hereby commanded to leave his guard at tree of life; and when he does, the whole creation will be consumed and appear infinite and holy, whereas it now appears finite and corrupt.

This will come to pass by an improvement of sensual enjoyment.

But first the notion that man has a body distinct from his soul is to be expunged; this I shall do by printing in the infernal method, by corrosives, which in Hell are salutary and medicinal, melting apparent surfaces away, and displaying the infinite which was hid.

If the doors of perception were cleansed everything would appear to man as it is, infinite.

For man has closed himself up till he sees all things thro' narrow chinks of his cavern.

A Memorable Fancy

I was in a Printing-house in Hell, and saw the method in which knowledge is transmitted from generation to generation.

In the first chamber was a Dragon-Man, clearing away the rubbish from a cave's mouth; within, a number of Dragons were hollowing the cave.

In the second chamber was a Viper folding round the rock and the cave, and others adorning it with gold, silver, and precious stones.

In the third chamber was an Eagle with wings and feathers of air: he caused the inside of the cave to be infinite. Around were numbers of Eagle-like men who built palaces in the immense cliffs.

In the fourth chamber were Lions of flaming fire, raging around and melting the metals into living fluids.

In the fifth chamber were Unnamed forms, which cast the metals into the expanse.

There they were received by Men who occupied the sixth chamber, and took the forms of books and were arranged in libraries.

The Giants who formed this world into its sensual existence, and now seem to live in it in chains, are in truth the causes of its life and the sources of all activity; but the chains are the cunning of weak and tame minds which have power to resist energy. According to the proverb, the weak in courage is strong in cunning.

Thus one portion of being is the Prolific, the other the Devouring. To the Devourer it seems as if the producer was in his chains; but it is not so, he only takes portions of existence and fancies that the whole.

But the Prolific would cease to be Prolific unless the Devourer, as a sea, received the excess of his delights.

Some will say: 'Is not God alone the Prolific?' I answer: 'God only Acts and Is, in existing beings or Men.'

These two classes of men are always upon earth, and they should be enemies: whoever tries to reconcile them seeks to destroy existence.

Religion is an endeavour to reconcile the two.

Note. Jesus Christ did not wish to unite, but to separate them, as in the Parable of sheep and goats! And He says: 'I came not to send Peace, but a Sword.'

Messiah or Satan or Tempter was formerly thought to be one of the Antediluvians who are our Energies.

A Memorable Fancy

An Angel came to me and said: 'O pitiable, foolish young man! O horrible! O dreadful state! Consider the hot, burning dungeon thou art preparing for thyself to all Eternity, to which thou art going in such career.'

I said, 'Perhaps you will be willing to show me my eternal lot, and we will contemplate together upon it, and see whether your lot or mine is most desirable.'

So he took me thro' a stable, and thro' a church, and down into the church vault, at the end of which was a mill. Thro' the mill we went, and came to a cave. Down the winding cavern we groped our tedious way, till a void boundless as a nether sky appear'd beneath us, and we held by the roots of trees, and hung over this immensity. But I said: 'If you please, we will commit ourselves to this void, and see whether Providence is here also. If you will not, I will.' But he answer'd: 'Do not presume, O young man, but as we here remain, behold thy lot which will soon appear when the darkness passes away.'

So I remain'd with him, sitting in the twisted root of an oak. He was suspended in a fungus, which hung with the head downward into the deep.

By degrees we beheld the infinite Abyss, fiery as the smoke of a burning city; beneath us, at an immense distance, was the sun, black but shining; round it were fiery tracks on which revolv'd vast spiders, crawling after their prey, which flew, or rather swum, in the infinite deep, in the most terrific shapes of animals sprung from corruption; and the air was full of them, and seem'd composed of them – these are Devils, and are called Powers of the Air. I now asked my companion which was my eternal lot? He said: 'Between the black and white spiders.'

But now, from between the black and white spiders, a cloud and fire burst and rolled thro' the deep, blackening all beneath; so that the nether deep grew black as a sea, and rolled with a terrible noise. Beneath us was nothing now to be seen but a black tempest, till looking East between the clouds and the waves we saw a cataract of blood mixed with fire, and not many stones' throw from us appear'd and sunk again the scaly fold of a monstrous serpent. At last, to the East, distant about three degrees, appear'd a fiery crest above the waves. Slowly it reared like a ridge of golden rocks, till we discover'd two globes of crimson fire, from which the sea fled away in clouds of smoke; and now we saw it was the head of Leviathan. His forehead was divided into streaks of green and purple like those on a tiger's forehead. Soon we saw his mouth and red gills hang just above the raging foam, tinging the black deep with beams of blood, advancing toward us with all the fury of a Spiritual Existence.

My friend the Angel climb'd up from his station into the mill: I remain'd alone, and then this appearance was no more; but I found myself sitting on a pleasant bank beside a river, by moonlight, hearing a harper, who sung to the harp; and his theme was: 'The man who never alters his opinion is like standing water, and breeds reptiles of the mind.'

But I arose and sought for the mill, and there I found my Angel, who, surprised, asked me how I escaped.

I answer'd: 'All that we saw was owing to your metaphysics; for when you ran away, I found myself on a bank by moonlight hearing a harper. But now we have seen my eternal lot, shall I show you yours?' He laugh'd at my proposal; but I, by force, suddenly caught him in my arms, and flew westerly thro' the night, till we were elevated above the earth's shadow; then I flung myself with him directly into the body of the sun. Here I clothed myself in white, and taking in my hand Swedenborg's volumes, sunk from the glorious clime, and passed all the planets till we came to Saturn. Here I stay'd to rest, and then leap'd into the void between Saturn and the fixed stars.

'Here,' said I, 'is your lot, in this space – if space it may be call'd.' Soon we saw the stable and the church, and I took him to the altar and open'd the Bible, and lo! it was a deep pit, into which I descended, driving the Angel before me. Soon we saw seven houses of brick. One we enter'd; in it were a number of monkeys, baboons, and all of that species, chain'd by the middle, grinning and snatching at one another, but withheld by the shortness of their chains. However, I saw that they sometimes grew numerous, and then the weak were caught by the strong, and with a grinning aspect, first coupled with, and then devour'd, by plucking off first one limb and then another, till the body was left a helpless trunk. This, after grinning and kissing it with seeming fondness, they devour'd too; and here and there I saw one savourily picking the flesh off of his own tail. As the stench terribly annoy'd us both, we went into the mill, and I in my hand brought the skeleton of a body, which in the mill was Aristotle's Analytics.

So the Angel said: 'Thy phantasy has imposed upon me, and thou oughtest to be ashamed.'

I answer'd: 'We impose on one another, and it is but lost time to converse with you whose works are only Analytics.'

Opposition is True Friendship.

I have always found that Angels have the vanity to speak of themselves as the Only Wise. This they do with a confident insolence sprouting from systematic reasoning.

Thus Swedenborg boasts that what he writes is new; tho' it is only the Contents or Index of already publish'd books.

A man carried a monkey about for a show, and because he was a little wiser than the monkey, grew vain, and conceiv'd himself as much wiser than seven men. It is so with Swedenborg: he shows the folly of churches, and exposes hypocrites, till he imagines that all are religious, and himself the single one on earth that ever broke a net.

Now hear a plain fact: Swedenborg has not written one new truth. Now hear another: he has written all the old falsehoods.

And now hear the reason. He conversed with Angels who are all religious, and conversed not with Devils who all hate religion, for he was incapable thro' his conceited notions.

Thus Swedenborg's writings are a recapitulation of all superficial opinions, and an analysis of the more sublime – but no further.

Have now another plain fact. Any man of mechanical talents may, from the writings of Paracelsus or Jacob Behmen, produce ten thousand volumes of equal value with Swedenborg's, and from those of Dante or Shakespear an infinite number.

But when he has done this, let him not say that he knows better than his master, for he only holds a candle in sunshine.

A Memorable Fancy

Once I saw a Devil in a flame of fire, who arose before an Angel that sat on a cloud, and the Devil utter'd these words: –

'The worship of God is: Honouring his gifts in other men, each according to his genius, and loving the greatest men best: those who envy or calumniate great men hate God; for there is no other God.'

The Angel hearing this became almost blue; but mastering himself he grew yellow, and at last white, pink, and smiling, and then replied: –

'Thou Idolater! is not God One? and is not he visible in Jesus Christ? and has not Jesus Christ given his sanction to the law of ten commandments? and are not all other men fools, sinners, and nothings?'

The Devil answer'd: 'Bray a fool in a mortar with wheat, yet shall not his folly be beaten out of him. If Jesus Christ is the greatest man, you ought to love Him in the greatest degree. Now hear how He has given His sanction to the law of ten commandments. Did He not mock at the sabbath, and so mock the sabbaths's God; murder those who were murder'd because of Him; turn away the law from the woman taken in adultery; steal the labour of others to support Him; bear false witness when he omitted making a defence before Pilate; covet when he pray'd for his disciples, and when He bid them shake off the dust of their feet against such as refused to lodge them? I tell you, no virtue can exist without breaking these ten commandments. Jesus was all virtue, and acted from impulse, not from rules.'

When he had so spoken, I beheld the Angel, who stretched out his arms, embracing the flame of fire, and he was consumed, and arose as Elijah.

Note. This Angel, who is now become a Devil, is my particular friend. We often read the Bible together in its infernal or diabolical sense, which the world shall have if they behave well.

I have also The Bible of Hell, which the world shall have whether they will or no.

One Law for the Lion and Ox is Oppression.

THE FRENCH REVOLUTION

The French Revolution (1791)   *The French Revolution*, the most overtly historical of Blake's mythic poems, presents an enactment of events in France in a prophetic manner, albeit with little actual realism. But even if he had had access to accurate knowledge, Blake would not have wanted merely to act as a mythic journalist. Instead, he uses the historical characters of the revolution as figures in his cosmic drama. Blake projected the poem in seven books but only the first exists (see General Introduction for details). It deals with the period of the revolution before the fall of the Bastille and shows the king and aristocracy threatening the common people and their representatives with the continued tyrannies and horrors of hierarchical government: its systematic oppressions are depicted in the seven towers of the Bastille in the form of unequal laws, standing armies, torture, organised religions, and the other elements of a vicious social order. One of the towers even has a man in it 'confin'd for a writing prophetic' (p. 210). Blake animates his historical characters with the eerily powerful, almost gothic qualities, which we find writ large in later prophetic works. He has the French king brooding and glowing gloomily like an eclipsed sun, urging that the old order should 'hide' until the tempests of change end (p. 212), while his advisers give him conflicting opinions. Nobles like Burgundy voice their contempt for the levelling forces of history: 'Shall this marble-built heaven become a clay cottage, this earth an oak stool, and these mowers/From the Atlantic mountains mow down all this great starry harvest of six thousand years?' (p. 213). On the other hand, ministers such as Necker facilitate the emergent democratic aspirations of the people through liberal reforms, while clergy in the form of the Archbishop of Paris urge a counter-revolutionary suppression: 'let the Bastille devour/These rebellious seditious; seal them up, O Anointed! in everlasting chains' (p. 216). Each of the characters is given the stage for speeches that achieve a terrific rhetorical

effectiveness. The speech by Abbé de Sieyès expressing the voice of the
people articulates Blake's deeply felt awareness of oppression, inequality
and the absolute need for social and political revolution as the basis for
his vision of human liberation:

> 'Hear, O heavens of France! the voice of the people, arising
>   from valley and hill,
> O'erclouded with power. Hear the voice of valleys, the voice of
>   meek cities,
> Mourning oppressèd on village and field, till the village and
>   field is a waste.
> For the husbandman weeps at blights of the fife, and blasting
>   of trumpets consume
> The souls of mild France; the pale mother nourishes her child
>   to the deadly slaughter [. . .]
> The millions of spirits immortal were bound in the ruins of
>   sulphur heaven
> To wander enslav'd; black, depress'd in dark ignorance, kept
>   in awe with the whip
> To worship terrors, bred from the blood of revenge and breath
>   of desire
> In bestial forms, or more terrible men; till the dawn of our
>   peaceful morning,
> Till dawn, till morning, till the breaking of clouds, and
>   swelling of winds, and the universal voice;
> Till man raise his darken'd limbs out of the caves of night.'

(p. 219)

THE FRENCH REVOLUTION
BOOK THE FIRST
Printed 1791

The dead brood over Europe: the cloud and vision descends over cheerful
    France;
O cloud well appointed! Sick, sick, the Prince on his couch! wreath'd in
    dim
And appalling mist; his strong hand outstretch'd, from his shoulder down
    the bone,
Runs aching cold into the sceptre, too heavy for mortal grasp – no more
To be swayèd by visible hand, nor in cruelty bruise the mild flourishing
    mountains.

Sick the mountains! and all their vineyards weep, in the eyes of the kingly
    mourner;
Pale is the morning cloud in his visage. Rise, Necker! the ancient dawn
    calls us
To awake from slumbers of five thousand years. I awake, but my soul is in
    dreams;
From my window I see the old mountains of France, like agèd men, fading
    away.

Troubled, leaning on Necker, descends the King to his chamber of council;
    shady mountains
In fear utter voices of thunder; the woods of France embosom the sound;
Clouds of wisdom prophetic reply, and roll over the palace roof heavy.
Forty men, each conversing with woes in the infinite shadows of his soul,
Like our ancient fathers in regions of twilight, walk, gathering round the
    King:
Again the loud voice of France cries to the morning; the morning
    prophesies to its clouds.

For the Commons convene in the Hall of the Nation. France shakes! And
    the heavens of France
Perplex'd vibrate round each careful countenance! Darkness of old times
    around them
Utters loud despair, shadowing Paris; her grey towers groan, and the
    Bastille trembles.

In its terrible towers the Governor stood, in dark fogs list'ning the horror;

A thousand his soldiers, old veterans of France, breathing red clouds of
    power and dominion.

Sudden seiz'd with howlings, despair, and black night, he stalk'd like a
    lion from tower

To tower; his howlings were heard in the Louvre; from court to court
    restless he dragg'd

His strong limbs; from court to court curs'd the fierce torment unquell'd,

Howling and giving the dark command; in his soul stood the purple
    plague,

Tugging his iron manacles, and piercing thro' the seven towers dark and
    sickly,

Panting over the prisoners like a wolf gorg'd. And the den nam'd Horror
    held a man

Chain'd hand and foot; round his neck an iron band, bound to the
    impregnable wall;

In his soul was the serpent coil'd round in his heart, hid from the light, as
    in a cleft rock:

And the man was confin'd for a writing prophetic. In the tower nam'd
    Darkness was a man

Pinion'd down to the stone floor, his strong bones scarce cover'd with
    sinews; the iron rings

Were forg'd smaller as the flesh decay'd: a mask of iron on his face hid the
    lineaments

Of ancient Kings, and the frown of the eternal lion was hid from the
    oppressèd earth.

In the tower namèd Bloody, a skeleton yellow remainèd in its chains on its
    couch

Of stone, once a man who refus'd to sign papers of abhorrence; the eternal
    worm

Crept in the skeleton. In the den nam'd Religion, a loathsome sick woman
    bound down

To a bed of straw; the seven diseases of earth, like birds of prey, stood on
    the couch

And fed on the body: she refus'd to be whore to the Minister, and with a
    knife smote him.

In the tower nam'd Order, an old man, whose white beard cover'd the
    stone floor like weeds

On margin of the sea, shrivell'd up by heat of day and cold of night; his
    den was short

And narrow as a grave dug for a child, with spiders' webs wove, and with
    slime
Of ancient horrors cover'd, for snakes and scorpions are his companions,
    harmless they breathe
His sorrowful breath: he, by conscience urg'd, in the city of Paris rais'd a
    pulpit,
And taught wonders to darken'd souls. In the den nam'd Destiny a strong
    man sat,
His feet and hands cut off, and his eyes blinded; round his middle a chain
    and a band
Fasten'd into the wall; fancy gave him to see an image of despair in his
    den,
Eternally rushing round, like a man on his hands and knees, day and night
    without rest:
He was friend to the favourite. In the seventh tower, nam'd the tower of
    God, was a man
Mad, with chains loose, which he dragg'd up and down; fed with hopes
    year by year, he pinèd
For liberty. – Vain hopes! his reason decay'd, and the world of attraction in
    his bosom
Centred, and the rushing of chaos overwhelm'd his dark soul: he was
    confin'd
For a letter of advice to a King, and his ravings in winds are heard over
    Versailles.

But the dens shook and trembled: the prisoners look up and assay to
    shout; they listen,
Then laugh in the dismal den, then are silent; and a light walks round the
    dark towers.
For the Commons convene in the Hall of the Nation; like spirits of fire in
    the beautiful
Porches of the Sun, to plant beauty in the desert craving abyss, they gleam
On the anxious city: all children new-born first behold them, tears are
    fled,
And they nestle in earth-breathing bosoms. So the city of Paris, their wives
    and children,
Look up to the morning Senate and visions of sorrow leave pensive streets.

But heavy-brow'd jealousies lour o'er the Louvre; and terrors of ancient
    Kings

Descend from the gloom and wander thro' the palace, and weep round the
   King and his Nobles;
While loud thunders roll, troubling the dead. Kings are sick throughout all
   the earth!
The voice ceas'd: the Nation sat; and the triple forg'd fetters of times were
   unloos'd.
The voice ceas'd: the Nation sat; but ancient darkness and trembling
   wander thro' the palace.

As in day of havoc and routed battle among thick shades of discontent,
On the soul-skirting mountains of sorrow cold waving, the Nobles fold
   round the King;
Each stern visage lock'd up as with strong bands of iron, each strong limb
   bound down as with marble,
In flames of red wrath burning, bound in astonishment a quarter of an
   hour.

Then the King glow'd: his Nobles fold round, like the sun of old time
   quench'd in clouds;
In their darkness the King stood; his heart flam'd, and utter'd a with'ring
   heat, and these words burst forth:

'The nerves of five thousand years' ancestry tremble, shaking the heavens
   of France;
Throbs of anguish beat on brazen war foreheads; they descend and look
   into their graves.
I see thro' darkness, thro' clouds rolling round me, the spirits of ancient
   Kings
Shivering over their bleachèd bones; round them their counsellors look up
   from the dust,
Crying: "Hide from the living! Our bonds and our prisoners shout in the
   open field.
Hide in the nether earth! Hide in the bones! Sit obscurèd in the hollow
   scull!
Our flesh is corrupted, and we wear away. We are not numberèd among
   the living. Let us hide
In stones, among roots of trees. The prisoners have burst their dens.
Let us hide! let us hide in the dust! and plague and wrath and tempest
   shall cease." '

He ceas'd, silent pond'ring; his brows folded heavy, his forehead was in
    affliction.
Like the central fire from the window he saw his vast armies spread over
    the hills,
Breathing red fires from man to man, and from horse to horse: then his
    bosom
Expanded like starry heaven; he sat down: his Nobles took their ancient
    seats.

Then the ancientest Peer, Duke of Burgundy, rose from the Monarch's
    right hand, red as wines
From his mountains; an odour of war, like a ripe vineyard, rose from his
    garments,
And the chamber became as a clouded sky; o'er the Council he stretch'd
    his red limbs
Cloth'd in flames of crimson; as a ripe vineyard stretches over sheaves of
    corn,
The fierce Duke hung over the Council; around him crowd, weeping in his
    burning robe,
A bright cloud of infant souls: his words fall like purple autumn on the
    sheaves:

'Shall this marble-built heaven become a clay cottage, this earth an oak
    stool, and these mowers
From the Atlantic mountains mow down all this great starry harvest of six
    thousand years?
And shall Necker, the hind of Geneva, stretch out his crook'd sickle o'er
    fertile France,
Till our purple and crimson is faded to russet, and the kingdoms of earth
    bound in sheaves,
And the ancient forests of chivalry hewn, and the joys of the combat burnt
    for fuel;
Till the power and dominion is rent from the pole, sword and sceptre from
    sun and moon,
The law and gospel from fire and air, and eternal reason and science
From the deep and the solid, and man lay his faded head down on the
    rock
Of eternity, where the eternal lion and eagle remain to devour?
This to prevent, urg'd by cries in day, and prophetic dreams hovering in
    night,

To enrich the lean earth that craves, furrow'd with ploughs, whose seed is
    departing from her,
Thy Nobles have gather'd thy starry hosts round this rebellious city,
To rouse up the ancient forests of Europe, with clarions of cloud-breathing
    war,
To hear the horse neigh to the drum and trumpet, and the trumpet and
    war shout reply.
Stretch the hand that beckons the eagles of heaven: they cry over Paris,
    and wait
Till Fayette point his finger to Versailles – the eagles of heaven must have
    their prey!'

He ceas'd, and burn'd silent: red clouds roll round Necker; a weeping is
    heard o'er the palace.
Like a dark cloud Necker paus'd, and like thunder on the just man's burial
    day he paus'd.
Silent sit the winds, silent the meadows; while the husbandman and
    woman of weakness
And bright children look after him into the grave, and water his clay with
    love,
Then turn towards pensive fields: so Necker paus'd, and his visage was
    cover'd with clouds.

The King lean'd on his mountains; then lifted his head and look'd on his
    armies, that shone
Thro' heaven, tinging morning with beams of blood; then turning to
    Burgundy, troubled: –
'Burgundy, thou wast born a lion! My soul is o'ergrown with distress
For the Nobles of France, and dark mists roll round me and blot the
    writing of God
Written in my bosom. Necker rise! leave the kingdom, thy life is
    surrounded with snares.
We have call'd an Assembly, but not to destroy; we have given gifts, not to
    the weak;
I hear rushing of muskets and bright'ning of swords; and visages,
    redd'ning with war,
Frowning and looking up from brooding villages and every dark'ning city.
Ancient wonders frown over the kingdom, and cries of women and babes
    are heard,

And tempests of doubt roll around me, and fierce sorrows, because of the
    Nobles of France.
Depart! answer not! for the tempest must fall, as in years that are passèd
    away.'

Dropping a tear the old man his place left, and when he was gone out
He set his face toward Geneva to flee; and the women and children of the
    city
Kneel'd round him and kissèd his garments and wept: he stood a short
    space in the street,
Then fled; and the whole city knew he was fled to Geneva, and the Senate
    heard it.

But the Nobles burn'd wrathful at Necker's departure, and wreath'd their
    clouds and waters
In dismal volumes; as, risen from beneath, the Archbishop of Paris arose
In the rushing of scales, and hissing of flames, and rolling of sulphurous
    smoke: –

'Hearken, Monarch of France, to the terrors of heaven, and let thy soul
    drink of my counsel!
Sleeping at midnight in my golden tower, the repose of the labours of men
Wav'd its solemn cloud over my head. I awoke; a cold hand passèd over
    my limbs, and behold!
An agèd form, white as snow, hov'ring in mist, weeping in the uncertain
    light.
Dim the form almost faded, tears fell down the shady cheeks; at his feet
    many cloth'd
In white robes, strewn in air censers and harps, silent they lay prostrated;
Beneath, in the awful void, myriads descending and weeping thro' dismal
    winds;
Endless the shady train shiv'ring descended, from the gloom where the
    agèd form wept.
At length, trembling, the vision sighing, in a low voice like the voice of the
    grasshopper, whisper'd:
"My groaning is heard in the abbeys, and God, so long worshipp'd, departs
    as a lamp
Without oil; for a curse is heard hoarse thro' the land, from a godless race
Descending to beasts; they look downward, and labour, and forget my holy
    law;

The sound of prayer fails from lips of flesh, and the holy hymn from
    thicken'd tongues;
For the bars of Chaos are burst; her millions prepare their fiery way
Thro' the orbèd abode of the holy dead, to root up and pull down and
    remove,
And Nobles and Clergy shall fail from before me, and my cloud and vision
    be no more;
The mitre become black, the crown vanish, and the sceptre and ivory staff
Of the ruler wither among bones of death; they shall consume from the
    thistly field,
And the sound of the bell, and voice of the sabbath, and singing of the
    holy choir
Is turn'd into songs of the harlot in day, and cries of the virgin in night.
They shall drop at the plough and faint at the harrow, unredeem'd,
    unconfess'd, unpardon'd;
The priest rot in his surplice by the lawless lover, the holy beside the
    accursèd,
The King, frowning in purple, beside the grey ploughman, and their worms
    embrace together."
The voice ceas'd: a groan shook my chamber. I slept, for the cloud of
    repose returnèd;
But morning dawn'd heavy upon me. I rose to bring my Prince heaven-
    utter'd counsel.
Hear my counsel, O King! and send forth thy Generals; the command of
    Heaven is upon thee!
Then do thou command, O King! to shut up this Assembly in their final
    home;
Let thy soldiers possess this city of rebels, that threaten to bathe their feet
In the blood of Nobility, trampling the heart and the head; let the Bastille
    devour
These rebellious seditious; seal them up, O Anointed! in everlasting
    chains.'
He sat down: a damp cold pervaded the Nobles, and monsters of worlds
    unknown
Swam round them, watching to be deliverèd – when Aumont, whose
    chaos-born soul
Eternally wand'ring, a comet and swift-falling fire, pale enter'd the
    chamber.
Before the red Council he stood, like a man that returns from hollow
    graves: –

'Awe-surrounded, alone thro' the army, a fear and a with'ring blight blown
    by the north,
The Abbé de Sieyes from the Nation's Assembly, O Princes and Generals of
    France,
Unquestionèd, unhinderèd! Awe-struck are the soldiers; a dark shadowy
    man in the form
Of King Henry the Fourth walks before him in fires; the captains like men
    bound in chains
Stood still as he pass'd: he is come to the Louvre, O King, with a message
    to thee!
The strong soldiers tremble, the horses their manes bow, and the guards of
    thy palace are fled!'

Uprose awful in his majestic beams Bourbon's strong Duke; his proud
    sword, from his thigh
Drawn, he threw on the earth: the Duke of Bretagne and the Earl of
    Bourgogne
Rose inflam'd, to and fro in the chamber, like thunder-clouds ready to
    burst.

'What damp all our fires, O spectre of Henry!' said Bourbon, 'and rend the
    flames
From the head of our King? Rise, Monarch of France! command me, and I
    will lead
This army of superstition at large, that the ardour of noble souls,
    quenchless,
May yet burn in France, nor our shoulders be plough'd with the furrows of
    poverty.'

Then Orleans, generous as mountains, arose and unfolded his robe, and
    put forth
His benevolent hand, looking on the Archbishop, who changèd as pale as
    lead,
Would have risen but could not: his voice issuèd harsh grating; instead of
    words harsh hissings
Shook the chamber; he ceas'd abash'd. Then Orleans spoke; all was silent.
He breath'd on them, and said: 'O Princes of fire, whose flames are for
    growth, not consuming,
Fear not dreams, fear not visions, nor be you dismay'd with sorrows which
    flee at the morning!
Can the fires of Nobility ever be quench'd, or the stars by a stormy night?

Is the body diseas'd when the members are healthful? can the man be
     bound in sorrow
Whose ev'ry function is fill'd with its fiery desire? can the soul, whose
     brain and heart
Cast their rivers in equal tides thro' the great Paradise, languish because
     the feet,
Hands, head, bosom, and parts of love follow their high breathing joy?
And can Nobles be bound when the people are free, or God weep when
     his children are happy?
Have you never seen Fayette's forehead, or Mirabeau's eyes, or the
     shoulders of Target,
Or Bailly the strong foot of France, or Clermont the terrible voice, and your
     robes
Still retain their own crimson? – Mine never yet faded, for fire delights in
     its form!
But go, merciless man, enter into the infinite labyrinth of another's brain
Ere thou measure the circle that he shall run. Go, thou cold recluse, into
     the fires
Of another's high flaming rich bosom, and return unconsum'd, and write
     laws.
If thou canst not do this, doubt thy theories, learn to consider all men as
     thy equals,
Thy brethren, and not as thy foot or thy hand, unless thou first fearest to
     hurt them.'

The Monarch stood up; the strong Duke his sword to its golden scabbard
     return'd;
The Nobles sat round like clouds on the mountains, when the storm is
     passing away: –
'Let the Nation's Ambassador come among Nobles, like incense of the
     valley!'

Aumont went out and stood in the hollow porch, his ivory wand in his
     hand;
A cold orb of disdain revolv'd round him, and coverèd his soul with snows
     eternal.
Great Henry's soul shudderèd, a whirlwind and fire tore furious from his
     angry bosom;
He indignant departed on horses of heav'n. Then the Abbé de Sieyès rais'd
     his feet

On the steps of the Louvre; like a voice of God following a storm, the Abbé
  follow'd
The pale fires of Aumont into the chamber; as a father that bows to his
son,
Whose rich fields inheriting spread their old glory, so the voice of the
  people bowèd
Before the ancient seat of the kingdom and mountains to be renewèd.

'Hear, O heavens of France! the voice of the people, arising from valley and
  hill,
O'erclouded with power. Hear the voice of valleys, the voice of meek cities,
Mourning oppressèd on village and field, till the village and field is a
  waste.
For the husbandman weeps at blights of the fife, and blasting of trumpets
  consume
The souls of mild France; the pale mother nourishes her child to the
  deadly slaughter.
When the heavens were seal'd with a stone, and the terrible sun clos'd in
  an orb, and the moon
Rent from the nations, and each star appointed for watchers of night,
The millions of spirits immortal were bound in the ruins of sulphur heaven
To wander enslav'd; black, depress'd in dark ignorance, kept in awe with
  the whip
To worship terrors, bred from the blood of revenge and breath of desire
In bestial forms, or more terrible men; till the dawn of our peaceful
  morning,
Till dawn, till morning, till the breaking of clouds, and swelling of winds,
  and the universal voice;
Till man raise his darken'd limbs out of the caves of night. His eyes and his
  heart
Expand – Where is Space? where, O Sun, is thy dwelling? where thy tent,
  O faint slumb'rous Moon?
Then the valleys of France shall cry to the soldier: "Throw down thy sword
  and musket,
And run and embrace the meek peasant." Her Nobles shall hear and shall
  weep, and put off
The red robe of terror, the crown of oppression, the shoes of contempt,
  and unbuckle
The girdle of war from the desolate earth. Then the Priest in his thund'rous
  cloud

Shall weep, bending to earth, embracing the valleys, and putting his hand
    to the plough,
Shall say: "No more I curse thee; but now I will bless thee: no more in
    deadly black
Devour thy labour; nor lift up a cloud in thy heavens, O laborious plough;
That the wild raging millions, that wander in forests, and howl in law-
    blasted wastes,
Strength madden'd with slavery, honesty bound in the dens of
    superstition,
May sing in the village, and shout in the harvest, and woo in pleasant
    gardens
Their once savage loves, now beaming with knowledge, with gentle awe
    adornèd;
And the saw, and the hammer, the chisel, the pencil, the pen, and the
    instruments
Of heavenly song sound in the wilds once forbidden, to teach the
    laborious ploughman
And shepherd, deliver'd from clouds of war, from pestilence, from night-
    fear, from murder,
From falling, from stifling, from hunger, from cold, from slander,
    discontent and sloth,
That walk in beasts and birds of night, driven back by the sandy desert,
Like pestilent fogs round cities of men; and the happy earth sing in its
    course,
The mild peaceable nations be openèd to heav'n, and men walk with their
    fathers in bliss."
Then hear the first voice of the morning: "Depart, O clouds of night, and
    no more
Return; be withdrawn cloudy war, troops of warriors depart, nor around
    our peaceable city
Breathe fires; but ten miles from Paris let all be peace, nor a soldier be
    seen!" '

He ended: the wind of contention arose, and the clouds cast their
    shadows; the Princes
Like the mountains of France, whose agèd trees utter an awful voice, and
    their branches
Are shatter'd; till gradual a murmur is heard descending into the valley,
Like a voice in the vineyards of Burgundy when grapes are shaken on
    grass,

Like the low voice of the labouring man, instead of the shout of joy;
And the palace appear'd like a cloud driven abroad; blood ran down the
    ancient pillars.
Thro' the cloud a deep thunder, the Duke of Burgundy, delivers the King's
    command: –

'Seest thou yonder dark castle, that moated around, keeps this city of Paris
    in awe?
Go, command yonder tower, saying: "Bastille, depart! and take thy
    shadowy course;
Overstep the dark river, thou terrible tower, and get thee up into the
    country ten miles.
And thou black southern prison, move along the dusky road to Versailles;
    there
Frown on the gardens" – and, if it obey and depart, then the King will
    disband
This war-breathing army; but, if it refuse, let the Nation's Assembly thence
    learn
That this army of terrors, that prison of horrors, are the bands of the
    murmuring kingdom.'

Like the morning star arising above the black waves, when a ship-wreck'd
    soul sighs for morning,
Thro' the ranks, silent, walk'd the Ambassador back to the Nation's
    Assembly, and told
The unwelcome message. Silent they heard; then a thunder roll'd round
    loud and louder;
Like pillars of ancient halls and ruins of times remote, they sat.
Like a voice from the dim pillars Mirabeau rose; the thunders subsided
    away;
A rushing of wings around him was heard as he brighten'd, and cried out
    aloud:
'Where is the General of the Nation?' The walls re-echo'd: 'Where is the
    General of the Nation?'

Sudden as the bullet wrapp'd in his fire, when brazen cannons rage in the
    field,
Fayette sprung from his seat saying 'Ready!' Then bowing like clouds, man
    toward man, the Assembly
Like a Council of Ardours seated in clouds, bending over the cities of men,

And over the armies of strife, where their children are marshall'd together
     to battle,
They murmuring divide; while the wind sleeps beneath, and the numbers
     are counted in silence,
While they vote the removal of War, and the pestilence weighs his red
     wings in the sky.

So Fayette stood silent among the Assembly, and the votes were given, and
     the numbers numb'red;
And the vote was that Fayette should order the army to remove ten miles
     from Paris.

The agèd Sun rises appall'd from dark mountains, and gleams a dusky
     beam
On Fayette; but on the whole army a shadow, for a cloud on the eastern
     hills
Hover'd, and stretch'd across the city, and across the army, and across the
     Louvre.
Like a flame of fire he stood before dark ranks, and before expecting
     captains:
On pestilent vapours around him flow frequent spectres of religious men,
     weeping
In winds; driven out of the abbeys, their naked souls shiver in keen open air;
Driven out by the fiery cloud of Voltaire, and thund'rous rocks of
     Rousseau,
They dash like foam against the ridges of the army, uttering a faint feeble
     cry.

Gleams of fire streak the heavens, and of sulphur the earth, from Fayette as
     he lifted his hand;
But silent he stood, till all the officers rush round him like waves
Round the shore of France, in day of the British flag, when heavy cannons
Affright the coasts, and the peasant looks over the sea and wipes a tear:
Over his head the soul of Voltaire shone fiery; and over the army Rousseau
     his white cloud
Unfolded, on souls of war, living terrors, silent list'ning toward Fayette.
His voice loud inspir'd by liberty, and by spirits of the dead, thus
     thunder'd: –

'The Nation's Assembly command that the Army remove ten miles from
     Paris;
Nor a soldier be seen in road or in field, till the Nation command return.'

Rushing along iron ranks glittering, the officers each to his station

Depart, and the stern captain strokes his proud steed, and in front of his
solid ranks

Waits the sound of trumpet; captains of foot stand each by his cloudy
drum:

Then the drum beats, and the steely ranks move, and trumpets rejoice in
the sky.

Dark cavalry, like clouds fraught with thunder, ascend on the hills, and
bright infantry, rank

Behind rank, to the soul-shaking drum and shrill fife, along the roads
glitter like fire.

The noise of trampling, the wind of trumpets, smote the Palace walls with
a blast.

Pale and cold sat the King in midst of his Peers, and his noble heart sunk,
and his pulses

Suspended their motion; a darkness crept over his eyelids, and chill cold
sweat

Sat round his brows faded in faint death; his Peers pale like mountains of
the dead,

Cover'd with dews of night, groaning, shaking forests and floods. The cold
newt,

And snake, and damp toad on the kingly foot crawl, or croak on the awful
knee,

Shedding their slime; in folds of the robe the crown'd adder builds and
hisses

From stony brows: shaken the forests of France, sick the kings of the
nations,

And the bottoms of the world were open'd, and the graves of archangels
unseal'd:

The enormous dead lift up their pale fires and look over the rocky cliffs.

A faint heat from their fires reviv'd the cold Louvre; the frozen blood
reflow'd.

Awful uprose the King; him the Peers follow'd; they saw the courts of the
Palace

Forsaken, and Paris without a soldier, silent. For the noise was gone up

And follow'd the army; and the Senate in peace sat beneath morning's
beam.

A SONG OF LIBERTY
Engraved circa 1792

'A Song of Liberty' (1792–3)   Written after *The Marriage of Heaven and Hell* but later added to that text, this is a visionary political poem. It presents Blake's whole myth in miniature, with direct reference to the revolutionary events of his day. It opens in the fallen experiential world of oppression, with Albion, Blake's representation of England, sick. The mention of America is a reminder of the American Revolution of 1775, and suddenly in response to revolutionary prophecy, France is commanded to 'rend down thy dungeon', a clear reference to the fall of the Bastille. With that, the fiery spirit of revolution is reborn. This is the 'new-born wonder' that Blake later names Orc, encompassing all forms of liberation. Here, he confronts the 'starry king' of England, George III, the representative of the repressive patriarchal law of Urizen. With his failure to stop revolution in America and his precarious position given the collapse of the French monarchy, George III is desperately regrouping the forces of reaction in order to repress liberation; but he is also doomed to failure, as the last section of the text shows. There, 'the stony law' is stamped to dust and with a ringing proclamation against imperial savagery, the chorus sounds Blake's resounding motto, '*Empire is no more! And now the lion and the wolf shall cease.* [. . .] For everything that lives is Holy!' (p. 226)

1. The Eternal Female groan'd! It was heard over all the Earth.
2. Albion's coast is sick, silent. The American meadows faint!
3. Shadows of Prophecy shiver along by the lakes and the rivers, and mutter across the ocean. France, rend down thy dungeon!
4. Golden Spain, burst the barriers of old Rome!
5. Cast thy keys, O Rome! into the deep, down falling, even to eternity down falling,
6. And weep.
7. In her trembling hands she took the new-born terror, howling.
8. On those infinite mountains of light, now barr'd out by the Atlantic sea, the new-born fire stood before the starry king!
9. Flagg'd with grey-brow'd snows and thunderous visages, the jealous wings wav'd over the deep.
10. The speary hand burnèd aloft, unbuckled was the shield; forth went the hand of Jealousy among the flaming hair, and hurl'd the new-born wonder thro' the starry night.
11. The fire, the fire, is falling!
12. Look up! look up! O citizen of London, enlarge thy countenance! O Jew, leave counting gold! return to thy oil and wine. O African! black African! Go, wingèd thought, widen his forehead!
13. The fiery limbs, the flaming hair, shot like the sinking sun into the western sea.
14. Wak'd from his eternal sleep, the hoary element, roaring, fled away.
15. Down rush'd, beating his wings in vain, the jealous King; his grey-brow'd counsellors, thunderous warriors, curl'd veterans, among helms, and shields, and chariots, horses, elephants, banners, castles, slings, and rocks,
16. Falling, rushing, ruining! buried in the ruins, on Urthona's dens;
17. All night beneath the ruins; then, their sullen flames faded, emerge round the gloomy King.
18. With thunder and fire, leading his starry hosts thro' the waste wilderness, he promulgates his ten commands, glancing his beamy eyelids over the deep in dark dismay,
19. Where the son of fire in his eastern cloud, while the morning plumes her golden breast,

20. Spurning the clouds written with curses, stamps the stony law to
    dust, loosing the eternal horses from the dens of night, crying
    Empire is no more! and now the lion and the wolf shall cease.

Chorus

Let the Priests of the Raven of dawn no longer, in deadly black, with
hoarse note curse the sons of joy! Nor his accepted brethren – whom,
tyrant, he calls free – lay the bound or build the roof! Nor pale
Religion's lechery call that Virginity that wishes but acts not!

For everything that lives is Holy!

VISIONS OF THE DAUGHTERS OF ALBION

Visions of the Daughters of Albion (1791–2) This short prophetic poem concerns three typically oddly-named characters – Oothoon, her lover Theotormon and his rival Bromion. The action is in three parts with a chorus of the Daughters of Albion to mark the end of each. In the first section (pp. 231–2), Oothoon overcomes the restraints of convention and determines to give herself in love to Theotormon – in other words, fearlessly accept sexual love. But while on her way to him, she is raped by Bromion who gloats over his possession of her. Instead of defending her, Theotormon rejects her as defiled, ties her back to back with Bromion and then wails with jealousy and torment (p. 232), a scene which forms the frontispiece image for the book. In the second section (pp. 232–4), each character speaks in turn giving their view of Oothoon's predicament, with Oothoon herself declaring her continued purity and arguing that sexual experience is no mark of defilement. The poem ends with an extraordinary speech by the manacled Oothoon (pp. 234–7), who rejects her oppression and asserts a vision of freedom. As with most of Blake's prophetic works, details and names (such as Leutha) remain obscure, but rather than worry about details, it is better to let the power of the imaginative drive carry the reader along.

Blake clearly links together two apparently separate social issues of his day – the oppression and exploitation of women (the daughters of Albion being the women of England), and the oppression and exploitation of black African slaves in America – and, as is the method of his prophetic works generally, he shows the interconnections between them. Take, for example, the passage which occurs after the rape of Oothoon by Bromion ('Bromion rent her with his thunders' p. 232): this reveals the link between the possession of women and possession of slaves as part of capitalism, showing how both are bolstered by a hypocritical ideology of religion and love. In fact the poem suggests that the lover Theotormon and the rapist Bromion are two sides of the possessive male attitude to women. It is the lover Theotormon with his possessive jealously who grossly labels his beloved a harlot, when she has been raped: he wanted to have her pure; she is raped and he blames her for it! In other words the idealisation of women as madonnas and their denigration as magdalens is a product of a male schizophrenia about women, of patriarchal ideology. There is a parallel here with Hardy's presentation of the same issue in *Tess of the D'Urbervilles*, where two male characters Alec D'Urberville and Angel Clare play similar roles to Bromion and Theotormon, depicting the exploitative hypocrisy of male attitudes to women. This possessive sexuality Blake links with the concurrent issue of racism and slavery, in order to achieve a double indictment of patriarchy and capitalism as part of an interlinked system of oppressions. Oothoon is described as the 'soft soul of America' as well as being one of the daughters of Albion. The male oppression of women is effectively a form of colonialism as was the exploitation of Africa and its peoples. For Blake, oppressions are indivisible, just as freedom is indivisible. As Shelley was to put it a generation later in *The Revolt of Islam*, 'Can man be free if woman be a slave?' (Canto 2, verse 43).

Both issues were live contemporary debates during the period when Blake wrote this work. There was an active campaign against the slave trade during the early 1790s, which culminated in a motion in the Commons on 23 April 1792, calling for its abolition. But not only was this form of colonial tyranny being debated while Blake was writing his poem; so was the colonisation of women by men. Blake knew Mary Wollstonecraft and must have known many of the arguments she put in her *Vindication of the Rights of Women* which appeared in the same year as Blake's poem. In that sense, Blake was responding to the feminist thinking of his day.

In a number of his writings Blake is evidently concerned with the issues of possessive love and the repression of sexuality (see 'The Garden of Love' and 'My Pretty Rose-Tree', p. 85). These are crucial in *Visions of the Daughters of Albion*. The third section of the poem is given over to Oothoon entirely. In the first part of her speech she analyses the oppressive male-dominated system of Urizen, the law-giver, who obliterates all individuality and joy in fixed relationships, like the legal bond of marriage, forcing women to 'turn the wheel of false desire' (p. 235) by being sexually owned by their husbands. It is this Urizenic view that Theotormon and Bromion have imposed on her. In rejecting this definition, Oothoon voices a classic Blakean indictment of jealous love, fixed by law or habit, as 'a creeping skeleton/With lamplike eyes watching around the frozen marriage bed'. Oothoon counteracts this with a remarkable assertion of free love in her vision of 'lovely copulation, bliss on bliss, with Theotormon' (p. 237).

But there are bound to be contradictions involved in any male's writing about the issue of sexual oppression, because, like it or not, men cannot just abdicate from complicity with that system of oppression and the values or behaviour which mediate it. Blake is no exception. This conception of freedom and of free love has Oothoon visualise it as an act of utter selflessness on her part. In response to her rape, all Theotormon could give her was jealous despair; she answers that by saying that she would not be jealous, but would adopt a model of selflessness, offering to find for Theotormon 'girls of mild silver, or of furious gold' and watch while he has a jolly good time. Well, attractive as this might seem to male readers, there are surely problems with it. David Aers points out that Oothoon's vision of free love 'actually reinforces the traditional culture of male discourse which Blake's poem sets out to undermine'.[5] There are similar problems to be found throughout Blake's work. Despite an ongoing critique of what he calls in *Jerusalem* 'cruel patriarchal pride' (Stevenson, p. 685), women are seen in the role of 'emanations' from the dominantly male forms of Blake's imagination: elsewhere in *Jerusalem* we are told, 'The Female searches sea and land for gratification to the / Male genius: who in return clothes her in gems of gold' (Stevenson, p. 783). Women are also seen as dangerous, jealous figures if not willing to submit to the male (see the extract 'Love and Jealousy' from *Milton*, p. 328). As Aers puts it, despite his radicalism, at times Blake 'relapses into startlingly conservative discourse' in his presentation of women.

According to Aers's reading, then, Oothoon's offer to Theotormon is, in effect, a male fantasy. But we may want to question whether the situation is so clear-cut. As Helen Bruder shows (Bruder, Chapters 2–3), like Thel, Oothoon speaks from within the frame of patriarchal restriction – she is still bound back to back with Bromion when she offers the vision of sexuality liberated from jealousy. At the same time, what she says subverts the outlooks of both of the male characters. This then is another example of Blake's productive indeterminacy over issues, his thought-provoking dialectic: in common with more recent views, Blake can perhaps be seen as presenting gender as not simply a conflict between different sexes but as a division within the individual, between the 'male' potentialities of the spectre and the 'female' potentialities of the emanation.

5 David Aers, 'Blake: Sex, Society and Ideology', in *Romanticism and Ideology: Studies in English Writing 1765–1830*, ed. D. Aers *et al*, Routledge and Kegan Paul, London 1981, pp. 38–40

Such contradictions are an indication that even visionaries don't escape history, and Blake is no exception. They makes him more human and gives us a sense of the man himself struggling with his own mind-forged manacles, at times with an endearing innocence. There is an apocryphal story attached to the song, 'My Pretty Rose-Tree' that helps reinforce this. We know that Blake's own marriage was idyllic, if a trifle imbalanced – Catherine dedicated herself to her husband's art and vision with an enthusiasm which matched his, and she must have contributed significantly to his output. It is said that at one point in the early 1790s, Blake joined a small society which was advocating free love; and that full of enthusiasm for this new manifestation of the revolutionary spirit, he rushed home to Catherine to convert her to its benefits and propose that he might partake of them. If it is true that this poem was the outcome, then perhaps reassuringly for us common readers even William Blake didn't quite have his cake and eat it.

VISIONS OF THE DAUGHTERS OF ALBION
Engraved 1793

The Argument

I loved Theotormon,
And I was not ashamed;
I trembled in my virgin fears
And I hid in Leutha's vale!

I plucked Leutha's flower,
And I rose up from the vale;
But the terrible thunders tore
My virgin mantle in twain.

Visions

Enslav'd, the Daughters of Albion weep; a trembling lamentation
Upon their mountains; in their valleys, sighs toward America.

For the soft soul of America, Oothoon, wander'd in woe
Along the vales of Leutha, seeking flowers to comfort her;
And thus she spoke to the bright Marigold of Leutha's vale: –

Art thou a flower? art thou a nymph? I see thee now a flower,
Now a nymph! I dare not pluck thee from thy dewy bed!'

The Golden nymph replied: 'Pluck thou my flower, Oothoon the mild!
Another flower shall spring, because the soul of sweet delight
Can never pass away.' She ceas'd, and clos'd her golden shrine.

Then Oothoon pluck'd the flower, saying: 'I pluck thee from thy bed,
Sweet flower, and put thee here to glow between my breasts;
And thus I turn my face to where my whole soul seeks.'

Over the waves she went in wing'd exulting swift delight,
And over Theotormon's reign took her impetuous course.

Bromion rent her with his thunders; on his stormy bed
Lay the faint maid, and soon her woes appall'd his thunders hoarse.

Bromion spoke: 'Behold this harlot here on Bromion's bed,
And let the jealous dolphins sport around the lovely maid!
Thy soft American plains are mine, and mine thy north and south:
Stamp'd with my signet are the swarthy children of the sun;
They are obedient, they resist not, they obey the scourge;
Their daughters worship terrors and obey the violent.
Now thou may'st marry Bromion's harlot, and protect the child
Of Bromion's rage, that Oothoon shall put forth in nine moons' time.'

Then storms rent Theotormon's limbs: he roll'd his waves around,
And folded his black jealous waters round the adulterate pair.
Bound back to back in Bromion's caves, terror and meekness dwell:

At entrance Theotormon sits, wearing the threshold hard
With secret tears; beneath him sound like waves on a desert shore
The voice of slaves beneath the sun, and children bought with money,
That shiver in religious caves beneath the burning fires
Of lust, that belch incessant from the summits of the earth.

Oothoon weeps not; she cannot weep, her tears are lockèd up;
But she can howl incessant, writhing her soft snowy limbs,
And calling Theotormon's Eagles to prey upon her flesh.

'I call with holy voice! Kings of the sounding air,
Rend away this defilèd bosom that I may reflect
The image of Theotormon on my pure transparent breast.'

The Eagles at her call descend and rend their bleeding prey:
Theotormon severely smiles; her soul reflects the smile,
As the clear spring, muddied with feet of beasts, grows pure and smiles.

The Daughters of Albion hear her woes, and echo back her sighs.

'Why does my Theotormon sit weeping upon the threshold,
And Oothoon hovers by his side, persuading him in vain?
I cry: Arise, O Theotormon! for the village dog
Barks at the breaking day; the nightingale has done lamenting;

The lark does rustle in the ripe corn, and the eagle returns
From nightly prey, and lifts his golden beak to the pure east,
Shaking the dust from his immortal pinions to awake
The sun that sleeps too long. Arise, my Theotormon! I am pure,
Because the night is gone that clos'd me in its deadly black.
They told me that the night and day were all that I could see;
They told me that I had five senses to enclose me up;
And they enclos'd my infinite brain into a narrow circle,
And sunk my heart into the Abyss, a red, round globe, hot burning,
Till all from life I was obliterated and erasèd.
Instead of morn arises a bright shadow, like an eye
In the eastern cloud; instead of night a sickly charnel-house,
That Theotormon hears me not. To him the night and morn
Are both alike; a night of sighs, a morning of fresh tears;
And none but Bromion can hear my lamentations.

'With what sense is it that the chicken shuns the ravenous hawk?
With what sense does the tame pigeon measure out the expanse?
With what sense does the bee form cells? Have not the mouse and frog
Eyes and ears and sense of touch? Yet are their habitations
And their pursuits as different as their forms and as their joys.
Ask the wild ass why he refuses burdens, and the meek camel
Why he loves man. Is it because of eye, ear, mouth, or skin,
Or breathing nostrils? No! for these the wolf and tiger have.
Ask the blind worm the secrets of the grave, and why her spires
Love to curl round the bones of death; and ask the rav'nous snake
Where she gets poison, and the wing'd eagle why he loves the sun;
And then tell me the thoughts of man, that have been hid of old.

'Silent I hover all the night, and all day could be silent,
If Theotormon once would turn his lovèd eyes upon me.
How can I be defil'd when I reflect thy image pure?
Sweetest the fruit that the worm feeds on, and the soul prey'd on by woe,
The new-wash'd lamb ting'd with the village smoke, and the bright swan
By the red earth of our immortal river. I bathe my wings,
And I am white and pure to hover round Theotormon's breast.'

Then Theotormon broke his silence, and he answerèd: –

'Tell me what is the night or day to one o'erflow'd with woe?

Tell me what is a thought, and of what substance is it made?
Tell me what is a joy, and in what gardens do joys grow?
And in what rivers swim the sorrows? And upon what mountains
Wave shadows of discontent? And in what houses dwell the wretched,
Drunken with woe, forgotten, and shut up from cold despair?

'Tell me where dwell the thoughts, forgotten till thou call them forth?
Tell me where dwell the joys of old, and where the ancient loves,
And when will they renew again, and the night of oblivion past,
That I might traverse times and spaces far remote, and bring
Comforts into a present sorrow and a night of pain?
Where goest thou, O thought? to what remote land is thy flight?
If thou returnest to the present moment of affliction,
Wilt thou bring comforts on thy wings, and dews and honey and balm,
Or poison from the desert wilds, from the eyes of the envier?'

Then Bromion said, and shook the cavern with his lamentation: –

'Thou knowest that the ancient trees seen by thine eyes have fruit;
But knowest thou that trees and fruits flourish upon the earth
To gratify senses unknown – trees, beasts, and birds unknown;
Unknown, not unperceiv'd, spread in the infinite microscope,
In places yet unvisited by the voyager, and in worlds
Over another kind of seas, and in atmospheres unknown?
Ah! are there other wars, beside the wars of sword and fire?
And are there other sorrows beside the sorrows of poverty?
And are there other joys beside the joys of riches and ease?
And is there not one law for both the lion and the ox?
And is there not eternal fire, and eternal chains
To bind the phantoms of existence from eternal life?'

Then Oothoon waited silent all the day and all the night;
But when the morn arose, her lamentation renew'd:
The Daughters of Albion hear her woes, and echo back her sighs.

'O Urizen! Creator of men! mistaken Demon of heaven!
Thy joys are tears, thy labour vain to form men to thine image.
How can one joy absorb another? Are not different joys
Holy, eternal, infinite? and each joy is a Love.

'Does not the great mouth laugh at a gift, and the narrow eyelids mock
At the labour that is above payment? And wilt thou take the ape
For thy counsellor, or the dog for a schoolmaster to thy children?
Does he who contemns poverty, and he who turns with abhorrence
From usury feel the same passion, or are they movèd alike?
How can the giver of gifts experience the delights of the merchant?
How the industrious citizen the pains of the husbandman?
How different far the fat fed hireling with hollow drum,
Who buys whole corn-fields into wastes, and sings upon the heath!
How different their eye and ear! How different the world to them!
With what sense does the parson claim the labour of the farmer?
What are his nets and gins and traps; and how does he surround him
With cold floods of abstraction, and with forests of solitude,
To build him castles and high spires, where kings and priests may dwell;
Till she who burns with youth, and knows no fixèd lot, is bound
In spells of law to one she loathes? And must she drag the chain
Of life in weary lust? Must chilling, murderous thoughts obscure
The clear heaven of her eternal spring; to bear the wintry rage
Of a harsh terror, driv'n to madness, bound to hold a rod
Over her shrinking shoulders all the day, and all the night
To turn the wheel of false desire, and longings that wake her womb
To the abhorrèd birth of cherubs in the human form,
That live a pestilence and die a meteor, and are no more;
Till the child dwell with one he hates, and do the deed he loathes,
And the impure scourge force his seed into its unripe birth,
Ere yet his eyelids can behold the arrows of the day?

'Does the whale worship at thy footsteps as the hungry dog;
Or does he scent the mountain prey because his nostrils wide
Draw in the ocean? Does his eye discern the flying cloud
As the raven's eye; or does he measure the expanse like the vulture?
Does the still spider view the cliffs where eagles hide their young;
Or does the fly rejoice because the harvest is brought in?
Does not the eagle scorn the earth, and despise the treasures beneath?
But the mole knoweth what is there, and the worm shall tell it thee.
Does not the worm erect a pillar in the mouldering churchyard
And a palace of eternity in the jaws of the hungry grave?
Over his porch these words are written: "Take thy bliss, O Man!
And sweet shall be thy taste, and sweet thy infant joys renew!"

'Infancy! fearless, lustful, happy, nestling for delight
In laps of pleasure: Innocence! honest, open, seeking
The vigorous joys of morning light, open to virgin bliss,
Who taught thee modesty, subtil modesty, child of night and sleep?
When thou awakest wilt thou dissemble all thy secret joys,
Or wert thou not awake when all this mystery was disclos'd?
Then com'st thou forth a modest virgin knowing to dissemble,
With nets found under thy night pillow, to catch virgin joy
And brand it with the name of whore, and sell it in the night
In silence, ev'n without a whisper, and in seeming sleep.
Religious dreams and holy vespers light thy smoky fires:
Once were thy fires lighted by the eyes of honest morn.
And does my Theotormon seek this hypocrite modesty,
This knowing, artful, secret, fearful, cautious, trembling hypocrite?
Then is Oothoon a whore indeed! and all the virgin joys
Of life are harlots; and Theotormon is a sick man's dream;
And Oothoon is the crafty slave of selfish holiness.

'But Oothoon is not so, a virgin fill'd with virgin fancies,
Open to joy and to delight wherever beauty appears:
If in the morning sun I find it, there my eyes are fix'd
In happy copulation; if in evening mild, wearièd with work,
Sit on a bank and draw the pleasures of this free-born joy.

'The moment of desire! the moment of desire! The virgin
That pines for man shall awaken her womb to enormous joys
In the secret shadows of her chamber: the youth shut up from
The lustful joy shall forget to generate, and create an amorous image
In the shadows of his curtains and in the folds of his silent pillow
Are not these the places of religion, the rewards of continence,
The self-enjoyings of self-denial? Why dost thou seek religion?
Is it because acts are not lovely that thou seekest solitude,
Where the horrible darkness is impressèd with reflections of desire?

'Father of Jealousy, be thou accursèd from the earth!
Why hast thou taught my Theotormon this accursèd thing,
Till beauty fades from off my shoulders, darken'd and cast out,
A solitary shadow wailing on the margin of nonentity?

'I cry: Love! Love! Love! happy happy Love! free as the mountain wind!

Can that be Love, that drinks another as a sponge drinks water,
That clouds with jealousy his nights, with weepings all the day,
To spin a web of age around him, grey and hoary, dark;
Till his eyes sicken at the fruit that hangs before his sight?
Such is self-love that envies all, a creeping skeleton,
With lamplike eyes watching around the frozen marriage bed!

'But silken nets and traps of adamant will Oothoon spread,
And catch for thee girls of mild silver, or of furious gold.
I'll lie beside thee on a bank, and view their wanton play
In lovely copulation, bliss on bliss, with Theotormon:
Red as the rosy morning, lustful as the first-born beam,
Oothoon shall view his dear delight; nor e'er with jealous cloud
Come in the heaven of generous love, nor selfish blightings bring.

'Does the sun walk, in glorious raiment, on the secret floor
Where the cold miser spreads his gold; or does the bright cloud drop
On his stone threshold? Does his eye behold the beam that brings
Expansion to the eye of pity; or will he bind himself
Beside the ox to thy hard furrow? Does not that mild beam blot
The bat, the owl, the glowing tiger, and the king of night?
The sea-fowl takes the wintry blast for a cov'ring to her limbs,
And the wild snake the pestilence to adorn him with gems and gold;
And trees, and birds, and beasts, and men behold their eternal joy.
Arise, you little glancing wings, and sing your infant joy!
Arise, and drink your bliss, for everything that lives is holy!'

Thus every morning wails Oothoon; but Theotormon sits
Upon the margin'd ocean conversing with shadows dire.

The Daughters of Albion hear her woes, and echo back her sighs.

AMERICA: A PROPHECY

America: A Prophecy (1793)   Blake's move from direct prophetic engagement with contemporary events in *The French Revolution* to the more mythological prophetic works in 'A Song of Liberty' and *Visions of the Daughters of Albion* is continued in this poem, in *Europe* and in *The Song of Los*. They depict the struggles of Orc, the spirit of liberation, against the tyranny of Urizen in all its forms, social, psychological, historical. The mythic framework which gradually unfolds through these poems is Blake's version of *Paradise Lost* and *Paradise Regained*, undertaken with his own distinctively individual conception; but it is a story which only ever gets told in fragments or with continually changing reconceptions, as in *The Four Zoas*. As a result, it is best to read these remarkable works for their immediate impact rather than try to piece together some kind of artificial coherence. For all their lingering obscurities, the longer prophetic works engage us in a tremendous drama, once the reader is attuned to Blake's ideas, and contain some of his most energetic writing and provocative ideas.

In *America*, Blake reflects the revolutionary optimism at the time of composition, before England's declaration of war on France and George III's governmental repression of radicalism made it increasingly dangerous to express such views. Blake translates contemporary history into a furious cosmic battle, with the actors in the American Revolution, like George Washington and Tom Paine, treading the boards alongside his mythic protagonists. In the prelude (pp. 240–1), Orc, named here for the first time, confronts the unnamed shadowy daughter of his tyrannical oppressor, Urthona (sometimes interpreted as a pun on 'earth owner'). Defying her father, she embraces the ferocious energy Orc embodies and the action of the main story begins. This dramatises George III, Guardian Prince of Albion, battling against the Orc-inspired revolution of Washington, and enacts the ensuing war. On the way we are treated to some of Blake's most powerfully articulated visions of tyranny and liberation, such as Orc's resounding reply to Albion's accusations:

The Terror answer'd: 'I am Orc, wreath'd round the accursèd tree:
The times are ended; shadows pass, the morning 'gins to break;
The fiery joy, that Urizen perverted to ten commands,
What night he led the starry hosts thro' the wide wilderness,
That stony Law I stamp to dust; and scatter Religion abroad
To the four winds as a torn book, and none shall gather the leaves;
But they shall rot on desert sands, and consume in bottomless deeps,
To make the deserts blossom, and the deeps shrink to their
     fountains,
And to renew the fiery joy, and burst the stony roof;
That pale religious lechery, seeking Virginity,
May find it in a harlot, and in coarse-clad honesty
The undefil'd, tho' ravish'd in her cradle night and morn;
For everything that lives is holy, life delights in life;
Because the soul of sweet delight can never be defil'd.

(pp. 242–3)

This recalls Oothoon's similar arguments in *Visions of the Daughters of Albion*. The last sections show how despite being almost 'o'erwhelmed' by English power, the American revolutionaries and the cleansing flames of Orc overthrow the repressive colonial system in all its forms, including the 'bonds of religion', leaving Urizen howling at the reversals of his totalitarian vision (pp. 246–7). Round one to the revolution, it seems; but Blake was on the verge of realising that Urizen was busy plotting revenge. In fact, in some copies, Blake added the following postscript verse to the prelude, expressing a brooding sense of disillusionment with his own prophetic role:

The stern bard ceas'd, asham'd of his own song: enrag'd he swung
His harp aloft sounding, then dashed its shining frame against
A ruin'd pillar in glitt'ring fragments: silent he turned away,
And wander'd down the vales of Kent in sick and drear lamentings.

(Stevenson, p. 190)

AMERICA: A PROPHECY
Engraved 1793

Preludium

The shadowy Daughter of Urthona stood before red Orc,
When fourteen suns had faintly journey'd o'er his dark abode:
His food she brought in iron baskets, his drink in cups of iron.
Crown'd with a helmet and dark hair the nameless Female stood;
A quiver with its burning stores, a bow like that of night,
When pestilence is shot from heaven – no other arms she need!
Invulnerable tho' naked, save where clouds roll round her loins
Their awful folds in the dark air: silent she stood as night;
For never from her iron tongue could voice or sound arise,
But dumb till that dread day when Orc assay'd his fierce embrace.

'Dark Virgin,' said the hairy Youth, 'thy father stern, abhorr'd,
Rivets my tenfold chains, while still on high my spirit soars;
Sometimes an eagle screaming in the sky, sometimes a lion
Stalking upon the mountains, and sometimes a whale, I lash
The raging fathomless abyss; anon a serpent folding
Around the pillars of Urthona, and round thy dark limbs
On the Canadian wilds I fold; feeble my spirit folds;
For chain'd beneath I rend these caverns: when thou bringest food
I howl my joy, and my red eyes seek to behold thy face –
In vain! these clouds roll to and fro, and hide thee from my sight.

Silent as despairing love, and strong as jealousy,
The hairy shoulders rend the links; free are the wrists of fire;
Round the terrific loins he seiz'd the panting, struggling womb;
It joy'd: she put aside her clouds and smilèd her first-born smile,
As when a black cloud shows its lightnings to the silent deep.

Soon as she saw the Terrible Boy, then burst the virgin cry: –

'I know thee, I have found thee, and I will not let thee go:
Thou art the image of God who dwells in darkness of Africa,
And thou art fall'n to give me life in regions of dark death.
On my American plains I feel the struggling afflictions

Endur'd by roots that writhe their arms into the nether deep.
I see a Serpent in Canada who courts me to his love,
In Mexico an Eagle, and a Lion in Peru;
I see a Whale in the South Sea, drinking my soul away.
O what limb-rending pains I feel! thy fire and my frost
Mingle in howling pains, in furrows by thy lightnings rent.
This is Eternal Death, and this the torment long foretold!'

A Prophecy

The Guardian Prince of Albion burns in his nightly tent:
Sullen fires across the Atlantic glow to America's shore,
Piercing the souls of warlike men who rise in silent night.
Washington, Franklin, Paine, and Warren, Gates, Hancock, and Green
Meet on the coast glowing with blood from Albion's fiery Prince.

Washington spoke: 'Friends of America! look over the Atlantic sea;
A bended bow is lifted in Heaven, and a heavy iron chain
Descends, link by link, from Albion's cliffs across the sea, to bind
Brothers and sons of America; till our faces pale and yellow,
Heads depress'd, voices weak, eyes downcast, hands work-bruis'd,
Feet bleeding on the sultry sands, and the furrows of the whip
Descend to generations, that in future times forget.'

The strong voice ceas'd; for a terrible blast swept over the heaving sea:
The eastern cloud rent: on his cliffs stood Albion's wrathful Prince,
A dragon form, clashing his scales: at midnight he arose,
And flam'd red meteors round the land of Albion beneath;
His voice, his locks, his awful shoulders, and his glowing eyes
Appear to the Americans upon the cloudy night.

Solemn heave the Atlantic waves between the gloomy nations,
Swelling, belching from its deeps red clouds and raging fires.
Albion is sick! America faints! Enrag'd the Zenith grew.
As human blood shooting its veins all round the orbèd heaven,
Red rose the clouds from the Atlantic in vast wheels of blood,
And in the red clouds rose a Wonder o'er the Atlantic sea –
Intense! naked! a Human fire, fierce glowing, as the wedge
Of iron heated in the furnace; his terrible limbs were fire,

With myriads of cloudy terrors, banners dark, and towers
Surrounded: heat but not light went thro' the murky atmosphere.

The King of England looking westward trembles at the vision.

Albion's Angel stood beside the Stone of Night, and saw
The Terror like a comet, or more like the planet red,
That once enclos'd the terrible wandering comets in its sphere.
Then, Mars, thou wast our centre, and the planets three flew round
Thy crimson disk; so, ere the Sun was rent from thy red sphere,
The Spectre glow'd, his horrid length staining the temple long
With beams of blood; and thus a voice came forth, and shook the temple: –

'The morning comes, the night decays, the watchmen leave their stations;
The grave is burst, the spices shed, the linen wrappèd up;
The bones of death, the cov'ring clay, the sinews shrunk and dry'd
Reviving shake, inspiring move, breathing, awakening,
Spring like redeemèd captives, when their bonds and bars are burst
Let the slave grinding at the mill run out into the field,
Let him look up into the heavens and laugh in the bright air;
Let the enchainèd soul, shut up in darkness and in sighing,
Whose face has never seen a smile in thirty weary years,
Rise and look out; his chains are loose, his dungeon doors are open;
And let his wife and children return from the oppressor's scourge.
They look behind at every step, and believe it is a dream,
Singing: "The Sun has left his blackness, and has found a fresher morning,
And the fair Moon rejoices in the clear and cloudless night;
For Empire is no more, and now the Lion and Wolf shall cease." '

In thunders ends the voice. Then Albion's Angel wrathful burnt
Beside the Stone of Night; and, like the Eternal Lion's howl
In famine and war, reply'd: 'Art thou not Orc, who serpent-form'd
Stands at the gate of Enitharmon to devour her children?
Blasphemous Demon, Antichrist, hater of Dignities,
Lover of wild rebellion, and transgressor of God's Law,
Why dost thou come to Angel's eyes in this terrific form?'

The Terror answer'd: 'I am Orc, wreath'd round the accursèd tree:
The times are ended; shadows pass, the morning 'gins to break;
The fiery joy, that Urizen perverted to ten commands,

What night he led the starry hosts thro' the wide wilderness,
That stony Law I stamp to dust; and scatter Religion abroad
To the four winds as a torn book, and none shall gather the leaves;
But they shall rot on desert sands, and consume in bottomless deeps,
To make the deserts blossom, and the deeps shrink to their fountains,
And to renew the fiery joy, and burst the stony roof;
That pale religious lechery, seeking Virginity,
May find it in a harlot, and in coarse-clad honesty
The undefil'd, tho' ravish'd in her cradle night and morn;
For everything that lives is holy, life delights in life;
Because the soul of sweet delight can never be defil'd.
Fires enwrap the earthly globe, yet Man is not consum'd;
Amidst the lustful fires he walks; his feet become like brass,
His knees and thighs like silver, and his breast and head like gold.

'Sound! sound! my loud war-trumpets, and alarm my Thirteen Angels!
Loud howls the Eternal Wolf! the Eternal Lion lashes his tail!
America is dark'ned; and my punishing Demons, terrifièd,
Crouch howling before their caverns deep, like skins dry'd in the wind.
They cannot smite the wheat, nor quench the fatness of the earth;
They cannot smite with sorrows, nor subdue the plough and spade;
They cannot wall the city, nor moat round the castle of princes;
They cannot bring the stubbèd oak to overgrow the hills;
For terrible men stand on the shores, and in their robes I see
Children take shelter from the lightnings: there stands Washington,
And Paine, and Warren, with their foreheads rear'd toward the East –
But clouds obscure my agèd sight. A vision from afar!
Sound! sound! my loud war-trumpets, and alarm my Thirteen Angels!
Ah, vision from afar! Ah, rebel form that rent the ancient
Heavens! Eternal Viper self-renew'd, rolling in clouds,
I see thee in thick clouds and darkness on America's shore,
Writhing in pangs of abhorrèd birth; red flames the crest rebellious
And eyes of death; the harlot womb, oft openèd in vain,
Heaves in enormous circles: now the times are return'd upon thee,
Devourer of thy parent, now thy unutterable torment renews.
Sound! sound! my loud war-trumpets, and alarm my Thirteen Angels!
Ah, terrible birth! a young one bursting! Where is the weeping mouth,
And where the mother's milk? Instead, those ever-hissing jaws
And parchèd lips drop with fresh gore: now roll thou in the clouds;
Thy mother lays her length outstretch'd upon the shore beneath.

Sound! sound! my loud war-trumpets, and alarm my Thirteen Angels!
Loud howls the Eternal Wolf! the Eternal Lion lashes his tail!'

Thus wept the Angel voice, and as he wept the terrible blasts
Of trumpets blew a loud alarm across the Atlantic deep.
No trumpets answer; no reply of clarions or of fifes:
Silent the Colonies remain and refuse the loud alarm.

On those vast shady hills between America and Albion's shore,
Now barr'd out by the Atlantic sea, call'd Atlantean hills,
Because from their bright summits you may pass to the Golden World,
An ancient palace, archetype of mighty Emperies,
Rears its immortal pinnacles, built in the forest of God
By Ariston, the King of Beauty, for his stolen bride.

Here on their magic seats the Thirteen Angels sat perturb'd,
For clouds from the Atlantic hover o'er the solemn roof.

Fiery the Angels rose, and as they rose deep thunder roll'd
Around their shores, indignant burning with the fires of Orc;
And Boston's Angel cried aloud as they flew thro' the dark night.

He cried: 'Why trembles honesty; and, like a murderer,
Why seeks he refuge from the frowns of his immortal station?
Must the generous tremble, and leave his joy to the idle, to the pestilence
That mock him? Who commanded this? What God? What Angel?
To keep the gen'rous from experience till the ungenerous
Are unrestrain'd performers of the energies of nature;
Till pity is become a trade, and generosity a science
That men get rich by; and the sandy desert is giv'n to the strong?
What God is he writes laws of peace, and clothes him in a tempest?
What pitying Angel lusts for tears, and fans himself with sighs?
What crawling villain preaches abstinence and wraps himself
In fat of lambs? No more I follow, no more obedience pay!'

So cried he, rending off his robe and throwing down his sceptre
In sight of Albion's Guardian; and all the Thirteen Angels
Rent off their robes to the hungry wind, and threw their golden sceptres
Down on the land of America; indignant they descended
Headlong from out their heav'nly heights, descending swift as fires

Over the land; naked and flaming are their lineaments seen
In the deep gloom; by Washington and Paine and Warren they stood;
And the flame folded, roaring fierce within the pitchy night,
Before the Demon red, who burnt towards America,
In black smoke, thunders, and loud winds, rejoicing in its terror,
Breaking in smoky wreaths from the wild deep, and gath'ring thick
In flames as of a furnace on the land from North to South,
What time the Thirteen Governors, that England sent, convene
In Bernard's house. The flames cover'd the land; they rouse; they cry;
Shaking their mental chains, they rush in fury to the sea
To quench their anguish; at the feet of Washington down fall'n
They grovel on the sand and writhing lie, while all
The British soldiers thro' the Thirteen States sent up a howl
Of anguish, threw their swords and muskets to the earth, and run
From their encampments and dark castles, seeking where to hide
From the grim flames, and from the visions of Orc, in sight
Of Albion's Angel; who, enrag'd, his secret clouds open'd
From North to South, and burnt outstretch'd on wings of wrath, cov'ring
The eastern sky, spreading his awful wings across the heavens.
Beneath him roll'd his num'rous hosts, all Albion's Angels camp'd
Darken'd the Atlantic mountains; and their trumpets shook the valleys,
Arm'd with diseases of the earth to cast upon the Abyss –
Their numbers forty millions, must'ring in the eastern sky.

In the flames stood and view'd the armies drawn out in the sky,
Washington, Franklin, Paine, and Warren, Allen, Gates, and Lee,
And heard the voice of Albion's Angel give the thunderous command;
His plagues, obedient to his voice, flew forth out of their clouds,
Falling upon America, as a storm to cut them off,
As a blight cuts the tender corn when it begins to appear.
Dark is the heaven above, and cold and hard the earth beneath:
And, as a plague-wind, fill'd with insects, cuts off man and beast,
And, as a sea o'erwhelms a land in the day of an earthquake,
Fury, rage, madness, in a wind swept through America;
And the red flames of Orc, that folded roaring, fierce, around
The angry shores; and the fierce rushing of th' inhabitants together!
The citizens of New York close their books and lock their chests;
The mariners of Boston drop their anchors and unlade;
The scribe of Pennsylvania casts his pen upon the earth;
The builder of Virginia throws his hammer down in fear.

Then had America been lost, o'erwhelm'd by the Atlantic,
And Earth had lost another portion of the Infinite;
But all rush together in the night in wrath and raging fire.
The red fires rag'd! The plagues recoil'd! Then roll'd they back with fury
On Albion's Angels: then the Pestilence began in streaks of red
Across the limbs of Albion's Guardian; the spotted plague smote Bristol's,
And the Leprosy London's Spirit, sickening all their bands:
The millions sent up a howl of anguish and threw off their hammer'd mail,
And cast their swords and spears to earth, and stood, a naked multitude:
Albion's Guardian writhèd in torment on the eastern sky,
Pale, quiv'ring toward the brain his glimmering eyes, teeth chattering,
Howling and shuddering, his legs quivering, convuls'd each muscle and
    sinew:
Sick'ning lay London's Guardian, and the ancient mitred York,
Their heads on snowy hills, their ensigns sick'ning in the sky.

The plagues creep on the burning winds, driven by flames of Orc,
And by the fierce Americans rushing together in the night,
Driven o'er the Guardians of Ireland, and Scotland and Wales.
They, spotted with plagues, forsook the frontiers; and their banners, sear'd
With fires of hell, deform their ancient Heavens with shame and woe.
Hid in his caves the Bard of Albion felt the enormous plagues,
And a cowl of flesh grew o'er his head, and scales on his back and ribs;
And, rough with black scales, all his Angels fright their ancient heavens.
The doors of marriage are open, and the Priests, in rustling scales,
Rush into reptile coverts, hiding from the fires of Orc,
That play around the golden roofs in wreaths of fierce desire,
Leaving the Females naked and glowing with the lusts of youth.

For the Female Spirits of the dead, pining in bonds of religion,
Run from their fetters; reddening, and in long-drawn arches sitting,
They feel the nerves of youth renew, and desires of ancient times
Over their pale limbs, as a vine when the tender grape appears.

Over the hills, the vales, the cities rage the red flames fierce:
The Heavens melted from North to South; and Urizen, who sat
Above all heavens, in thunders wrapp'd, emerg'd his leprous head
From out his holy shrine, his tears in deluge piteous
Falling into the deep sublime; flagg'd with grey-brow'd snows
And thunderous visages, his jealous wings wav'd over the deep;

Weeping in dismal howling woe, he dark descended, howling
Around the smitten bands, clothèd in tears and trembling, shudd'ring,
    cold.
His storèd snows he pourèd forth, and his icy magazine,
He open'd on the deep, and on the Atlantic sea, white, shiv'ring;
Leprous his limbs, all over white, and hoary was his visage;
Weeping in dismal howlings before the stern Americans,
Hiding the Demon red with clouds and cold mists from the earth;
Till Angels and weak men twelve years should govern o'er the strong;
And then their end should come, when France receiv'd the Demon's light.

Stiff shudderings shook the heav'nly thrones! France, Spain, and Italy
In terror view'd the bands of Albion, and the ancient Guardians,
Fainting upon the elements, smitten with their own plagues!
They slow advance to shut the five gates of their law-built Heaven,
Fillèd with blasting fancies and with mildews of despair,
With fierce disease and lust, unable to stem the fires of Orc,
But the five gates were consum'd, and their bolts and hinges melted;
And the fierce flames burnt round the heavens, and round the abodes
    of men.

EUROPE: A PROPHECY
Engraved 1794

Europe: A Prophecy (1794)   In *Europe*, Blake adds gender warfare to
the problems which beset Orc and liberation: here he is captured and
corrupted by Enitharmon, a possessively maternal female figure who
goes through a number of incarnations in later works. We are also
introduced to the important figure of Los, Blake's embodiment of the
creative energies of the prophetic artist. Los aids Orc in his continuing
confrontation with Albion's Angel and his tyrannical mentor Urizen.
Less clearly structured or focused than *America*, the poem is more
confusing for its variety of characters who are sometimes difficult to
place. *Europe* is perhaps most notable for its inclusion of Blake's famous
design 'Ancient of Days' as its frontispiece, in which an Old Testament
figure, enclosed in a fiery globe and often associated with Urizen,
circumscribes and limits the horizons of the universe with a pair of
mathematical compasses or dividers, the extensions of his own fingers,
to 'bind the Infinite' (p. 250) as the poem has it. The section beginning
'In thoughts peturb'd' (p. 253) describes this process of sensory
restriction in perhaps the most vivid passage of the poem, reminding us
that Blake is simultaneously addressing the psychological and physical
body of individual humanity as well as social history and the cosmos.

'Five windows light the cavern'd Man: thro' one he breathes the air;
Thro' one hears music of the spheres; thro' one the Eternal Vine
Flourishes, that he may receive the grapes; thro' one can look
And see small portions of the Eternal World that ever groweth;
Thro' one himself pass out what time he please, but he will not;
For stolen joys are sweet, and bread eaten in secret pleasant.'

So sang a Fairy, mocking, as he sat on a streak'd tulip,
Thinking none saw him: when he ceas'd I started from the trees,
And caught him in my hat, as boys knock down a butterfly.
'How know you this,' said I, 'small Sir? where did you learn this
    song?'
Seeing himself in my possession, thus he answer'd me:
'My Master, I am yours! command me, for I must obey.'

'Then tell me, what is the Material World, and is it dead?'
He, laughing, answer'd: 'I will write a book on leaves of flowers,
If you will feed me on love-thoughts, and give me now and then
A cup of sparkling poetic fancies; so, when I am tipsy,
I'll sing to you to this soft lute, and show you all alive
The World, when every particle of dust breathes forth its joy.'

I took him home in my warm bosom: as we went along
Wild flowers I gather̀d; and he show'd me each Eternal Flower:
He laugh'd aloud to see them whimper because they were pluck'd.
They hover'd round me like a cloud of incense. When I came
Into my parlour and sat down, and took my pen to write,
My Fairy sat upon the table, and dictated EUROPE.

Preludium

The nameless Shadowy Female rose from out the breast of Orc,
Her snaky hair brandishing in the winds of Enitharmon;

And thus her voice arose: –

'O mother Enitharmon, wilt thou bring forth other sons,
To cause my name to vanish, that my place may not be found?
For I am faint with travel,
Like the dark cloud disburden'd in the day of dismal thunder.

'My roots are brandish'd in the heavens, my fruits in earth beneath
Surge, foam, and labour into life, first born and first consum'd!
Consumèd and consuming!
Then why shouldst thou, Accursèd Mother, bring me into life?

'I wrap my turban of thick clouds around my lab'ring head,
And fold the sheety waters as a mantle round my limbs;
Yet the red sun and moon
And all the overflowing stars rain down prolific pains.

'Unwilling I look up to heaven, unwilling count the stars:
Sitting in fathomless abyss of my immortal shrine
I seize their burning power,
And bring forth howling terrors, all-devouring fiery kings,

'Devouring and devourèd, roaming on dark and desolate
    mountains,
In forests of Eternal Death, shrieking in hollow trees.
Ah, mother Enitharmon!
Stamp not with solid form this vig'rous progeny of fires.

'I bring forth from my teeming bosom myriads of flames,
And thou dost stamp them with a signet; then they roam abroad,
And leave me void as death.
Ah! I am drown'd in shady woe and visionary joy.

'And who shall bind the Infinite with an eternal band
To compass it with swaddling bands? and who shall cherish it
With milk and honey?
I see it smile, and I roll inward, and my voice is past.'

        She ceas'd, and roll'd her shady clouds
        Into the secret place.

A Prophecy

The deep of winter came,
What time the Secret Child
Descended through the orient gates of the Eternal day:
War ceas'd, and all the troops like shadows fled to their abodes.

Then Enitharmon saw her sons and daughters rise around;
Like pearly clouds they meet together in the crystal house;
And Los, possessor of the Moon, joy'd in the peaceful night,
Thus speaking, while his num'rous sons shook their bright fiery wings: –

'Again the night is come,
That strong Urthona takes his rest;
And Urizen, unloos'd from chains,
Glows like a meteor in the distant North.
Stretch forth your hands and strike the elemental strings!
Awake the thunders of the deep!

'The shrill winds wake,
Till all the sons of Urizen look out and envy Los.
Seize all the spirits of life, and bind
Their warbling joys to our loud strings!
Bind all the nourishing sweets of earth
To give us bliss, that we may drink the sparkling wine of Los!
And let us laugh at war,
Despising toil and care,
Because the days and nights of joy in lucky hours renew.

'Arise, O Orc, from thy deep den!
First-born of Enitharmon, rise!
And we will crown thy head with garlands of the ruddy vine;
For now thou art bound,
And I may see thee in the hour of bliss, my eldest-born.'

The horrent Demon rose, surrounded with red stars of fire,
Whirling about in furious circles round the Immortal Fiend.

Then Enitharmon down descended into his red light,
And thus her voice rose to her children: the distant heavens reply: –

'Now comes the night of Enitharmon's joy!
Who shall I call? Who shall I send,
That Woman, lovely Woman, may have dominion?
Arise, O Rintrah! thee I call, and Palamabron, thee!
Go! tell the Human race that Woman's love is Sin;
That an Eternal life awaits the worms of sixty winters,
In an allegorical abode, where existence hath never come.
Forbid all Joy; and, from her childhood, shall the little Female
Spread nets in every secret path.

'My weary eyelids draw towards the evening; my bliss is yet but new.

'Arise! O Rintrah, eldest-born, second to none but Orc!
O lion Rintrah, raise thy fury from thy forests black!
Bring Palamabron, hornèd priest, skipping upon the mountains,
And silent Elynittria, the silver-bowèd queen.
Rintrah, where hast thou hid thy bride?
Weeps she in desert shades?
Alas! my Rintrah, bring the lovely jealous Ocalythron.

'Arise, my son! bring all thy brethren, O thou King of Fire!
Prince of the Sun! I see thee with thy innumerable race,
Thick as the summer stars;
But each, ramping, his golden mane shakes,
And thine eyes rejoice because of strength, O Rintrah, furious King!'

Enitharmon slept
Eighteen hundred years. Man was a dream,
The night of Nature and their harps unstrung!
She slept in middle of her nightly song
Eighteen hundred years, a Female dream.

Shadows of men in fleeting bands upon the winds
Divide the heavens of Europe;
Till Albion's Angel, smitten with his own plagues, fled with his bands.
The cloud bears hard on Albion's shore,
Fill'd with immortal Demons of futurity:
In council gather the smitten Angels of Albion;
The cloud bears hard upon the council-house, down rushing
On the heads of Albion's Angels.

One hour they lay burièd beneath the ruins of that hall;
But as the stars rise from the Salt Lake, they arise in pain,
In troubled mists, o'erclouded by the terrors of struggling times.

In thoughts perturb'd they rose from the bright ruins, silent following
The fiery King, who sought his ancient temple, serpent-form'd,
That stretches out its shady length along the Island white.
Round him roll'd his clouds of war; silent the Angel went
Along the infinite shores of Thames to golden Verulam.
There stand the venerable porches, that high-towering rear
Their oak-surrounded pillars, form'd of massy stones, uncut
With tool, stones precious! – such eternal in the heavens,
Of colours twelve (few known on earth) give light in the opaque,
Plac'd in the order of the stars; when the five senses whelm'd
In deluge o'er the earth-born man, then turn'd the fluxile eyes
Into two stationary orbs, concentrating all things:
The ever-varying spiral ascents to the Heavens of Heavens
Were bended downward, and the nostrils' golden gates shut,
Turn'd outward, barr'd, and petrify'd against the Infinite.

Thought chang'd the Infinite to a Serpent, that which pitieth
To a devouring flame; and Man fled from its face and hid
In forests of night: then all the eternal forests were divided
Into earths, rolling in circles of Space, that like an ocean rush'd
And overwhelmèd all except this finite wall of flesh.
Then was the Serpent temple form'd, image of Infinite,
Shut up in finite revolutions, and Man became an Angel,
Heaven a mighty circle turning, God a tyrant crown'd.

Now arriv'd the ancient Guardian at the southern porch,
That planted thick with trees of blackest leaf, and in a vale
Obscure enclos'd the Stone of Night; oblique it stood, o'erhung
With purple flowers and berries red, image of that sweet South,
Once open to the heavens, and elevated on the human neck,
Now overgrown with hair, and cover'd with a stony roof
Downward 'tis sunk beneath th' attractive North, that round the feet,
A raging whirlpool, draws the dizzy enquirer to his grave.

> Albion's Angel rose upon the Stone of Night.
> He saw Urizen on the Atlantic;

And his brazen Book,
That Kings and Priests had copièd on Earth,
Expanded from North to South.

And the clouds and fires pale roll'd round in the night of Enitharmon,
Round Albion's cliffs and London's walls: still Enitharmon slept.
Rolling volumes of grey mist involve Churches, Palaces, Towers;
For Urizen unclasp'd his Book, feeding his soul with pity.
The youth of England, hid in gloom, curse the pain'd heavens, compell'd
Into the deadly night to see the form of Albion's Angel.
Their parents brought them forth, and Agèd Ignorance preaches, canting,
On a vast rock, perceiv'd by those senses that are clos'd from thought –
Bleak, dark, abrupt it stands, and overshadows London city.
They saw his bony feet on the rock, the flesh consum'd in flames;
They saw the Serpent temple lifted above, shadowing the Island white;
They heard the voice of Albion's Angel, howling in flames of Orc,
Seeking the trump of the Last Doom.

Above the rest the howl was heard from Westminster, louder and louder:
The Guardian of the secret codes forsook his ancient mansion,
Driven out by the flames of Orc; his furr'd robes and false locks
Adherèd and grew one with his flesh and nerves, and veins shot thro'
      them.
With dismal torment sick, hanging upon the wind, he fled
Grovelling, along Great George Street, thro' the Park gate: all the soldiers
Fled from his sight: he dragg'd his torments to the wilderness.

Thus was the howl thro' Europe!
For Orc rejoic'd to hear the howling shadows;
But Palamabron shot his lightnings, trenching down his wide back;
And Rintrah hung with all his legions in the nether deep.

Enitharmon laugh'd in her sleep to see (O woman's triumph!)
Every house a den, every man bound: the shadows are fill'd
With spectres, and the windows wove over with curses of iron:
Over the doors 'Thou shalt not', and over the chimneys 'Fear' is written:
With bands of iron round their necks fasten'd into the walls
The citizens, in leaden gyves the inhabitants of suburbs
Walk heavy; soft and bent are the bones of villagers.

Between the clouds of Urizen the flames of Orc roll heavy
Around the limbs of Albion's Guardian, his flesh consuming:
Howlings and hissings, shrieks and groans, and voices of despair
Arise around him in the cloudy heavens of Albion. Furious,
The red-limb'd Angel seiz'd in horror and torment
The trump of the Last Doom; but he could not blow the iron tube!
Thrice he assay'd presumptuous to awake the dead to Judgement.
A mighty Spirit leap'd from the land of Albion,
Nam'd Newton: he seiz'd the trump, and blow'd the enormous blast!
Yellow as leaves of autumn, the myriads of Angelic hosts
Fell thro' the wintry skies, seeking their graves,
Rattling their hollow bones in howling and lamentation.

Then Enitharmon woke, nor knew that she had slept;
And eighteen hundred years were fled
As if they had not been.
She call'd her sons and daughters
To the sports of night
Within her crystal house,
And thus her song proceeds: –

'Arise, Ethinthus! tho' the earth-worm call,
Let him call in vain,
Till the night of holy shadows
And human solitude is past!

'Ethinthus, Queen of Waters, how thou shinest in the sky!
My daughter, how do I rejoice! for thy children flock around,
Like the gay fishes on the wave, when the cold moon drinks the dew.
Ethinthus! thou art sweet as comforts to my fainting soul,
For now thy waters warble round the feet of Enitharmon.

'Manatha-Varcyon! I behold thee flaming in my halls.
Light of thy mother's soul! I see thy lovely eagles round;
Thy golden wings are my delight, and thy flames of soft delusion.

'Where is my luring bird of Eden? Leutha, silent love!
Leutha, the many-colour'd bow delights upon thy wings!
Soft soul of flowers, Leutha!
Sweet smiling Pestilence! I see thy blushing light;
Thy daughters, many changing,
Revolve like sweet perfumes ascending, O Leutha, Silken Queen!

'Where is the youthful Antamon, Prince of the Pearly Dew?
O Antamon! why wilt thou leave thy mother Enitharmon?
Alone I see thee, crystal form,
Floating upon the bosom'd air,
With lineaments of gratified desire.
My Antamon! the seven churches of Leutha seek thy love.

'I hear the soft Oothoon in Enitharmon's tents;
Why wilt thou give up woman's secrecy, my melancholy child?
Between two moments Bliss is ripe.
O Theotormon! robb'd of joy, I see thy salt tears flow
Down the steps of my crystal house.

'Sotha and Thiralatha! secret dwellers of dreamful caves,
Arise and please the horrent Fiend with your melodious songs;
Still all your thunders, golden-hoof'd, and bind your horses black.
Orc! smile upon my children,
Smile, son of my afflictions!
Arise, O Orc, and give our mountains joy of thy red light!'

She ceas'd; for all were forth at sport beneath the solemn moon
Waking the stars of Urizen with their immortal songs;
That Nature felt thro' all her pores the enormous revelry,
Till Morning oped the eastern gate;
Then every one fled to his station, and Enitharmon wept.

But terrible Orc, when he beheld the morning in the East,
Shot from the heights of Enitharmon,
And in the vineyards of red France appear'd the light of his fury.

The Sun glow'd fiery red!
The furious Terrors flew around
On golden chariots, raging with red wheels, dropping with blood
The Lions lash their wrathful tails!
The Tigers couch upon the prey and suck the ruddy tide;
And Enitharmon groans and cries in anguish and dismay.

Then Los arose: his head he rear'd, in snaky thunders clad;
And with a cry that shook all Nature to the utmost pole,
Call'd all his sons to the strife of blood.

THE BOOK OF URIZEN
Engraved 1794

The Book of Urizen (1794)   It is fitting that in the year after the execution of Louis XVI, when England declared war on revolutionary France, the guillotine-fuelled Terror began and Tom Paine was outlawed, Blake should give Urizen his own albeit incomplete prophetic poem. Often seen as the beginnings of the 'Bible of Hell', projected in *The Marriage of Heaven and Hell* (p. 206) and followed up in *The Book of Ahania* and *The Book of Los*, this text describes the 'Genesis' of Blake's mythic cycle, a fall from Eternity into division in which the organic republic of the Immortals fragments because of an egocentric lust for power and domination by Urizen. The result is the initiation of the historical cycles of tyranny and social inequality in a limited material universe, along with the moral and psychological divisions and restrictions of humanity. As well as punning on 'your reason', the word 'Urizen' puns on 'horizon', with its implications of limited viewpoints and what Blake calls 'single vision' in 'With Happiness stretch'd' ('To Thomas Butts', p. 146). The poem is more gnomic in form and effect than the expansive verse of other prophetic works as it tracks the mutating forms of Urizen from Chapter IV onwards. Against Urizen is set Los, the blacksmith-prophet, embodiment of the prophetic imagination, who himself is split by gender division into a female self, Enitharmon (p. 268). Their child, Orc, familiar from earlier works, is here chained in Oedipal bonds by his parents (pp. 270–1), suggesting that in the Urizen system, the institution of the family itself produces and perpetuates the repression of free energies.

THE FIRST BOOK OF URIZEN

Preludium to the First Book of Urizen

Of the primeval Priest's assum'd power,
When Eternals spurn'd back his Religion,
And gave him a place in the North,
Obscure, shadowy, void, solitary.

Eternals! I hear your call gladly.
Dictate swift wingèd words, and fear not
To unfold your dark visions of torment.

CHAPTER I

1. Lo, a Shadow of horror is risen
In Eternity! unknown, unprolific,
Self-clos'd, all-repelling. What Demon
Hath form'd this abominable Void,
This soul-shudd'ring Vacuum? Some said
It is Urizen. But unknown, abstracted,
Brooding, secret, the dark Power hid.

2. Times on times he divided, and measur'd
Space by space in his ninefold darkness,
Unseen, unknown; changes appear'd
Like desolate mountains, rifted furious
By the black winds of perturbation.

3. For he strove in battles dire,
In unseen conflictions with Shapes,
Bred from his forsaken wilderness,
Of beast, bird, fish, serpent, and element,
Combustion, blast, vapour, and cloud.

4. Dark, revolving in silent activity,
Unseen in tormenting passions,
An Activity unknown and horrible,
A self-contemplating Shadow,
In enormous labours occupièd.

5. But Eternals beheld his vast forests;
Ages on ages he lay, clos'd, unknown,
Brooding, shut in the deep; all avoid
The petrific, abominable Chaos.

6. His cold horrors, silent, dark Urizen
Prepar'd; his ten thousands of thunders,
Rang'd in gloom'd array, stretch out across
The dread world; and the rolling of wheels,
As of swelling seas, sound in his clouds,

In his hills of stor'd snows, in his mountains
Of hail and ice; voices of terror
Are heard, like thunders of autumn,
When the cloud blazes over the harvests.

CHAPTER II

1. Earth was not, nor globes of attraction;
The will of the Immortal expanded
Or contracted his all-flexible senses;
Death was not, but Eternal life sprung.

2. The sound of a trumpet the heavens
Awoke, and vast clouds of blood roll'd
Round the dim rocks of Urizen, so nam'd
That solitary one in Immensity.

3. Shrill the trumpet! and myriads of Eternity
Muster around the bleak deserts,
Now fill'd with clouds, darkness, and waters,
That roll'd perplex'd, lab'ring; and utter'd
Words articulate, bursting in thunders,
That roll'd on the tops of his mountains: –

4. 'From the depths of dark solitude, from
The Eternal abode in my Holiness,
Hidden, set apart, in my stern counsels,
Reserv'd for the days of futurity,
I have sought for a joy without pain,
For a solid without fluctuation.
Why will you die, O Eternals?
Why live in unquenchable burnings?

5. 'First I fought with the fire, consum'd
Inwards into a deep world within,
A Void immense, wild, dark and deep,
Where nothing was – Nature's wide womb;
And self-balanc'd, stretch'd o'er the void,
I alone, even I! the winds merciless
Bound; but condensing in torrents
They fall and fall; strong I repell'd
The vast waves, and arose on the waters
A wide World of solid obstruction.

6. 'Here alone I, in books form'd of metals,
Have written the secrets of Wisdom,
The secrets of dark Contemplation,
By fightings and conflicts dire
With terrible monsters sin-bred,
Which the bosoms of all inhabit –
Seven deadly Sins of the Soul.

7. 'Lo! I unfold my darkness, and on
This rock place, with strong hand, the Book
Of Eternal brass, written in my solitude:

8. 'Laws of peace, of love, of unity,
Of pity, compassion, forgiveness;
Let each choose one habitation,
His ancient infinite mansion,
One command, one joy, one desire,
One curse, one weight, one measure,
One King, one God, one Law.'

CHAPTER III

1. The voice ended: they saw his pale visage
Emerge from the darkness, his hand
On the rock of Eternity unclasping
The Book of brass. Rage seiz'd the strong –

2. Rage, fury, intense indignation,
In cataracts of fire, blood, and gall,
In whirlwinds of sulphurous smoke,
And enormous forms of energy,
In living creations appear'd,
In the flames of eternal fury.

3. Sund'ring, dark'ning, thund'ring,
Rent away with a terrible crash,
Eternity roll'd wide apart,
Wide asunder rolling;
Mountainous, all around
Departing, departing, departing,
Leaving ruinous fragments of life,
Hanging, frowning cliffs, and, all between,
An Ocean of voidness unfathomable.

4. The roaring fires ran o'er the heav'ns
In whirlwinds and cataracts of blood,
And o'er the dark deserts of Urizen
Fires pour thro' the void, on all sides,
On Urizen's self-begotten armies.

5. But no light from the fires! all was darkness
In the flames of Eternal fury.

6. In fierce anguish and quenchless flames
To the deserts and rocks he ran raging,
To hide; but he could not. Combining,
He dug mountains and hills in vast strength,
He pilèd them in incessant labour,
In howlings and pangs and fierce madness,
Long periods in burning fires labouring;
Till hoary, and age-broke, and agèd,
In despair and the shadows of death

7. And a roof vast, petrific, around
On all sides he fram'd, like a womb,
Where thousands of rivers, in veins
Of blood, pour down the mountains to cool
The eternal fires, beating without
From Eternals; and like a black Globe,
View'd by sons of Eternity, standing
On the shore of the infinite ocean,,
Like a human heart, struggling and beating,
The vast world of Urizen appear'd.

8. And Los, round the dark globe of Urizen,
Kept watch for Eternals to confine
The obscure separation alone;
For Eternity stood wide apart,
As the stars are apart from the earth,

9. Los wept, howling around the dark Demon,
And cursing his lot; for in anguish
Urizen was rent from his side,
And a fathomless Void for his feet,
And intense fires for his dwelling.

10. But Urizen, laid in a stony sleep,
Unorganis'd, rent from Eternity.

11. The Eternals said: 'What is this? Death?
Urizen is a clod of clay!'

12. Los howl'd in a dismal stupor,
Groaning, gnashing, groaning,
Till the wrenching apart was healèd.

13. But the wrenching of Urizen heal'd not.
Cold, featureless, flesh or clay,
Rifted with direful changes,
He lay in a dreamless night,

14. Till Los rous'd his fires, affrighted
At the formless, unmeasurable Death.

CHAPTER IV

1. Los, smitten with astonishment,
Frighten'd at the hurtling bones

2. And at the surging, sulphureous,
Perturbèd, immortal, mad raging

3. In whirlwinds, and pitch, and nitre
Round the furious limbs of Los.

4. And Los formèd nets and gins,
And threw the nets round about.

5. He watch'd in shudd'ring fear
The dark changes, and bound every change
With rivets of iron and brass.

6. And these were the changes of Urizen: –

CHAPTER IV A

1. Ages on ages roll'd over him;
In stony sleep ages roll'd over him,
Like a dark waste stretching, changeable,
By earthquakes riv'n, belching sullen fires:
On ages roll'd ages in ghastly
Sick torment; around him in whirlwinds
Of darkness the Eternal Prophet howl'd,
Beating still on his rivets of iron,
Pouring solder of iron; dividing
The horrible night into watches.

2. And Urizen (so his eternal name)
His prolific delight obscur'd more and more,
In dark secrecy hiding in surging
Sulphureous fluid his phantasies.
The Eternal Prophet heav'd the dark bellows,
And turn'd restless the tongs, and the hammer
Incessant beat, forging chains new and new,
Numb'ring with links hours, days, and years.

3. The Eternal mind, bounded, began to roll
Eddies of wrath, ceaseless, round and round,
And the sulphureous foam, surging thick,
Settled, a lake, bright and shining clear,
White as the snow on the mountains cold.

4. Forgetfulness, dumbness, necessity,
In chains of the mind lockèd up,
Like fetters of ice shrinking together,
Disorganis'd, rent from Eternity,
Los beat on his fetters of iron;
And heated his furnaces, and pour'd
Iron solder and solder of brass.

5. Restless turn'd the Immortal, enchain'd,
Heaving dolorous, anguish'd, unbearable;
Till a roof, shaggy, wild, enclos'd
In an orb his fountain of thought.

6. In a horrible, dreamful slumber,
Like the linkèd infernal chain,
A vast Spine writh'd in torment
Upon the winds, shooting pain'd
Ribs, like a bending cavern;
And bones of solidness froze
Over all his nerves of joy –
And a first Age passèd over,
And a state of dismal woe.

7. From the caverns of his jointed Spine
Down sunk with fright a red
Round Globe, hot, burning, deep,
Deep down into the Abyss;
Panting, conglobing, trembling,
Shooting out ten thousand branches
Around his solid bones –
And a second Age passèd over,
And a state of dismal woe.

8. In harrowing fear rolling round,
His nervous Brain shot branches
Round the branches of his Heart,
On high, into two little orbs,
And fixèd in two little caves,
Hiding carefully from the wind,
His Eyes beheld the deep –
And a third Age passèd over,
And a state of dismal woe.

9. The pangs of hope began.
In heavy pain, striving, struggling,
Two Ears, in close volutions,
From beneath his orbs of vision
Shot spiring out, and petrified
As they grew – And a fourth Age passèd,
And a state of dismal woe.

10. In ghastly torment sick,
Hanging upon the wind,
Two Nostrils bent down to the deep –
And a fifth Age passèd over,
And a state of dismal woe.

11. In ghastly torment sick,
Within his ribs bloated round
A craving, hungry Cavern;
Thence arose his channell'd Throat,
And, like a red flame, a Tongue
Of thirst and of hunger appear'd –
And a sixth Age passèd over,
And a state of dismal woe.

12. Enragèd and stifled with torment,
He threw his right Arm to the North,
His left Arm to the South,
Shooting out in anguish deep,
And his Feet stamp'd the nether Abyss
In trembling and howling and dismay –
And a seventh Age passèd over,
And a state of dismal woe.

CHAPTER V

1. In terrors Los shrunk from his task:
His great hammer fell from his hand;
His fires beheld, and sickening
Hid their strong limbs in smoke;
For with noises, ruinous, loud,
With hurtlings and clashings and groans,
The Immortal endur'd his chains,
Tho' bound in a deadly sleep.

2. All the myriads of Eternity,
All the wisdom and joy of life
Roll like a sea around him;
Except what his little orbs
Of sight by degrees unfold.

3. And now his Eternal life,
Like a dream, was obliterated.

4. Shudd'ring, the Eternal Prophet smote
With a stroke from his North to South region.
The bellows and hammer are silent now;
A nerveless silence his prophetic voice
Seiz'd; a cold Solitude and dark Void
The Eternal Prophet and Urizen clos'd.

5. Ages on ages roll'd over them,
Cut off from life and light, frozen
Into horrible forms of deformity.
Los suffer'd his fires to decay;
Then he look'd back with anxious desire,
But the Space, undivided by existence,
Struck horror into his soul.

6. Los wept, obscur'd with mourning,
His bosom earthquak'd with sighs;
He saw Urizen, deadly, black,
In his chains bound; and Pity began,

7. In anguish dividing and dividing –
For Pity divides the soul –
In pangs, Eternity on Eternity,
Life in cataracts pour'd down his cliffs.
The Void shrunk the lymph into Nerves,
Wand'ring wide on the bosom of night,
And left a round globe of blood
Trembling upon the Void.
Thus the Eternal Prophet was divided
Before the death image of Urizen;
For in changeable clouds and darkness,
In a winterly night beneath,
The Abyss of Los stretch'd immense;
And now seen, now obscur'd, to the eyes
Of Eternals the visions remote
Of the dark separation appear'd:
As glasses discover Worlds
In the endless Abyss of space,
So the expanding eyes of Immortals
Beheld the dark visions of Los,
And the globe of life-blood trembling.

8. The globe of life-blood trembled,
Branching out into roots,
Fibrous, writhing upon the winds,
Fibres of blood, milk, and tears,
In pangs, Eternity on Eternity.
At length in tears and cries embodièd,
A Female form, trembling and pale,
Waves before his deathy face.

9. All Eternity shudder'd at sight
Of the first Female, now separate,
Pale as a cloud of snow,
Waving before the face of Los.

10. Wonder, awe, fear, astonishment
Petrify the Eternal myriads
At the first Female form now separate.
They call'd her Pity, and fled.

11. 'Spread a Tent with strong curtains around them!
Let cords and stakes bind in the Void,
That Eternals may no more behold them.'

12. They began to weave curtains of darkness,
They erected large pillars round the Void,
With golden hooks fasten'd in the pillars;
With infinite labour the Eternals
A woof wove, and callèd it Science.

CHAPTER VI

1. But Los saw the Female, and pitièd;
He embrac'd her; she wept, she refus'd;
In perverse and cruel delight
She fled from his arms, yet he follow'd.

2. Eternity shudder'd when they saw
Man begetting his likeness
On his own Divided Image!

3. A time passèd over: the Eternals
Began to erect the tent,
When Enitharmon, sick,
Felt a Worm within her womb.

4. Yet helpless it lay, like a Worm
In the trembling womb,
To be moulded into existence.

5. All day the Worm lay on her bosom;
All night within her womb
The Worm lay till it grew to a Serpent,
With dolorous hissings and poisons
Round Enitharmon's loins folding.

6. Coil'd within Enitharmon's womb
The Serpent grew, casting its scales;
With sharp pangs the hissings began

To change to a grating cry –
Many sorrows and dismal throes,
Many forms of fish, bird, and beast
Brought forth an Infant form
Where was a Worm before.

7. The Eternals their tent finishèd,
Alarm'd with these gloomy visions,
When Enitharmon, groaning,
Produc'd a Man-Child to the light.

8. A shriek ran thro' Eternity,
And a paralytic stroke,
At the birth of the Human Shadow.

9. Delving earth in his resistless way,
Howling, the Child with fierce flames
Issu'd from Enitharmon.

10. The Eternals closèd the tent;
They beat down the stakes, the cords
Stretch'd for a work of Eternity –
No more Los beheld Eternity!

11. In his hands he seiz'd the Infant,
He bathèd him in springs of sorrow,
He gave him to Enitharmon.

CHAPTER VII

1. They namèd the child Orc; he grew,
Fed with milk of Enitharmon.

2. Los awoke her. O sorrow and pain!
A tight'ning girdle grew
Around his bosom. In sobbings
He burst the girdle in twain;
But still another girdle
Oppress'd his bosom. In sobbings

Again he burst it. Again
Another girdle succeeds.
The girdle was form'd by day;
By night was burst in twain.

3. These falling down on the Rock
Into an iron Chain,
In each other link by link lock'd.

4. They took Orc to the top of a mountain.
O how Enitharmon wept!
They chain'd his young limbs to the Rock
With the Chain of Jealousy,
Beneath Urizen's deathful Shadow.

5. The Dead heard the voice of the Child,
And began to awake from sleep;
All things heard the voice of the Child,
And began to awake to life.

6. And Urizen, craving with hunger,
Stung with the odours of Nature,
Explor'd his dens around.

7. He form'd a line and a plummet
To divide the Abyss beneath;
He form'd a dividing rule;

8. He formèd scales to weigh,
He formèd massy weights;
He formèd a brazen quadrant;
He formèd golden compasses,
And began to explore the Abyss;
And he planted a garden of fruits.

9. But Los encircled Enitharmon
With fires of Prophecy
From the sight of Urizen and Orc.

10. And she bore an enormous race.

CHAPTER VIII

1. Urizen explor'd his dens,
Mountain, moor, and wilderness,
With a globe of fire lighting his journey –
A fearful journey, annoy'd
By cruel enormities, forms
Of life on his forsaken mountains.

2. And his World teem'd vast enormities,
Fright'ning, faithless, fawning,
Portions of life, similitudes
Of a foot, or a hand, or a head,
Or a heart, or an eye; they swam mischievous,
Dread terrors, delighting in blood!

3. Most Urizen sicken'd to see
His eternal creations appear,
Sons and daughters of sorrow, on mountains,
Weeping, wailing. First Thiriel appear'd,
Astonish'd at his own existence,
Like a man from a cloud born; and Utha,
From the waters emerging, laments;
Grodna rent the deep earth, howling,
Amaz'd; his heavens immense crack
Like the ground parch'd with heat; then Fuzon
Flam'd out, first begotten, last born;
All his Eternal sons in like manner;
His daughters, from green herbs and cattle,
From monsters and worms of the pit.

4. He in darkness clos'd view'd all his race,
And his soul sicken'd! He curs'd
Both sons and daughters; for he saw
That no flesh nor spirit could keep
His iron laws one moment.

5. For he saw that Life liv'd upon Death:
The Ox in the slaughter-house moans;
The Dog at the wintry door;
And he wept, and he callèd it Pity,
And his tears flowèd down on the winds.

6. Cold he wander'd on high, over their Cities,
In weeping and pain and woe;
And wherever he wander'd, in sorrows
Upon the agèd Heavens,
A cold Shadow follow'd behind him
Like a spider's web, moist, cold, and dim,
Drawing out from his sorrowing soul,
The dungeon-like heaven dividing,
Wherever the footsteps of Urizen
Walkèd over the cities in sorrow;

7. Till a Web, dark and cold, throughout all
The tormented element stretch'd
From the sorrows of Urizen's soul.
And the Web is a Female in embryo;
None could break the Web, no wings of fire,

8. So twisted the cords, and so knotted
The meshes, twisted like to the human brain.

9. And all call'd it the Net of Religion.

CHAPTER IX

1. Then the Inhabitants of those Cities
Felt their Nerves change into Marrow,
And hardening Bones began
In swift diseases and torments,
In throbbings and shootings and grindings,
Thro' all the coasts; till weaken'd
The Senses inward rush'd, shrinking
Beneath the dark Net of infection;

2. Till the shrunken eyes, clouded over,
Discern'd not the woven Hypocrisy;
But the streaky slime in their heavens,
Brought together by narrowing perceptions,
Appear'd transparent air; for their eyes
Grew small like the eyes of a man,
And, in reptile forms shrinking together,
Of seven feet stature they remain'd.

3. Six days they shrunk up from existence,
And on the seventh day they rested,
And they bless'd the seventh day, in sick hope,
And forgot their Eternal life.

4. And their Thirty Cities divided
In form of a Human Heart.
No more could they rise at will
In the infinite Void, but bound down
To earth by their narrowing perceptions,
They livèd a period of years;
Then left a noisome body
To the jaws of devouring darkness.

5. And their children wept, and built
Tombs in the desolate places,
And form'd Laws of Prudence, and call'd them
The Eternal Laws of God.

6. And the Thirty Cities remain'd,
Surrounded by salt floods, now call'd
Africa: its name was then Egypt.

7. The remaining sons of Urizen
Beheld their brethren shrink together
Beneath the Net of Urizen.
Persuasion was in vain;
For the ears of the inhabitants
Were wither'd and deafen'd and cold,
And their eyes could not discern
Their brethren of other cities.

8. So Fuzon call'd all together
The remaining children of Urizen,
And they left the pendulous earth.
They callèd it Egypt, and left it.

9. And the salt Ocean rollèd englob'd.

THE SONG OF LOS
Engraved 1795

The Song of Los (1795)   Here Blake extends his vision of international revolution from America and Europe to Africa and Asia, in an effort to fulfil the prophetic task of creating his own mythology: as he later asserts in *Jerusalem*, 'I must Create a System or be enslav'd by another Man's' (p. 336). While the obscurity of the mythic stories may partly be due to this being Blake's 'work in progress', the speech of the Kings of Asia (pp. 278–9) is a reminder that Blake has not left the tangible oppressions of a divided society behind in his search for a comprehensive expression of his vision: the mention of 'Fires in the City' (p. 279), for example, has been linked to the Anti-Catholic Gordon Riots in 1780 which Blake witnessed, and to the burning of radical scientist and clergyman Joseph Priestley's house by an anti-revolutionary mob in 1791.

Africa

I Will sing you a song of Los, the Eternal Prophet:
He sung it to four harps, at the tables of Eternity,
      In heart-formèd Africa.
Urizen faded! Ariston shudder'd!
         And thus the Song began: –

Adam stood in the garden of Eden,
And Noah on the mountains of Ararat;
They saw Urizen give his Laws to the Nations
By the hands of the children of Los.

Adam shudder'd! Noah faded! Black grew the sunny African
When Rintrah gave Abstract Philosophy to Brahma in the East.
(Night spoke to the Cloud:
'Lo! these Human-form'd spirits, in smiling hypocrisy, war
Against one another; so let them war on, slaves to the eternal
    elements.')
Noah shrunk beneath the waters,
Abram fled in fires from Chaldaea;
Moses beheld upon Mount Sinai forms of dark delusion.

To Trismegistus, Palamabron gave an abstract Law;
To Pythagoras, Socrates, and Plato.

Times rollèd on o'er all the sons of Har: time after time
Orc on Mount Atlas howl'd, chain'd down with the Chain of
    Jealousy;
Then Oothoon hover'd over Judah and Jerusalem,
And Jesus heard her voice – a Man of Sorrows! – He receiv'd
A Gospel from wretched Theotormon.

The human race began to wither; for the healthy built
Secluded places, fearing the joys of Love,

And the diseasèd only propagated.
So Antamon call'd up Leutha from her valleys of delight,
And to Mahomet a loose Bible gave;
But in the North, to Odin, Sotha gave a Code of War,
Because of Diralada, thinking to reclaim his joy.

These were the Churches, Hospitals, Castles, Palaces,
Like nets and gins and traps, to catch the joys of Eternity,
                And all the rest a desert;
Till, like a dream, Eternity was obliterated and erasèd,

Since that dread day when Har and Heva fled,
Because their brethren and sisters liv'd in War and Lust;
And, as they fled, they shrunk
Into two narrow doleful forms,
Creeping in reptile flesh upon
The bosom of the ground;
And all the vast of Nature shrunk
Before their shrunken eyes.

Thus the terrible race of Los and Enitharmon gave
Laws and Religions to the sons of Har, binding them more
And more to Earth, closing and restraining;
Till a Philosophy of Five Senses was complete:
Urizen wept, and gave it into the hands of Newton and Locke.

Clouds roll heavy upon the Alps round Rousseau and Voltaire,
And on the mountains of Lebanon round the deceasèd Gods
Of Asia, and on the deserts of Africa round the Fallen Angels.
The Guardian Prince of Albion burns in his nightly tent.

Asia

The Kings of Asia heard
The howl rise up from Europe,
And each ran out from his Web,
From his ancient woven Den;
For the darkness of Asia was startled
At the thick-flaming, thought-creating fires of Orc.

And the Kings of Asia stood
And cri èd in bitterness of soul: –

'Shall not the King call for Famine from the heath,
Nor the Priest for Pestilence from the fen,
To restrain, to dismay, to thin
The inhabitants of mountain and plain,
In the day of full-feeding prosperity
And the night of delicious songs?

Shall not the Counsellor throw his curb
Of Poverty on the laborious,
To fix the price of labour,
To invent allegoric riches?

And the privy admonishers of men
Call for Fires in the City,
For heaps of smoking ruins,
In the night of prosperity and wantonness,

To turn man from his path,
To restrain the child from the womb,
To cut off the bread from the city;
That the remnant may learn to obey,

That the pride of the heart may fail,
That the lust of the eyes may be quench'd,
That the delicate ear in its infancy
May be dull'd, and the nostrils clos'd up,
To teach Mortal Worms the path
That leads from the gates of the Grave?'

Urizen heard them cry,
And his shudd'ring, waving wings
Went enormous above the red flames,
Drawing clouds of despair thro' the Heavens
Of Europe as he went.
And his Books of brass, iron, and gold
Melted over the land as he flew,
Heavy-waving, howling, weeping.

And he stood over Judaea,
And stay'd in his ancient place,
And stretch'd his clouds over Jerusalem;

For Adam, a mouldering skeleton,
Lay bleach'd on the garden of Eden;
And Noah, as white as snow,
On the mountains of Ararat.

Then the thunders of Urizen bellow'd aloud
From his woven darkness above.

Orc, raging in European darkness,
Arose like a pillar of fire above the Alps,
Like a serpent of fiery flame!
          The sullen Earth
          Shrunk!

Forth from the dead dust, rattling bones to bones
Join. Shaking, convuls'd, the shiv'ring Clay breathes,
And all Flesh naked stands: Fathers and Friends,
Mothers and Infants, Kings and Warriors.

The Grave shrieks with delight, and shakes
Her hollow womb, and clasps the solid stem:
Her bosom swells with wild desire;
And milk and blood and glandous wine
In rivers rush, and shout and dance,
On mountain, dale, and plain.

          The Song of Los is ended.
               Urizen Wept.

THE BOOK OF LOS
Engraved 1795

The Book of Los (1795)   The amazing productiveness of Blake during the first half of this decade was almost a race against time as governmental restrictions began to impact on the creative artists sympathetic to radical views. Here, as if in a kind of desperation at the repressive times, Blake attempts another version of his creation and fall-into-division story, even more fragmented and unfinished, and this time more abstract and less easy to see as engaged with social or historical reality. As Los hurls his chains in fury and stamps his feet in verse 7 (p. 284), we can imagine Blake's own frustrations as the tides of revolution hit the banks of repression and are turned back. In the face of this fall, Los's task as the prophetic artist-blacksmith is to reformulate and recast the world through the works of the imagination, and he starts by beating out a body and a habitation from the unsuppressed fires of energy and desire, in order to contain Urizen and his effects.

CHAPTER I

1. Eno, agèd Mother,
Who the chariot of Leutha guides,
Since the day of thunders in old time,

2. Sitting beneath the eternal Oak,
Trembled and shook the steadfast Earth,
And thus her speech broke forth: –

3. 'O Times remote!
When Love and Joy were adoration,
And none impure were deem'd,
Not eyeless Covet,
Nor thin-lipp'd Envy,
Nor bristled Wrath,
Nor Curlèd Wantonness;

4. 'But Covet was pourèd full,
Envy fed with fat of lambs,
Wrath with lion's gore,
Wantonness lull'd to sleep
With the virgin's lute,
Or sated with her love;

5. 'Till Covet broke his locks and bars,
And slept with open doors;
Envy sung at the rich man's feast;
Wrath was follow'd up and down
By a little ewe lamb;
And Wantonness on his own true love
Begot a giant race.

6. Raging furious, the flames of desire
Ran thro' heaven and earth, living flames,
Intelligent, organis'd, arm'd
With destruction and plagues. In the midst
The Eternal Prophet, bound in a chain,
Compell'd to watch Urizen's shadow,

7. Rag'd with curses and sparkles of fury:
Round the flames roll, as Los hurls his chains,
Mounting up from his fury, condens'd,
Rolling round and round, mounting on high
Into Vacuum, into nonentity,
Where nothing was; dash'd wide apart,
His feet stamp the eternal fierce-raging
Rivers of wide flame; they roll round
And round on all sides, making their way
Into darkness and shadowy obscurity.

8. Wide apart stood the fires: Los remain'd
In the Void between fire and fire:
In trembling and horror they beheld him;
They stood wide apart, driv'n by his hands
And his feet, which the nether Abyss
Stamp'd in fury and hot indignation.

9. But no light from the fires! all was
Darkness round Los: heat was not; for bound up
Into fiery spheres from his fury,
The gigantic flames trembled and hid.

10. Coldness, darkness, obstruction, a Solid
Without fluctuation, hard as adamant,
Black as marble of Egypt, impenetrable,
Bound in the fierce raging Immortal;
And the separated fires, froze in
A vast Solid, without fluctuation,
Bound in his expanding clear senses.

CHAPTER II

1. The Immortal stood frozen amidst
The vast Rock of Eternity, times
And times, a night of vast durance,
Impatient, stifled, stiffen'd, hard'ned;

2. Till impatience no longer could bear
The hard bondage: rent, rent, the vast Solid,
With a crash from Immense to Immense,

3. Crack'd across into numberless fragments.
The Prophetic wrath, struggling for vent,
Hurls apart, stamping furious to dust,
And crumbling with bursting sobs, heaves
The black marble on high into fragments.

4. Hurl'd apart on all sides as a falling
Rock, the innumerable fragments away
Fell asunder; and horrible Vacuum
Beneath him, and on all sides round,

5. 'Falling! falling! Los fell and fell,
Sunk precipitant, heavy, down! down!
Times on times, night on night, day on day –
Truth has bounds, Error none – falling, falling,
Years on years, and ages on ages;
Still he fell thro' the Void, still a Void
Found for falling, day and night without end;
For tho' day or night was not, their spaces
Were measur'd by his incessant whirls
In the horrid Vacuity bottomless.

6. The Immortal revolving, indignant,
First in wrath threw his limbs, like the babe
New-born into our world: wrath subsided,
And contemplative thoughts first arose;
Then aloft his head rear'd in the Abyss,
And his downward-borne fall chang'd oblique.

7. Many ages of groans! till there grew
Branchy forms, organising the Human
Into finite inflexible organs;

8. Till in process from falling he bore
Sidelong on the purple air, wafting
The weak breeze in efforts o'erwearièd:

9. Incessant the falling Mind labour'd,
Organising itself, till the Vacuum
Became Element, pliant to rise,
Or to fall, or to swim, or to fly,
With ease searching the dire Vacuity.

CHAPTER III

1. The Lungs heave incessant, dull, and heavy;
For as yet were all other parts formless,
Shiv'ring, clinging around like a cloud,
Dim and glutinous as the white Polypus,
Driv'n by waves and englob'd on the tide.

2. And the unformèd part crav'd repose;
Sleep began; the Lungs heave on the wave:
Weary, overweigh'd, sinking beneath
In a stifling black fluid, he woke.

3. He arose on the waters; but soon
Heavy falling, his organs like roots
Shooting out from the seed, shot beneath,
And a vast World of Waters around him
In furious torrents began.

4. Then he sunk, and around his spent Lungs
Began intricate pipes that drew in
The spawn of the waters, outbranching
An immense Fibrous Form, stretching out
Thro' the bottoms of Immensity: raging.

5. He rose on the floods; then he smote
The wild deep with his terrible wrath,
Separating the heavy and thin.

6. Down the heavy sunk, cleaving around
To the fragments of Solid: uprose
The thin, flowing round the fierce fires
That glow'd furious in the Expanse.

CHAPTER IV

1. Then Light first began: from the fires,
Beams, conducted by fluid so pure,
Flow'd around the Immense. Los beheld
Forthwith, writhing upon the dark Void,
The Backbone of Urizen appear,
Hurtling upon the wind,
Like a serpent, like an iron chain,
Whirling about in the Deep.

2. Upfolding his Fibres together
To a Form of impregnable strength,
Los, astonish'd and terrifièd, built
Furnaces; he formed an Anvil,
A Hammer of adamant: then began
The binding of Urizen day and night.

3. Circling round the dark Demon with howlings,
Dismay, and sharp blightings, the Prophet
Of Eternity beat on his iron links.

4. And first from those Infinite fires,
The light that flow'd down on the winds
He seiz'd, beating incessant, condensing
The subtil particles in an Orb.

5. Roaring indignant, the bright sparks
Endur'd the vast Hammer; but unwearièd
Los beat on the Anvil, till glorious
An immense Orb of fire he fram'd.

6. Oft he quench'd it beneath in the Deeps;
Then survey'd the all-bright mass. Again
Seizing fires from the terrific Orbs,
He heated the round Globe, then beat;
While, roaring, his Furnaces endur'd
The chain'd Orb in their infinite wombs.

7. Nine ages completed their circles,
When Los heated the glowing mass, casting
It down into the Deeps: the Deeps fled
Away in redounding smoke: the Sun
Stood self-balanc'd. And Los smil'd with joy
He the vast Spine of Urizen seiz'd,
And bound down to the glowing Illusion.

8. But no light! for the Deep fled away
On all sides, and left an unform'd
Dark Vacuity: here Urizen lay
In fierce torments on his glowing bed;

9. Till his Brain in a rock, and his Heart
In a fleshy slough, formèd four rivers,
Obscuring the immense Orb of fire,
Flowing down into night; till a Form
Was completed, a Human Illusion,
In darkness and deep clouds involv'd.

THE BOOK OF AHANIA
Engraved 1795

The Book of Ahania (1795)   Ahania is Urizen's female counterpart, the division into male and female epitomising the divided psyche, while Fuzon is their rebellious son. Perhaps the most notable section of the poem is the last chapter, in which Ahania laments lost joy in a moving elegy (pp. 296–8). With this 1795 sequence of prophetic fragments, Blake finally admits defeat and goes into voluntary exile and silence as the dark years of political repression and war take their toll: he doesn't print any major new work of his own until *Milton* in 1810.

CHAPTER I

1. Fuzon, on a chariot iron-wing'd,
On spikèd flames rose; his hot visage
Flam'd furious; sparkles his hair and beard
Shot down his wide bosom and shoulders.
On clouds of smoke rages his chariot,
And his right hand burns red in its cloud,
Moulding into a vast Globe his wrath,
As the thunder-stone is moulded,
Son of Urizen's silent burnings.

2. 'Shall we worship this Demon of smoke,'
Said Fuzon, 'this abstract Nonentity,
This cloudy God seated on waters,
Now seen, now obscur'd, King of Sorrow?'

3. So he spoke in a fiery flame,
On Urizen frowning indignant,
The Globe of wrath shaking on high.
Roaring with fury, he threw
The howling Globe; burning it flew,
Length'ning into a hungry beam. Swiftly

4. Oppos'd to the exulting flam'd beam,
The broad Disk of Urizen upheav'd
Across the Void many a mile.

5. It was forg'd in mills where the winter
Beats incessant: ten winters the disk,
Unremitting, endur'd the cold hammer.

6. But the strong arm that sent it remember'd
The sounding beam: laughing, it tore through
That beaten mass, keeping its direction,
The cold loins of Urizen dividing.

7. Dire shriek'd his invisible Lust!
Deep groan'd Urizen; stretching his awful hand,
Ahania (so name his parted Soul)
He seiz'd on his mountains of Jealousy.
He groan'd, anguish'd, and callèd her Sin,
Kissing her and weeping over her;
Then hid her in darkness, in silence,
Jealous, tho' she was invisible.

8. She fell down, a faint Shadow, wand'ring
In Chaos, and circling dark Urizen,
As the moon, anguish'd, circles the earth,
Hopeless! abhorr'd! a death-shadow,
Unseen, unbodièd, unknown,
The mother of Pestilence!

9. But the fiery beam of Fuzon
Was a pillar of fire to Egypt,
Five hundred years wand'ring on earth,
Till Los seiz'd it, and beat in a mass
With the body of the sun.

CHAPTER II

1. But the forehead of Urizen gathering,
And his eyes pale with anguish, his lips
Blue and changing, in tears and bitter
Contrition he prepar'd his Bow,

2. Form'd of Ribs, that in his dark solitude,
When obscur'd in his forests, fell monsters
Arose. For his dire Contemplations
Rush'd down like floods from his mountains,
In torrents of mud settling thick,
With eggs of unnatural production:
Forthwith hatching, some howl'd on his hills,
Some in vales, some aloft flew in air.

3. Of these, an enormous dread Serpent,
Scalèd and poisonous, hornèd,
Approach'd Urizen, even to his knees,
As he sat on his dark-rooted Oak.

4. With his horns he push'd furious:
Great the conflict and great the jealousy
In cold poisons; but Urizen smote him!

5. First he poison'd the rocks with his blood,
Then polish'd his ribs, and his sinews
Drièd, laid them apart till winter;
Then a Bow black prepar'd: on this Bow
A poisonèd Rock plac'd in silence.
He utter'd these words to the Bow: –

6. 'O Bow of the clouds of Secrecy!
O nerve of that lust-form'd monster!
Send this Rock swift, invisible, thro'
The black clouds on the bosom of Fuzon.'

7. So saying, in torment of his wounds
He bent the enormous ribs slowly –
A circle of darkness! – then fixèd
The sinew in its rest; then the Rock,
Poisonous source, plac'd with art, lifting difficult
Its weighty bulk. Silent the Rock lay,

8. While Fuzon, his tigers unloosing,
Thought Urizen slain by his wrath.
'I am God!' said he, 'eldest of things.'

9. Sudden sings the Rock; swift and invisible
On Fuzon flew, enter'd his bosom;
His beautiful visage, his tresses,
That gave light to the mornings of heaven,
Were smitten with darkness, deform'd,
And outstretch'd on the edge of the forest.

10. But the Rock fell upon the Earth,
Mount Sinai, in Arabia.

CHAPTER III

1. The Globe shook, and Urizen, seated
On black clouds, his sore wound anointed;
The ointment flow'd down on the Void
Mix'd with blood – here the snake gets her poison!

2. With difficulty and great pain Urizen
Lifted on high the dead corse:
On his shoulders he bore it to where
A Tree hung over the Immensity.

3. For when Urizen shrunk away
From Eternals, he sat on a Rock,
Barren – a Rock which himself,
From redounding fancies, had petrifièd.
Many tears fell on the Rock,
Many sparks of vegetation.
Soon shot the painèd root
Of Mystery under his heel:
It grew a thick tree: he wrote
In silence his Book of Iron;
Till the horrid plant bending its boughs,
Grew to roots when it felt the earth,
And again sprung to many a tree,

4. Amaz'd started Urizen when
He beheld himself compassèd round
And high-roofèd over with trees.
He arose, but the stems stood so thick,
He with difficulty and great pain
Brought his Books – all but the Book
Of Iron – from the dismal shade.

5. The Tree still grows over the Void,
Enrooting itself all around,
An endless labyrinth of woe!

6. The corse of his first begotten
On the accursèd Tree of Mystery,
On the topmost stem of this Tree
Urizen nail'd Fuzon's corse.

CHAPTER IV

1. Forth flew the arrows of Pestilence
Round the pale living Corse on the Tree.

2. For in Urizen's slumbers of abstraction,
In the infinite ages of Eternity,
When his Nerves of Joy melted and flow'd,
A white Lake on the dark blue air,
In perturb'd pain and dismal torment,
Now stretching out, now swift conglobing,

3. Effluvia vapour'd above
In noxious clouds; these hover'd thick
Over the disorganis'd Immortal,
Till petrific pain scurf'd o'er the Lakes,
As the bones of Man, solid and dark.

4. The clouds of Disease hover'd wide
Around the Immortal in torment,
Perching around the hurtling bones –
Disease on disease, shape on shape,
Wingèd, screaming in blood and torment!

5. The Eternal Prophet beat on his Anvils,
Enrag'd in the desolate darkness;
He forg'd Nets of iron around,
And Los threw them around the bones.

6. The Shapes, screaming, flutter'd vain:
Some combin'd into muscles and glands,
Some organs for craving and lust;
Most remain'd on the tormented Void –
Urizen's army of horrors!

7. Round the pale living Corse on the Tree.
Forty years, flew the arrows of Pestilence.

8. Wailing and terror and woe
Ran thro' all his dismal world;

Forty years all his sons and daughters
Felt their skulls harden; then Asia
Arose in the pendulous deep.

  9. They reptilise upon the Earth.

10. Fuzon groan'd on the Tree.

CHAPTER V

1. The lamenting voice of Ahania,
Weeping upon the Void!
And round the Tree of Fuzon,
Distant in solitary night,
Her voice was heard, but no form
Had she; but her tears from clouds
Eternal fell round the Tree.

2. And the voice cried: 'Ah, Urizen! Love!
Flower of morning! I weep on the verge
Of Nonentity – how wide the Abyss
Between Ahania and thee!

3. 'I lie on the verge of the deep;
I see thy dark clouds ascend;
I see thy black forests and floods,
A horrible waste to my eyes!

4. 'Weeping I walk over rocks,
Over dens, and thro' valleys of death.
Why didst thou despise Ahania,
To cast me from thy bright presence
Into the World of Loneness?

5. 'I cannot touch his hand,
Nor weep on his knees, nor hear
His voice and bow, nor see his eyes
And joy; nor hear his footsteps, and
My heart leap at the lovely sound!

I cannot kiss the place
Whereon his bright feet have trod;
But I wander on the rocks
With hard necessity.

6. 'Where is my golden palace?
Where my ivory bed?
Where the joy of my morning hour?
Where the Sons of Eternity singing,

7. 'To awake bright Urizen, my King,
To arise to the mountain sport,
To the bliss of eternal valleys;

8. 'To awake my King in the morn,
To embrace Ahania's joy
On the breath of his open bosom,
From my soft cloud of dew to fall
In showers of life on his harvests?

9. 'When he gave my happy soul
To the Sons of Eternal Joy;
When he took the Daughters of Life
Into my chambers of love;

10. 'When I found Babes of bliss on my beds,
And bosoms of milk in my chambers,
Fill'd with eternal seed –
O! eternal births sung round Ahania,
In interchange sweet of their joys!

11. 'Swell'd with ripeness and fat with fatness,
Bursting on winds, my odours,
My ripe figs and rich pomegranates,
In infant joy at thy feet,
O Urizen! sported and sang.

12. 'Then thou with thy lap full of seed,
With thy hand full of generous fire,
Walkèd forth from the clouds of morning;

On the virgins of springing joy,
On the Human soul to cast
The seed of eternal Science.

13. 'The sweat pourèd down thy temples,
To Ahania return'd in evening;
The moisture awoke to birth
My mother's joys, sleeping in bliss.

14. 'But now alone! over rocks, mountains,
Cast out from thy lovely bosom!
Cruel Jealousy, selfish Fear,
Self-destroying! how can delight
Renew in these chains of darkness,
Where bones of beasts are strown
On the bleak and snowy mountains,
Where bones from the birth are burièd
Before they see the light?'

THE FOUR ZOAS

Selections from *The Four Zoas* **(1797–1804)** *The Four Zoas* is Blake's longest and most experimental work. Even the title-page is confusing. Blake's original title, dated 1797, was *Vala, Or The Death and Judgement of the Ancient Man, A Dream of Nine Nights,* but this has his second thoughts superimposed above it, *The Four Zoas: The Torments of Love and Jealousy in the Death and Judgement of Albion the Ancient Man.* First drafted up to 1800, Blake continued working on it for many years afterwards, but never finished it, raiding it for passages for the later long poems, *Milton* and *Jerusalem.*

The Four Zoas contains some of Blake's most fascinating writing, but the whole conception is difficult to follow because of the many changes he made to his developing mythic story in response to contemporary events. As in the other prophetic works, Blake depicts cosmic history, contemporary events, and the psychological state of the individual simultaneously. Blake imagines the whole universe, human history and all human individuals as one giant Universal Man, named Albion (the old name for Britain). Albion falls sick and his wholeness divides into a war of opposing faculties. At one level, the four Zoas (from the Greek word meaning 'lives') are the four main human elements: Urizen embodies conscious thought; Luvah embodies passion and desire; Urthona, imagination and wrath; Tharmas, compassion. During Albion's sickness, these 'Eternals' divide from each other and within themselves in a power battle for supremacy: they split into male and female, or in Blake's terms 'spectre' and 'emanation'. As we saw with *Visions of the Daughters of Albion,* Blake's examination of gender division has its contradictions, which emerge again here, not least because part of Blake's story involves seeing Albion's sickness as the product of his seduction by Vala, the wilful, sensual emanation of Luvah.

Urthona, the Zoa of imagination and wrath, has a spectre called Los, the blacksmith-prophet who epitomises Blake's own artistic activity. His emanation is Enitharmon, modelled on Blake's wife Catherine according to some commentators. They have a son, Orc, who is the spectre of Luvah (passion), and the representative of revolution; but at the same time their relationship in its fallen and divided state is riven with Oedipal jealousy, which leads Los to chain Orc down to 'the iron mountain's top' in Night 5 (lines 95–103; Stevenson p. 356). Both Los and Orc confront the obsessive rationalism and authoritarianism of Urizen, who attempts to rule the universe, history and the individual with his repressive laws and a society based on materialism, war and tyranny. The extract here ironically titled 'Urizen's Words of Wisdom' outlines the social inequalities, moral hypocrisies and psychological divisions enforced by Urizen's desire for tyranny: Urizen exhorts his followers to

Compel the Poor to live upon a crust of bread by soft mild arts:
So shall you govern over all. Let Moral Duty tune your tongue,
But be your hearts harder than the nether millstone   (p. 309)

No doubt part of Blake's target here was the quietism preached by Methodists and evangelicals such as William Wilberforce in his *Practical View of the Prevailing Religious System*, 1797, in which, with a wily and vicious logic characteristic of such right-wing thinking, he argued that by

softening the glare of wealth, and moderating the insolence of power, [Christianity] renders the inequalities of the social state less galling to the lower orders, whom she also instructs, in their turn, to be diligent, humble, patient: reminding them that their more lowly path has been allotted to them by the hand of God; that it is their part faithfully to discharge its duties, and contentedly to bear its inconveniences; that the present state of things is very short; that the objects about which worldly men conflict so eagerly, are not worth the contest; that the peace of mind, which Religion affords indiscriminately to all ranks, affords more true satisfaction than all the expensive pleasures which are beyond the poor man's reach; that in this view the poor have the advantage; that, if their superiors enjoy more abundant comforts, they are also exposed to many temptations from which the inferior classes are happily exempted; that 'having food and raiment, they should be therewith content', since their situation in life, with all its evils, is better than they have deserved at the hands of God; and finally, that all human distinctions will soon be done away, and the true followers of Christ will all, as children of the same Father, be alike admitted to the possession of the same heavenly inheritance. Such are the blessed effects of Christianity on the temporal well-being of political communities.[6]

It was precisely against such hypocrisy that Blake's social critique was made.

Later, the sons of Urizen are depicted abandoning the plough, harrow and loom and 'the arts of life' for 'the arts of death', in the form of instruments of warfare, and inventing 'intricate wheels' 'To perplex youth in their outgoings and to bind to labours': these are both the wheels of morality and of industrial capitalism which demands 'laborious workmanship [. . .] to obtain a scanty pittance of bread' (Night 7, lines 495–508; Stevenson, p. 392). This narrative struggle is finally resolved when Urizen is won over by Los to realise that life cannot be planned out rationally without creating death and repression. In keeping with Blake's belief in 'kissing joy as it flies', Urizen finally realises he cannot bind life to his fears and 'dark futurity' since 'futurity is in the moment' (Night 9, lines 178–81; Stevenson, p. 438). In the extract titled 'The Tillage of Urizen' (p. 313), Urizen's sons reject war and set about reviving the arts of life and energy in an apocalyptic vision of renewal.

The Four Zoas is, then, simultaneously

(i) an account of the fluctuations of the individual psyche and relationships (the quarrels between Los and Enitharmon embody the struggles between the sexes but also within each unstable gender identity; see 'The Song of Enitharmon over Los', pp. 303–4)

(ii) an epic depiction of the events of contemporary history – in Night 7, lines 162–5, Orc, spirit of revolution, is corrupted by Urizen into a serpent 'that he might draw all human forms/Into submission to his will' (Stevenson, p. 379; see 'The Serpent Orc', p. 310), an episode which Erdman argues Blake developed after Napoleon, the child of the Revolution, undertook the *coup d'etat* of the 18th of Brumaire and proclaimed himself First Consul (Erdman, pp. 316–7)

(iii) a satirical attack on social injustices coupled with a prophetic vision of social revolution: at the opening of Night 9 ('The Last Judgement', pp. 311–12), the newly-liberated poor 'smite their oppressors' and take a terrible revenge, only to be forced into the apocalyptic wine-press themselves in order to be purged of the distortions which led them to their violent vengeance

(iv) an ultimately utopian vision of the cosmic processes of the universe.

This multiple viewpoint epitomises Blake's prophetic capacity to see 'present, past, and future' simultaneously (p. 74), seeing all things in a 'fourfold' manner (p. 148).

The following selection cannot do justice to the full extent of the poem's conception and interested readers should consult *Blake – The Complete Poems*, ed. W. H. Stevenson (second edition), for the complete text. The extracts here aim to give some glimpses of the action and landscape of Blake's imaginary universe, and the reader is best advised to let the images and language impact on their own imaginations, rather than seek fixed allegorical explanations for all the characters or events.

Selections from THE FOUR ZOAS[38]
sometimes called 'Vala'
Manuscript *circa* 1797–1804

Introduction to Night the First [59]

The song of the Agèd Mother, which shook the heavens with
    wrath,
Hearing the march of long-resounding, strong, heroic Verse,
Marshall'd in order for the day of Intellectual Battle.

Four Mighty Ones are in every Man: a perfect Unity
Cannot exist but from the Universal Brotherhood of Eden,
The Universal Man, to Whom be glory evermore. Amen.
What are the Natures of those Living Creatures the Heavenly
    Father only
Knoweth: no Individual knoweth, nor can know in all Eternity.

The Wanderer [60]

Enion brooded o'er the rocks: the rough rocks groaning vegetate –
Such power was given to the solitary Wanderer –
The barkèd Oak, the long-limb'd Beech, the Chestnut-tree, the Pine,
The Pear-tree mild, the frowning Walnut, the sharp Crab, and Apple sweet
The rough bark opens, twittering peep forth little beaks and wings,
The Nightingale, the Goldfinch, Robin, Lark, Linnet and Thrush;
The Goat leap'd from the craggy cliff, the Sheep awoke from the mould;
Upon its green stalk rose the Corn, waving innumerable,
Enfolding the bright infants from the desolating winds.

A Vision of Eternity [61]

Eternity appear'd above them as One Man, enfolded
In Luvah's robes of blood, and bearing all his afflictions:
As the sun shines down on the misty earth, such was the Vision.
But purple Night, and crimson Morning, and golden Day, descending

Thro' the clear changing atmosphere, display'd green fields among
The varying clouds, like Paradises stretch'd in the expanse,
With towns, and villages, and temples, tents, sheep-folds and pastures,
Where dwell the children of the Elemental worlds in harmony.

The Song sung at the Feast of Los and Enitharmon[62]

The Mountain callèd out to the Mountain: 'Awake, O Brother
                                                                    Mountain!
Let us refuse the Plough and Spade, the heavy Roller and spikèd
Harrow; burn all these corn-fields; throw down all these fences!

Fatten'd on human blood, and drunk with wine of life is better far
Than all these labours of the harvest and the vintage. See the river,
Red with the blood of Men, swells lustful round my rocky knees:
My clouds are not the clouds of verdant fields and groves of fruit,
But Clouds of Human Souls: my nostrils drink the Lives of Men.

'The Villages lament, they faint, outstretch'd upon the plain:
Wailing runs round the Valleys from the mill and from the barn:
But most the polish'd Palaces, dark, silent, bow with dread,
Hiding their books and pictures underneath the dens of Earth.

'The Cities send to one another saying: "My sons are mad
With wine of cruelty! Let us plait a scourge, O Sister City!
Children are nourish'd for the slaughter. Once the child was fed
With milk; but wherefore now are children fed with blood?" '

The Song of Enitharmon over Los[63]

I seize the sphery harp, strike the strings!

At the first sound the golden Sun arises from the deep,
And shakes his awful hair;
The Echo wakes the moon to unbind her silver locks:
The golden Sun bears on my song,
And nine bright Spheres of harmony rise round the fiery king.

The joy of Woman is the death of her most best-belovèd,
Who dies for love of her
In torments of fierce jealousy and pangs of adoration:
The Lovers' night bears on my song,
And the nine Spheres rejoice beneath my powerful control.

They sing unceasing to the notes of my immortal hand.
The solemn, silent Moon
Reverberates the living harmony upon my limbs;
The birds and beasts rejoice and play,
And every one seeks for his mate to prove his inmost joy.

Furious and terrible they sport and rend the nether Deep;
The Deep lifts up his rugged head,
And, lost in infinite humming wings, vanishes with a cry.
The fading cry is ever dying:
The living voice is ever living in its inmost joy.

Arise, you little glancing wings and sing your infant joy!
Arise and drink your bliss!
For everything that lives is holy; for the Source of Life
Descends to be a Weeping Babe;
For the Earthworm renews the moisture of the sandy plain.

Now my left hand I stretch to Earth beneath,
And strike the terrible string.
I wake sweet joy in dens of sorrow, and I plant a smile
In forests of affliction,
And wake the bubbling springs of life in regions of dark death.

O, I am weary! Lay thine hand upon me, or I faint.
I faint beneath these beams of thine;
For thou hast touchèd my five Senses, and they answer'd thee.
Now I am nothing, and I sink,
And on the bed of silence sleep, till thou awakest me.

The Wail of Enion [64]

I am made to sow the thistle for wheat, the nettle for a nourishing dainty:
I have planted a false oath in the earth, it has brought forth a Poison Tree:
I have chosen the serpent for a counsellor, and the dog
For a schoolmaster to my children:
I have blotted out from light and living the dove and nightingale,
And I have causèd the earthworm to beg from door to door:
I have taught the thief a secret path into the house of the just:
I have taught pale Artifice to spread his nets upon the morning
My heavens are brass, my earth is iron, my moon a clod of clay,
My sun a pestilence burning at noon, and a vapour of death in night.

What is the price of Experience? Do men buy it for a song,
Or Wisdom for a dance in the street? No! it is bought with the price
Of all that a man hath – his house, his wife, his children.
Wisdom is sold in the desolate market where none come to buy,
And in the wither'd field where the farmer ploughs for bread in vain.

It is an easy thing to triumph in the summer's sun,
And in the vintage, and to sing on the waggon loaded with corn:
It is an easy thing to talk of patience to the afflicted,
To speak the laws of prudence to the houseless wanderer,
To listen to the hungry raven's cry in wintry season,
When the red blood is fill'd with wine and with the marrow of lambs:

It is an easy thing to laugh at wrathful elements;
To hear the dog howl at the wintry door, the ox in the slaughter-house
    moan;
To see a God on every wind and a blessing on every blast;
To hear sounds of Love in the thunderstorm that destroys our enemy's
    house;
To rejoice in the blight that covers his field, and the sickness that cuts
    off his children,
While our olive and vine sing and laugh round our door, and our
    children bring fruits and flowers.

Then the groan and the dolour are quite forgotten, and the slave
    grinding at the mill,

And the captive in chains, and the poor in the prison, and the soldier
    in the field
When the shatter'd bone hath laid him groaning among the happier dead:
It is an easy thing to rejoice in the tents of prosperity –
Thus would I sing and thus rejoice; but it is not so with me.

Winter [65]

Still the faint harps and silver voices calm the weary couch;
But from the caves of deepest Night, ascending in clouds of mist,
The Winter spread his wide black wings across from pole to pole;
Grim Frost beneath and terrible Snow, link'd in a marriage chain,
Began a dismal dance. The Winds around on pointed rocks
Settled like bats innumerable, ready to fly abroad.

The Woes of Urizen in the Dens of Urthona [66]

Ah! how shall Urizen the King submit to this dark mansion?
Ah! how is this? Once on the heights I stretch'd my throne sublime.
The mountains of Urizen, once of silver, where the sons of wisdom dwelt,
And on whose tops the virgins sang, are rocks of Desolation.

My fountains, once the haunt of swans, now breed the scaly tortoise,
The houses of my harpers are become a haunt of crows,
The gardens of Wisdom are become a field of horrid graves,
And on the bones I drop my tears, and water them in vain.

Once how I walkèd from my Palace in gardens of delight!
The sons of wisdom stood around, the harpers follow'd with harps,
Nine virgins, cloth'd in light, compos'd the song to their immortal voices,
And at my banquets of new wine my head was crown'd with joy.

Then in my ivory pavilions I slumber'd in the noon,
And walkèd in the silent night among sweet-smelling flowers,
Till on my silver bed I slept, and sweet dreams round me hover'd;
But now my land is darken'd and my wise men are departed.

My songs are turnèd to cries of lamentation
Heard on my mountains, and deep sighs under my palace roof;
Because the steeds of Urizen, once swifter than the light,
Were kept back from my Lord and from his chariot of mercies.

O! did I keep the horses of the Day in silver pastures!
O! I refus'd the Lord of Day the horses of his Prince!
O! did I close my treasuries with roofs of solid stone,
And darken all my palace walls with envyings and hate!

O fool! to think that I could hide from his all-piercing eyes
The gold and silver and costly stones, his holy workmanship.
O fool! could I forget the light that fillèd my bright spheres
Was a reflection of his face who call'd me from the deep!

I well remember, for I heard the mild and holy voice
Saying: 'O Light, spring up and shine,' and I sprang up from the deep.
He gave to me a silver sceptre, and crown'd me with a golden crown,
And said: 'Go forth and guide my Son who wanders on the ocean.'

I went not forth: I hid myself in black clouds of my wrath:
I call'd the stars around my feet in the night of councils dark;
The stars threw down their spears, and fled naked away.
We fell: I seiz'd thee, dark Urthona, in my left hand, falling,

I seiz'd thee, beauteous Luvah; thou art faded like a flower,
And like a lily thy wife Vala, wither'd by winds.
When thou didst bear the golden cup at the immortal tables,
Thy children smote their fiery wings, crown'd with the gold of Heaven.

Thy pure feet stept on the steps divine, too pure for other feet,
And thy fair locks shadow'd thine eyes from the divine effulgence.
Then thou didst keep with strong Urthona the living gates of Heaven;
But now thou art bow'd down with him, even to the gates of Hell.

Because thou gavest Urizen the wine of the Almighty
For steeds of Light, that they might run in thy golden chariot of pride,
I gave to thee the steeds. I pour'd the stolen wine,
And, drunken with the immortal draught, fell from my throne sublime.

I will arise, explore these dens, and find that deep pulsation
That shakes my caverns with strong shudders. Perhaps this is the Night
Of Prophecy, and Luvah hath burst his way from Enitharmon.
When Thought is clos'd in Caves, then Love shall show its root in
    deepest Hell.

Los in his Wrath [67]

Los rear'd his mighty stature: on Earth stood his feet; above
The Moon his furious forehead, circled with black bursting
    thunders;
His naked limbs glitt'ring upon the dark blue sky, his knees
Bathèd in bloody clouds; his loins in fires of War, where spears
And swords rage, where the Eagles cry and Vultures laugh, saying:

'Now comes the night of carnage, now the flesh of Kings and
    Princes
Pamper'd in palaces for our food, the blood of Captains nurtur'd
With lust and murder for our drink. The drunken Raven shall
    wander
All night among the slain, and mock the wounded that groan in
    the field.'

The War-Song of Orc [68]

Loud sounds the war-song round red Orc in his fury,
And round the nameless Shadowy Female in her howling terror,
When all the Elemental Gods join'd in the wondrous song: –
'Sound the war-trumpet terrific, souls clad in attractive steel!
Sound the shrill fife, Serpents of War! I hear the northern drum
Awake! I hear the flappings of the folding banners!
The Dragons of the North put on their armour;
Upon the eastern sea direct they take their course;
The glitt'ring of their horses' trappings stains the vault of night.

'Stop we the rising of the glorious King! spur, spur your clouds
Of death! O northern drum, awake! O hand of iron, sound
The northern drum! Now give the charge! bravely obscur'd

With darts of wintry hail! Again the black bow draw;
Again the elemental strings to your right breasts draw;
And let the thund'ring drum speed on the arrows black!

Vala's Going Forth [69]

And she went forth and saw the forms of Life and of Delight
Walking on mountains, or flying in the open expanse of heaven.
She heard sweet voices in the winds, and in the voices of birds
That rose from waters; for the waters were as the voice of Luvah,
Not seen to her like waters, or like this dark world of death;
Tho' all those fair perfections, which men know only by name.
In beautiful substantial forms appear'd, and servèd her
As food or drink or ornament, or in delightful works
To build her bowers. For the elements brought forth abundantly
The living Soul in glorious forms; and every one came forth,
Walking before her Shadowy face and bowing at her feet.
But, in vain, delights were pourèd forth on the howling Melancholy!
For her delight the Horse his proud neck bow'd, and his white mane;
And the strong Lion deign'd in his mouth to wear the golden bit;
While the far-beaming Peacock waited on the fragrant wind
To bring her fruits of sweet delight from trees of richest wonders;
And the strong-pinion'd Eagle bore the fire of Heaven in the night-season.

Urizen's Words of Wisdom [70]

And Urizen read in his Book of Brass in sounding tones: —
'Listen, O Daughters, to my voice! listen to the words of wisdom!
Compel the Poor to live upon a crust of bread by soft mild arts:
So shall you govern over all. Let Moral Duty tune your tongue,
But be your hearts harder than the nether millstone;
To bring the Shadow of Enitharmon beneath our wondrous Tree,
That Los may evaporate like smoke, and be no more.
Draw down Enitharmon to the Spectre of Urthona,
And let him have dominion over Los, the terrible Shade.
Smile when they frown, frown when they smile; and when a man looks
    pale
With labour and abstinence, say he looks healthy and happy;

And when his children sicken, let them die: there are enough
Born, even too many, and our earth will soon be overrun
Without these arts. If you would make the Poor live with temper,
With pomp give every crust of bread you give; with gracious cunning
Magnify small gifts; reduce the man to want a gift, and then give with
    pomp.
Say he smiles, if you hear him sigh; if pale, say he is ruddy
Preach temperance: say he is overgorg'd, and drowns his wit
In strong drink, tho' you know that bread and water are all
He can afford. Flatter his wife, pity his children, till we can
Reduce all to our will, as spaniels are taught with art.'

The Shade of Enitharmon [71]

Her Shadow went forth and return'd. Now she was pale as snow,
  When the mountains and hills are cover'd over, and the paths of
    men shut up;
  But, when her Spirit return'd, as ruddy as a morning when
  The ripe fruit blushes into joy in Heaven's eternal halls.

The Serpent Orc [72]

He saw Orc, a Serpent form, augmenting times on times
In the fierce battle; and he saw the Lamb of God, and the
  world of Los
Surrounded by his dark machines; for Orc augmented swift
In fury, a Serpent wondrous, among the constellations of Urizen.
A crest of fire rose on his forehead, red as the carbuncle;
Beneath, down to his eyelids, scales of pearl; then gold and silver,
Immingled with the ruby, overspread his visage; down
His furious neck, writhing contortive in dire budding pains,
The scaly armour shot out. Stubborn, down his back and bosom,
The emerald, onyx, sapphire, jasper, beryl, amethyst,
Strove in terrific emulation which should gain a place
Upon the mighty fiend – the fruit of the Mysterious Tree
Kneaded in Uvith's kneading-trough.

The Last Judgement [73]

                    Terrifièd at Non-Existence –
For such they deem'd the death of the body – Los his vegetable hands
Outstretch'd; his right hand, branching out in fibrous strength,
Seiz'd the Sun; his left hand, like dark roots, cover'd the Moon,
And tore them down, cracking the heavens across from immense to
    immense.
Then fell the fires of Eternity, with loud and shrill
Sound of loud Trumpet, thundering along from heaven to heaven,
A mighty sound articulate: 'Awake! ye Dead, and come
To Judgement from the four winds! awake, and come away!'
Folding like scrolls of the enormous volume of Heaven and Earth,
With thunderous noise and dreadful shakings, rocking to and fro,
The Heavens are shaken, and the Earth removèd from its place;
The foundations of the eternal hills discover'd.
The thrones of Kings are shaken, they have lost their robes and crowns;
The Poor smite their oppressors, they awake up to the harvest;
The naked warriors rush together down to the seashore,
Trembling before the multitudes of slaves now set at liberty:
They are become like wintry flocks, like forests stripp'd of leaves.
The Oppressèd pursue like the wind; there is no room for escape . . .
The Books of Urizen unroll with dreadful noise! The folding Serpent
Of Orc began to consume in fierce raving fire; his fierce flames
Issu'd on all sides, gathering strength in animating volumes,
Roaring abroad on all the winds, raging intense, reddening
Into resistless pillars of fire, rolling round and round, gathering
Strength from the earths consum'd, and heavens, and all hidden abysses,
Where'er the Eagle has explor'd, or Lion or Tiger trod,
Or where the comets of the night, or stars of day
Have shot their arrows or long-beamèd spears in wrath and fury.

And all the while the Trumpet sounds.
From the clotted gore, and from the hollow den
Start forth the trembling millions into flames of mental fire,
Bathing their limbs in the bright visions of Eternity.

Then, like the doves from pillars of smoke, the trembling families
Of women and children throughout every nation under heaven
Cling round the men in bands of twenties and of fifties, pale

As snow that falls round a leafless tree upon the green.
Their oppressors are fall'n; they have stricken them; they awake to life.
Yet, pale, the Just man stands erect, and looking up to Heav'n.
Trembling and strucken by the universal stroke, the trees unroot;
The rocks groan horrible and run about; the mountains and
Their rivers cry with a dismal cry; the cattle gather together,
Lowing they kneel before the heavens; the wild beasts of the forests
Tremble. The Lion, shuddering, asks the Leopard: 'Feelest thou
The dread I feel, unknown before? My voice refuses to roar,
And in weak moans I speak to thee. This night,
Before the morning's dawn, the Eagle call'd the Vulture,
The Raven call'd the Hawk. I heard them from my forests,
Saying: "Let us go up far, for soon I smell upon the wind
A terror coming from the South." The Eagle and Hawk fled away
At dawn, and ere the sun arose, the Raven and Vulture follow'd.
Let us flee also to the North.' They fled. The Sons of Men
Saw them depart in dismal droves. The trumpets sounded loud,
And all the Sons of Eternity descended into Beulah.

The Lament of Albion [74]

O weakness and O weariness! O war within my members!
My sons, exilèd from my breast, pass to and fro before me.
My birds are silent in my hills; flocks die beneath my branches;
My tents are fallen; my trumpets and the sweet sounds of my harp
Is silent on my clouded hills that belch forth storms and fires;
My milk of cows, and honey of bees, and fruit of golden harvest
Are gather'd in the scorching heat and in the driving rain.
My robe is turnèd to confusion, and my bright gold to stone.
Where once I sat, I weary walk in misery and pain;
For from within my wither'd breast, grown narrow with my woes,
The corn is turn'd to thistles, and the apples into poison;
The birds of song to murderous crows, my joys to bitter groans;
The voices of children in my tents to cries of helpless infants.
And all exilèd from the face of light and shine of morning,
In this dark World, a narrow house! I wander up and down:
I hear Mystery howling in these flames of Consummation.
When shall the Man of future times become as in days of old?
O weary life! why sit I here and give up all my powers

To indolence, to the night of death, when indolence and mourning
Sit hovering over my dark threshold? Tho' I arise, look out
And scorn the war within my members, yet my heart is weak
And my head faint. – Yet will I look again into the morning!
Whence is this sound of rage of men drinking each other's blood,
Drunk with the smoking gore, and red, but not with nourishing wine.

Accuser and Accused[75]

They see him whom they have pierc'd; they wail because of him;
They magnify themselves no more against Jerusalem, nor
Against her little ones. The Innocent, accusèd before the judges,
Shines with immortal glory: trembling, the Judge springs from his throne,
Hiding his face in the dust beneath the prisoner's feet, and saying:
'Brother of Jesus, what have I done? Entreat thy Lord for me!
Perhaps I may be forgiven.'

The Tillage of Urizen[76]

Then seiz'd the sons of Urizen the plough: they polish'd it
From rust of ages: all its ornament of gold and silver and ivory
Re-shone across the field immense, where all the nations
Darken'd like mould in the divided fallows, where the weed
Triumphs in its own destruction. They took down the harness
From the blue walls of Heaven, starry, jingling, ornamented
With beautiful art, the study of Angels, the workmanship of Demons,
When Heaven and Hell in emulation strove in sports of glory.
The noise of rural work resounded thro' the heavens of heavens:
The horses neigh from the battle, the wild bulls from the sultry waste,
The tigers from the forests, and the lions from the sandy deserts.
They sing; they seize the instruments of harmony; they throw away
The spear, the bow, the gun, the mortar; they level the fortifications;
They beat the iron engines of destruction into wedges;
They give them to Urthona's sons. Ringing, the hammers sound
In dens of death, to forge the spade, the mattock, and the axe,
The heavy roller to break the clods, to pass over the nations.

Song of the Sinless Soul[77]

'Come forth, O Vala! from the grass and from the silent dew;
Rise from the dews of death, for the Eternal Man is risen!'

She rises among flowers and looks toward the eastern clearness;
She walks, yea runs – her feet are wing'd – on the tops of the bending
    grass;
Her garments rejoice in the vocal wind, and her hair glistens with dew.

She answer'd thus: 'Whose voice is this in the voice of the nourishing air,
In the spirit of the morning, awaking the Soul from its grassy bed?
Where dost thou dwell? for it is thee I seek, and but for thee
I must have slept eternally, nor have felt the dew of thy morning.
Look how the opening dawn advances with vocal harmony!
Look how the beams foreshow the rising of some glorious power!
The Sun is thine; he goeth forth in his majestic brightness.
O thou creating voice that callest! and who shall answer thee?

'Where dost thou flee, O Fair One! where dost thou seek thy happy place?
To yonder brightness? There I haste, for sure I came from thence;
Or I must have slept eternally, nor have felt the dew of morning.'

'Eternally thou must have slept, nor have felt the morning dew,
But for yon nourishing Sun: 'tis that by which thou art arisen.
The birds adore the Sun; the beasts rise up and play in his beams,
And every flower and every leaf rejoices in his light.
Then, O thou Fair One, sit thee down, for thou art as the grass,
Thou risest in the dew of morning, and at night art folded up.'

'Alas! am I but as a flower? Then will I sit me down;
Then will I weep; then I'll complain, and sigh for immortality,
And chide my maker, thee O Sun, that raisedst me to fall.'

So saying she sat down and wept beneath the apple-trees.

'O! be thou blotted out, thou Sun, that raisedst me to trouble,
That gavest me a heart to crave, and raisedst me, thy phantom,
To feel thy heart, and see thy light, and wander here alone,
Hopeless, if I am like the grass, and so shall pass away.'

'Rise, sluggish Soul! Why sitt'st thou here? why dost thou sit and weep?
Yon Sun shall wax old and decay, but thou shalt ever flourish.
The fruit shall ripen and fall down, and the flowers consume away,
But thou shalt still survive. Arise! O dry thy dewy tears!'

'Ha! shall I still survive? Whence came that sweet and comforting voice,
And whence that voice of sorrow? O Sun! thou art nothing now to me:
Go on thy course rejoicing, and let us both rejoice together!
I walk among His flocks and hear the bleating of His lambs.
O! that I could behold His face and follow His pure feet!
I walk by the footsteps of His flocks. Come hither, tender flocks!
Can you converse with a pure Soul that seeketh for her Maker?
You answer not: then am I set your mistress in this garden.
I'll watch you and attend your footsteps. You are not like the birds
That sing and fly in the bright air; but you do lick my feet,
And let me touch your woolly backs: follow me as I sing;
For in my bosom a new Song arises to my Lord:

'Rise up, O Sun! most glorious minister and light of day!
Flow on, ye gentle airs, and bear the voice of my rejoicing!
Wave freshly, clear waters, flowing around the tender grass;
And thou, sweet-smelling ground, put forth thy life in fruit and flowers!
Follow me, O my flocks, and hear me sing my rapturous song!
I will cause my voice to be heard on the clouds that glitter in the sun.
I will call, and who shall answer me? I shall sing; who shall reply?
For, from my pleasant hills, behold the living, living springs,
Running among my green pastures, delighting among my trees!
I am not here alone: my flocks, you are my brethren;
And you birds, that sing and adorn the sky, you are my sisters.
I sing, and you reply to my song; I rejoice, and you are glad.
Follow me, O my flocks! we will now descend into the valley.
O, how delicious are the grapes, flourishing in the sun!
How clear the spring of the rock, running among the golden sand!
How cool the breezes of the valley! And the arms of the branching trees
Cover us from the sun: come and let us sit in the shade.
My Luvah here hath plac'd me in a sweet and pleasant land,
And given me fruits and pleasant waters, and warm hills and cool valleys.
Here will I build myself a house, and here I'll call on His name;
Here I'll return, when I am weary, and take my pleasant rest.'

Vala in Lower Paradise[78]

So saying, she arose and walkèd round her beautiful house;
And then from her white door she look'd to see her bleating lambs,
But her flocks were gone up from beneath the trees into the hills.

'I see the hand that leadeth me doth also lead my flocks.'
She went up to her flocks, and turnèd oft to see her shining house.
She stopp'd to drink of the clear spring, and eat the grapes and apples;
She bore the fruits in her lap; she gather'd flowers for her bosom.
She callèd to her flocks, saying: 'Follow me, O my flocks!'

They follow'd her to the silent valley beneath the spreading trees,
And on the river's margin she ungirded her golden girdle;
She stood in the river and view'd herself within the wat'ry glass,
And her bright hair was wet with the waters. She rose up from the river,
And as she rose her eyes were open'd to the world of waters;
She saw Tharmas sitting upon the rocks beside the wavy sea.

MILTON

Selections from *Milton* (1800–4; engraved 1809–10)   *Milton* begins
with a Preface attacking the enemies of true inspiration which Blake
sees as tied down by classicism and memory, a reaction which is
understandable when we recall the attacks on Blake's own artistic
practices around this time. In resounding voice, Blake calls on the
young to 'Set your foreheads against the ignorant hirelings! For we have
hirelings in the Camp, the Court, and the University' (p. 319). In
retaliation, Blake offers his most famous lyric, 'And did those feet in
ancient time', in which the blighted state of England, with its 'dark
Satanic mills' of morality, authority and mental enslavement, is contrasted
to the rebuilding of Jerusalem, the vision of a new heaven and earth in
England, which can be renewed through the 'mental fight' of artistic
energy and visionary desire.

Milton has its origins in two moments of inspiration during Blake's
stay at Felpham, one being a rapturous instant in which a lark's song
mingled with the odours of wild thyme. The other was a shaft of
sunlight which struck Blake's shoe as he was fastening it, which led him
to imagine the great Republican poet Milton undergoing a prophetic
journey from heaven back into the world to enter Blake via his foot and
transmit to him a renewed vision. The poem itself takes place between
these two moments, fulfilling Blake's visionary sense that eternity lies in
the here and now, while the redemption Milton achieves is cosmic,
personal and national, renewing Milton's own poetic vision, the lapsed
state of England, and Blake himself.

On the way we encounter some of Blake's most expansive imaginings
as Milton journeys through space and time, like Satan in *Paradise Lost*.
Rather than action, much of the poem is taken up with description and
explanation of the Blakean universe. This makes the poem somewhat
static by comparison with the furious if confusing action of *The Four
Zoas*, and it perhaps lacks the sense of historical and social engagement
to be found there. But it does have remarkable inventive energy as Blake
populates his visionary landscape and reveals the fabric of his cosmos in
a manner we now tend to associate with fantasy literature or science
fiction. In the extracts given here, for example, we are introduced to
Blake's view of the nature of infinity, time and space, which strangely
has much in common with the adventurous speculations of recent

astronomers and physicists about black holes and multiple universes ('The Nature of Infinity' p. 322; 'The Building of Time', p. 326). We visit the 'Mundane Shell' (p. 323), the vegetative world of the physical universe which has fallen from Eternity or Eden, but which is saved from the ultimate chaos of Ulro by, among other things, the labours of the creative artist. Unusually for Blake, this leads him into some uncharacteristic celebrations of nature and natural phenomena. In his annotations to Wordsworth's poems, Blake notes that 'Natural Objects always did and now do weaken, deaden and obliterate Imagination in Me', since in itself, the material world tends to deaden the spiritual eye of the imagination. Contrary to many other Romantic poets, nature was never the object of Blake's attention, and what is 'Valuable is Not to be found in Nature' alone (Keynes, p. 783). Towards the end of *Milton*, he is scathing about those writers 'Who pretend to Poetry that they may destroy Imagination / By imitation of Nature's Images drawn from Remembrance' ('Reason and Imagination' p. 329). Yet perhaps because of the original inspiration, we find the wonderfully celebratory passage about the lark ('The Birds and the Flowers', p. 327), as well as vivid descriptions of the armies of animals and insects which inhabit the apocalyptic landscape surrounding 'The Wine-Press of Los' (p. 325).

As this indicates, we also meet characters familiar from the earlier prophetic works. The sick and divided Albion is portrayed again as in the grip of a deathly sleep, this time so profound that he cannot even recognise the partial truths of misguided visionaries such as Swedenborg, or the Methodist evangelists George Whitefield and John Wesley (p. 324). Meanwhile at his forge in Bowlahoola, the prophetic blacksmith Los struggles against chaos and death to rebuild the city of art and vision, Golgonooza ('The Forge of Los', p. 324). Undoubtedly part of Blake's drive, as the extract entitled 'Reason and Imagination' indicates (p. 329), was to revenge himself on the 'paltry rhymes' of the uninspired, those who 'dare to mock with the aspersion of Madness/Cast on the Inspirèd by the tame high finisher of paltry Blots'. The bitter humiliations recorded in the shorter verses and epigrams here bear fuller fruit, but Blake's overriding concern was to celebrate the living moment of life itself and of inspiration:

> For in this Period the Poet's Work is done; and all the great
> Events of Time start forth and are conceiv'd in such a Period,
> Within a Moment, a Pulsation of the Artery.
>
> ('The Building of Time', p. 326)

Selections from MILTON [79]
Engraved 1809–1810

Preface

The stolen and perverted writings of Homer and Ovid, of Plato and Cicero, which all men ought to contemn, are set up by artifice against the Sublime of the Bible; but when the New Age is at leisure to pronounce, all will be set right, and those grand works of the more ancient, and consciously and professedly Inspired men will hold their proper rank, and the Daughters of Memory shall become the Daughters of Inspiration. Shakspeare and Milton were both curb'd by the general malady and infection from the silly Greek and Latin slaves of the sword.

Rouse up, O Young Men of the New Age! Set your foreheads against the ignorant hirelings! For we have hirelings in the Camp, the Court, and the University, who would, if they could, for ever depress mental, and prolong corporeal war. Painters! on you I call. Sculptors! Architects! suffer not the fashionable fools to depress your powers by the prices they pretend to give for contemptible works, or the expensive advertising boasts that they make of such works: believe Christ and His Apostles that there is a class of men whose whole delight is in destroying. We do not want either Greek or Roman models if we are but just and true to our own Imaginations, those Worlds of Eternity in which we shall live for ever, in Jesus our Lord.

> And did those feet in ancient time
> Walk upon England's mountains green?
> And was the holy Lamb of God
> On England's pleasant pastures seen?
>
> And did the Countenance Divine
> Shine forth upon our clouded hills?
> And was Jerusalem builded here
> Among these dark Satanic Mills?
>
> Bring me my bow of burning gold!
> Bring me my arrows of desire!
> Bring me my spear! O clouds, unfold!
> Bring me my chariot of fire!

I will not cease from mental fight,
Nor shall my sword sleep in my hand,
Till we have built Jerusalem
In England's green and pleasant land.

Would to God that all the Lord's people were Prophets.
                                        Numbers xi: 29

The Invocation [80]

Daughters of Beulah! Muses who inspire the Poet's Song,
Record the journey of immortal Milton thro' your realms
Of terror and mild moony lustre, in soft Sexual delusions
Of varièd beauty, to delight the wanderer, and repose
His burning thirst and freezing hunger! Come into my hand,
By your mild power descending down the nerves of my right arm
From out the portals of my Brain, where by your ministry
The Eternal Great Humanity Divine planted His Paradise,
And in it caus'd the Spectres of the Dead to take sweet form
In likeness of Himself. Tell also of the False Tongue, vegetated
Beneath your land of Shadows, of its sacrifices and
Its offerings; even till Jesus, the image of the Invisible God,
Became its prey; a curse, an offering, and an atonement
For Death Eternal, in the Heavens of Albion, and before the Gates
Of Jerusalem his Emanation, in the Heavens beneath Beulah!

The Mills of Satan [81]

And the Mills of Satan were separated into a moony Space
Among the rocks of Albion's Temples, and Satan's Druid Sons
Offer the Human Victims throughout all the Earth; and Albion's
Dread Tomb, immortal on his Rock, overshadow'd the whole
    Earth,
Where Satan, making to himself Laws from his own identity,
Compell'd others to serve him in moral gratitude and submission,
Being call'd God, setting himself above all that is callèd God.
And all the Spectres of the Dead, calling themselves Sons of God,
In his Synagogues worship Satan under the Unutterable Name.

The Sin of Leutha [82]

The Sin was begun in Eternity, and will not rest to Eternity,
Till two Eternities meet together. Ah! lost! lost! lost for ever!

Milton's Journey to Eternal Death [83]

Then Milton rose up from the Heavens of Albion ardorous:
The whole Assembly wept prophetic, seeing in Milton's face
And in his lineaments divine the shades of Death and Ulro;
He took off the robe of the Promise, and ungirded himself from the
     oath of God.

And Milton said: 'I go to Eternal Death! The Nations still
Follow after the detestable Gods of Priam, in pomp
Of warlike Selfhood, contradicting and blaspheming.
When will the Resurrection come to deliver the sleeping body
From corruptibility? O when, Lord Jesus! wilt Thou come?
Tarry no longer, for my soul lies at the gates of death.
I will arise and look forth for the morning of the grave;
I will go down to the sepulchre to see if morning breaks;
I will go down to self-annihilation and Eternal Death;
Lest the Last Judgement come and find me unannihilate,
And I be seiz'd and giv'n into the hands of my own Selfhood.
The Lamb of God is seen thro' mists and shadows, hov'ring
Over the sepulchres, in clouds of Jehovah and winds of Elohim,
A disk of blood, distant; and Heav'ns and Earths roll dark between.
What do I here before the Judgement without my Emanation,
With the Daughters of Memory, and not with the Daughters of
     Inspiration?
I, in my Selfhood, am that Satan! I am that Evil One!
He is my Spectre! In my obedience to loose him from my Hells,
To claim the Hells, my Furnaces, I go to Eternal Death.'

And Milton said: 'I go to Eternal Death!' Eternity shudder'd;
For he took the outside course, among the graves of the dead,
A mournful Shade. Eternity shudder'd at the image of Eternal Death.

Then on the verge of Beulah he beheld his own Shadow,

A mournful form, double, hermaphroditic, male and female
In one wonderful body, and he enter'd into it
In direful pain; for the dread Shadow, twenty-seven-fold,
Reach'd to the depths of direst Hell, and thence to Albion's land,
Which is this Earth of Vegetation on which now I write.

The Nature of Infinity [84]

The nature of Infinity is this: That every thing has its
Own Vortex; and when once a traveller thro' Eternity
Has pass'd that Vortex, he perceives it roll backward behind
His path, into a Globe itself enfolding, like a sun,
Or like a moon, or like a universe of starry majesty,
While he keeps onwards in his wondrous journey on the Earth,
Or like a human form, a friend with whom he liv'd benevolent.
As the eye of man views both the East and West, encompassing
Its vortex, and the North and South with all their starry host,
Also the rising sun and setting moon he views, surrounding
His corn-fields and his valleys of five hundred acres square.
Thus is the Earth one infinite plane, and not as apparent
To the weak traveller confin'd beneath the moony shade.
Thus is the Heaven a Vortex pass'd already, and the Earth
A Vortex not yet pass'd by the traveller thro' Eternity.

The Sea of Time and Space [85]

First Milton saw Albion upon the Rock of Ages,
Deadly pale, outstretch'd, and snowy cold, storm-cover'd –
A Giant form of perfect beauty, outstretch'd on the Rock
In solemn death: the Sea of Time and Space thunder'd aloud
Against the Rock, which was enwrappèd with the weeds of Death.
Hovering over the cold bosom in its vortex, Milton bent down
To the bosom of Death: what was underneath soon seem'd above,
A cloudy heaven mingled with stormy seas in loudest ruin;
But as a wintry globe descends precipitant, thro' Beulah bursting,
With thunders loud and terrible, so Milton's Shadow fell
Precipitant, loud thund'ring, into the Sea of Time and Space.

The Mundane Shell [86]

The Mundane Shell is a vast Concave Earth, an immense
Harden'd Shadow of all things upon our Vegetated Earth,
Enlarg'd into Dimension and deform'd into indefinite Space,
In Twenty-seven Heavens and all their Hells, with Chaos
And Ancient Night and Purgatory. It is a cavernous Earth
Of labyrinthine intricacy, twenty-seven folds of Opaqueness,
And finishes where the lark mounts.

A River in Eden [87]

There is in Eden a sweet River of milk and liquid pearl
Nam'd Ololon, on whose mild banks dwelt those who Milton
    drove
Down into Ulro; and they wept in long-resounding song
For seven days of Eternity, and the River's living banks,
The mountains wail'd, and every plant that grew, in solemn
    sighs, lamented.

Los [88]

I am that Shadowy Prophet, who, six thousand years ago,
Fell from my station in the Eternal bosom. Six thousand years
Are finish'd. I return! Both Time and Space obey my will.
I in six thousand years walk up and down; for not one moment
Of Time is lost, nor one event of Space unpermanent;
But all remain; every fabric of six thousand years
Remains permanent: tho' on the Earth, where Satan
Fell and was cut off, all things vanish and are seen no more,
They vanish not from me and mine; we guard them first and last.
The Generations of Men run on in the tide of Time,
But leave their destin'd lineaments permanent for ever and ever.

Swedenborg [89]

O Swedenborg! strongest of men, the Samson shorn by the Churches;
Showing the Transgressors in Hell, the proud Warriors in Heaven,
Heaven as a Punisher, and Hell as One under Punishment;
With Laws from Plato and his Greeks to renew the Trojan Gods
In Albion, and to deny the value of the Saviour's blood.

Whitefield and Wesley [90]

He sent his two Servants, Whitefield and Wesley: were they Prophets,
Or were they Idiots or Madmen? – Show us Miracles!
Can you have greater Miracles than these? Men who devote
Their life's whole comfort to entire scorn and injury and death?
Awake! thou sleeper on the Rock of Eternity, Albion, awake!
The trumpet of Judgement hath twice sounded: all Nations are awake,
But thou art still heavy and dull. Awake, Albion, awake!

The Forge of Los [91]

In Bowlahoola Los's Anvils stand and his Furnaces rage;
Thundering the Hammers beat, and the Bellows blow loud,
Living, self-moving, mourning, lamenting, and howling incessantly
Bowlahoola thro' all its porches feels, tho' too fast founded,
Its pillars and porticoes to tremble at the force
Of mortal or immortal arm; and softly lilling flutes,
Accordant with the horrid labours, make sweet melody
The Bellows are the Animal Lungs, the Hammers the Animal Heart,
The Furnaces the Stomach for digestion; terrible their fury!
Thousands and thousands labour, thousands play on instruments,
Stringèd or fluted, to ameliorate the sorrows of slavery.
Loud sport the dancers in the Dance of Death, rejoicing in carnage.
The hard dentant Hammers are lull'd by the flutes' lula lula,
The bellowing Furnaces' blare by the long-sounding clarion,
The double drum drowns howls and groans, the shrill fife shrieks and
   cries,
The crooked horn mellows the hoarse raving serpent – terrible but
   harmonious.

The Wine-Press of Los [92]

But the Wine-press of Los is eastward of Golgonooza, before the Seat
Of Satan: Luvah laid the foundation, and Urizen finish'd it in howling
    woe.
How red the Sons and Daughters of Luvah! here they tread the grapes,
Laughing and shouting, drunk with odours; many fall, o'erwearièd;
Drown'd in the wine is many a youth and maiden: those around
Lay them on skins of tigers and of the spotted leopard and the wild ass,
Till they revive, or bury them in cool grots, making lamentation.

This Wine-press is call'd War on Earth: it is the Printing-Press
Of Los; and here he lays his words in order above the mortal brain,
As cogs are form'd in a wheel to turn the cogs of the adverse wheel.

Timbrels and violins sport round the Wine-presses; the little Seed,
The sportive Root, the Earth-worm, the Gold-beetle, the wise Emmet
Dance round the Wine-presses of Luvah; the Centipede is there,
The Ground-spider with many eyes, the Mole clothèd in velvet,
The ambitious Spider in his sullen web, the lucky Golden-spinner,
The Earwig arm'd, the tender Maggot, emblem of immortality,
The Flea, Louse, Bug, the Tape-worm; all the Armies of Disease,
Visible or invisible to the slothful, Vegetating Man;
The slow Slug, the Grasshopper, that sings and laughs and drinks –
Winter comes: he folds his slender bones without a murmur.

The cruel Scorpion is there, the Gnat, Wasp, Hornet, and the Honey-bee,
The Toad and venomous Newt, the Serpent cloth'd in gems and gold:
They throw off their gorgeous raiment: they rejoice with loud jubilee,
Around the Wine-presses of Luvah, naked and drunk with wine.

There is the Nettle that stings with soft down, and there
The indignant Thistle, whose bitterness is bred in his milk,
Who feeds on contempt of his neighbour; there all the idle Weeds,
That creep around the obscure places, show their various limbs
Naked in all their beauty, dancing round the Wine-presses.

But in the Wine-presses the Human grapes sing not nor dance!
They howl and writhe in shoals of torment, in fierce flames consuming,
In chains of iron and in dungeons, circled with ceaseless fires,

In pits and dens and shades of death, in shapes of torment and woe –
The plates, and screws, and racks, and saws, and cords, and fires and
    cisterns,
The cruel joys of Luvah's Daughters, lacerating with knives
And whips their Victims, and the deadly sport of Luvah's Sons.

They dance around the dying, and they drink the howl and groan;
They catch the shrieks in cups of gold, they hand them to one another:
These are the sports of love, and these the sweet delights of amorous play,
Tears of the grape, the death-sweat of the cluster, the last sigh
Of the mild youth who listens to the luring songs of Luvah.

The Building of Time [93]

But others of the Sons of Los build Moments and Minutes and Hours,
And Days and Months and Years, and Ages and Periods: wondrous
    buildings!
And every Moment has a Couch of gold for soft repose –
A Moment equals a pulsation of the artery –
And between every two Moments stands a Daughter of Beulah,
To feed the Sleepers on their Couches with maternal care.
And every Minute has an azure Tent with silken Veils;
And every Hour has a bright golden Gate carvèd with skill;
And every Day and Night has Walls of brass and Gates of adamant,
Shining like precious stones, and ornamented with appropriate signs;
And every Month a silver-pavèd Terrace, buildèd high;
And every Year invulnerable Barriers with high Towers;
And every Age is moated deep with Bridges of silver and gold;
And every Seven Ages is encircled with a Flaming Fire.
Now Seven Ages is amounting to Two Hundred Years:
Each has its Guard, each Moment, Minute, Hour, Day, Month and Year;
All are the work of Fairy hands of the Four Elements:
The Guard are Angels of Providence on duty evermore.
Every Time less than a pulsation of the artery
Is equal in its period and value to Six Thousand Years;
For in this Period the Poet's Work is done; and all the great
Events of Time start forth and are conceiv'd in such a Period,
Within a Moment, a Pulsation of the Artery.

The Heavens and the Earth [94]

The Sky is an immortal Tent built by the Sons of Los;
And every Space that a Man views around his dwelling-place,
Standing on his own roof, or in his garden on a mount
Of twenty-five cubits in height, such Space is his Universe:
And on its verge the Sun rises and sets, the Clouds bow
To meet the flat Earth and the Sea in such an order'd Space;
The Starry Heavens reach no further, but here bend and set
On all sides, and the two Poles turn on their valves of gold;
And if he move his dwelling-place, his Heavens also move
Where'er he goes, and all his neighbourhood bewail his loss.
Such are the Spaces callèd Earth, and such its dimension.
As to that false appearance which appears to the reasoner,
As of a Globe rolling thro' Voidness, it is a delusion of Ulro.

The Birds and the Flowers [95]

Thou hearest the Nightingale begin the Song of Spring:
The Lark, sitting upon his earthy bed, just as the morn
Appears, listens silent; then, springing from the waving
        corn-field, loud
He leads the Choir of Day – trill! trill! trill! trill!
Mounting upon the wings of light into the great Expanse,
Re-echoing against the lovely blue and shining heavenly Shell;
His little throat labours with inspiration; every feather
On throat and breast and wings vibrates with the effluence Divine
All Nature listens silent to him, and the awful Sun
Stands still upon the mountain looking on this little Bird
With eyes of soft humility and wonder, love and awe.
Then loud from their green covert all the Birds begin their song:
The Thrush, the Linnet and the Goldfinch, Robin and the Wren
Awake the Sun from his sweet revery upon the mountain:
The Nightingale again assays his song, and thro' the day
And thro' the night warbles luxuriant; every Bird of song
Attending his loud harmony with admiration and love.
This is a Vision of the lamentation of Beulah over Ololon.

Thou perceivest the Flowers put forth their precious Odours;

And none can tell how from so small a centre comes such sweet,
Forgetting that within that centre Eternity expands
Its ever-during doors, that Og and Anak fiercely guard.
First, ere the morning breaks, joy opens in the flowery bosoms,
Joy even to tears, which the Sun rising dries: first the Wild Thyme
And Meadow-sweet, downy and soft, waving among the reeds,
Light springing on the air, lead the sweet dance; they wake
The Honeysuckle sleeping on the oak; the flaunting beauty
Revels along upon the wind; the White-thorn, lovely May,
Opens her many lovely eyes; listening the Rose still sleeps –
None dare to wake her; soon she bursts her crimson-curtain'd bed
And comes forth in the majesty of beauty. Every Flower,
The Pink, the Jessamine, the Wallflower, the Carnation.
The Jonquil, the mild Lily opes her heavens; every Tree
And Flower and Herb soon fill the air with an innumerable dance,
Yet all in order sweet and lovely. Men are sick with love!
Such is a Vision of the lamentation of Beulah over Ololon.

Love and Jealousy [96]

And the Divine Voice was heard in the Songs of Beulah, saying:
'When I first married you, I gave you all my whole soul;
I thought that you would love my loves and joy in my delights,
Seeking for pleasures in my pleasures, O Daughter of Babylon!
Then thou wast lovely, mild, and gentle; now thou art terrible
In Jealousy and unlovely in my sight, because thou hast cruelly
Cut off my loves in fury, till I have no Love left for thee.
Thy Love depends on him thou lovest, and on his dear loves
Depend thy pleasures, which thou hast cut off by Jealousy:
Therefore I show my Jealousy, and set before you Death.
Behold Milton, descended to redeem the Female Shade
From Death Eternal! such your lot to be continually redeem'd
By Death and misery of those you love, and by Annihilation.
When the Sixfold Female perceives that Milton annihilates
Himself, that seeing all his loves by her cut off, he leaves
Her also, entirely abstracting himself from Female loves,
She shall relent in fear of death; she shall begin to give
Her maidens to her husband, delighting in his delight.
And then, and then alone, begins the happy Female joy,

As it is done in Beulah; and thou, O Virgin Babylon! Mother of
   Whoredoms,
Shalt bring Jerusalem in thine arms in the night watches; and
No longer turning her a wandering Harlot in the streets,
Shalt give her into the arms of God, your Lord and Husband.'
Such are the Songs of Beulah, in the Lamentations of Ololon.

Reason and Imagination [97]

The Negation is the Spectre, the Reasoning Power in Man:
This is a false Body, an Incrustation over my Immortal
Spirit, a Selfhood which must be put off and annihilated alway.
To cleanse the Face of my Spirit by self-examination,
To bathe in the waters of Life, to wash off the Not Human,
I come in Self-annihilation and the grandeur of Inspiration;
To cast off Rational Demonstration by Faith in the Saviour,
To cast off the rotten rags of Memory by Inspiration,
To cast off Bacon, Locke, and Newton from Albion's covering,
To take off his filthy garments and clothe him with Imagination;
To cast aside from Poetry all that is not Inspiration,
That it no longer shall dare to mock with the aspersion of Madness
Cast on the Inspirèd by the tame high finisher of paltry Blots
Indefinite or paltry Rhymes, or paltry Harmonies,
Who creeps into State Government like a caterpillar to destroy;
To cast off the idiot Questioner, who is always questioning,
But never capable of answering; who sits with a sly grin
Silent plotting when to question, like a thief in a cave;
Who publishes Doubt and calls it Knowledge; whose Science is Despair,
Whose pretence to knowledge is Envy, whose whole Science is
To destroy the wisdom of ages, to gratify ravenous Envy
That rages round him like a Wolf, day and night, without rest.
He smiles with condescension; he talks of Benevolence and Virtue,
And those who act with Benevolence and Virtue they murder time on
   time.
These are the destroyers of Jerusalem! these are the murderers
Of Jesus! who deny the Faith and mock at Eternal Life,
Who pretend to Poetry that they may destroy Imagination
By imitation of Nature's Images drawn from Remembrance.
These are the Sexual Garments, the Abomination of Desolation,

Hiding the Human Lineaments, as with an Ark and Curtains
Which Jesus rent, and now shall wholly purge away with Fire,
Till Generation is swallow'd up in Regeneration.

The Song of the Shadowy Female [98]

My Garments shall be woven of sighs and heart-broken
    lamentations:
The misery of unhappy Families shall be drawn out into its
    border,
Wrought with the needle, with dire sufferings, poverty, pain,
    and woe,
Along the rocky Island and thence throughout the whole Earth.
There shall be the sick Father and his starving Family; there
The Prisoner in the stone Dungeon, and the Slave at the Mill.
I will have writings written all over it in Human words,
That every Infant that is born upon the Earth shall read
And get by rote, as a hard task of a life of sixty years.
I will have Kings inwoven upon it, and Counsellors and
    Mighty Men:
The Famine shall clasp it together with buckles and clasps,
And the Pestilence shall be its fringe, and the War its girdle;
To divide into Rahab and Tirzah, that Milton may come to
    our tents.
For I will put on the Human Form, and take the Image of God,
Even Pity and Humanity; but my clothing shall be Cruelty.
And I will put on Holiness as a breastplate and as a helmet,
And all my ornaments shall be of the gold of broken hearts,
And the precious stones of anxiety and care, and desperation
    and death,
And repentance for sin, and sorrow, and punishment and fear;
To defend me from thy terrors, O Orc! my only belovèd!

JERUSALEM

Selections from *Jerusalem* (1804–1820) *Jerusalem* opens each chapter with short essays and poems. In the first, shaking off the soporific effects of his stay at Felpham, Blake proclaims endearingly, 'After my three years' slumber on the banks of the Ocean, I again display my Giant forms to the Public' (p.334). He also explains the artistic and formal integrity of his verse-writing, arguing that his poetry is carefully 'studied'. His metrical form he sees as liberated from the 'bondage' of rhyme and blank verse. Blake invents for himself a seven-stress line which hovers around an iambic rhythm but is flexible enough to vary according to the needs of the moment, since 'Poetry fetter'd, fetters the Human Race' (p. 335).

This opening passage also provides the key theme for the poem itself, 'continual Forgiveness of Sin' (p. 334), which Blake had already explored in 'The Everlasting Gospel'. As the passage titled 'The Remembrance of Sin' suggests (p. 345), retribution for sin is to be seen as part of the cycle of law and violence which can only be broken by an acceptance of the other which is nothing less than a transformation of consciousness. The Preface to Chapter 3 states, 'Friendship cannot exist without Forgiveness of Sins continually' (p. 346). For Blake, this is the revolutionary message of Jesus, which, if taken literally, would instantly transform society and human relations. As before, he offers a psycho-social vision encompassing the different levels of experience dialectically: in a later passage, not represented here, the Voice of the Atlantic asserts, 'Are not Religion and Politics the same thing? Brotherhood is Religion' (Stevenson, p. 751). At the same time there is evidence of the inner struggle in Blake to maintain his vision in the face of hostility, indifference and the savage reactionary times:

> Trembling I sit day and night; my friends are astonish'd at me.
> Yet they forgive my wanderings. I rest not from my great task –
> To open the eternal worlds, to open the immortal eyes
> Of man inward into the worlds of thought, into Eternity
> Ever expanding in the bosom of God, the human imagination.
>
> (Stevenson, p. 636)

In the extract from Chapter 2 titled 'Fourfold and Twofold Vision' (p. 345), we get a sense of how much in retreat Blake felt himself to be in the face of the reversals of revolutionary hopes.

Jerusalem is the most fully finished of Blake's longer prophetic works. Many elements of his mythic vision are familiar from earlier poems, and some passages derive from the incomplete *The Four Zoas*; but he also builds in a more intricate cast of minor characters from British and biblical history as well as from his own times, all populating Britain as the actual stage for his 'Giant forms' (p. 334). In the extracts given here, we begin with a call to 'Awake' and overcome the limited vision of material existence ('Introduction', p. 335). That state is partly explained in a passage describing the divisions of the human psyche and social body ('The Reasoning Power', p. 335), in terms which are reminiscent of the 'contraries' in *The Marriage of Heaven and Hell* (p. 196). 'The Words of Los' (p. 336) are often taken as Blake's own statement of intent in his prophetic works. We then encounter the building of Golgonooza, the city of visionary art to counteract the effects of the divided human condition, in a London Blake knew intimately and names affectionately (p. 336): Tyburn, London's arena of public executions, is linked to Calvary and Golgotha, the names given to the site of Christ's crucifixion. The Blakean narrator then expands his vision of the alienated condition of Albion or England, represented by the dominance of rationalism (Locke and Newton) in 'the Schools and Universities', and explains his prophetic role to overthrow it ('A Vision of Albion', pp. 336–7). Albion's own lament for his divided self is articulated as his alienation from his female emanation, Jerusalem, who herself is defined as 'Liberty' (pp. 337–8). In the opening poem to Chapter 2, 'The fields from Islington to Marybone' become the scene for an enactment of Blake's whole myth of fall and redemption in miniature (pp. 338–41). As in *Milton*, the 'Satan' here is the spectre of selfhood, an element of self-alienated humanity, which needs to be reclaimed and reintegrated. The passage titled 'A Female Will' (p. 341), along with two later passages (pp. 351–2), present images of dominant possessive females as emblems of that self-division, but are also a reminder of some of the problems with Blake's portrayal of gender issues which we met in *Visions of the Daughters of Albion*.

Throughout the poem, Blake insists that humanity has it within its own grasp to achieve a revolutionary vision and a vision of revolution, as evidenced in the extract from Chapter 2 titled here 'The Fury of Los' (pp. 342–4): Los, the visionary blacksmith, berates the hypocrisies of the fallen Albion, allowing Blake to launch a vitriolic attack on his contemporaries who had already earned his wrath in his shorter satirical works. Instead of calling on God for help, Los insists humanity should redeem itself since God dwells in humanity. This radical Christianity leads Blake to a 'Vision of Joseph and Mary' (pp. 349–50), in which Mary's pregnancy is seen as the result of adultery and the theme of forgiveness of sins is given a twist as subversive as anything in Shelley's atheistic essays. In the Preface to Chapter 4 of *Jerusalem*, we find this Blakean redefinition of the nature of Christianity: 'I know of no other Christianity and of no other Gospel than the liberty of both body and mind to exercise the Divine Arts of Imagination – Imagination, the real and Eternal world of which this Vegetable Universe is but a faint shadow [. . .] What is the Life of Man but Art and Science? [. . .] Let every Christian, as much as in him lies, engage himself openly and publicly, before all the World, in some mental pursuit for the Building up of Jerusalem' (pp. 352–3). In contradiction to the hypocrisies of the self-righteous which Blake parodies in the opening of this passage, Blake offers us his thread of 'golden string' (p. 352) to lead to salvation: 'to obey [our] Humanities, and not pretend Holiness' (p. 356), to 'put off Holiness,/ And put on Intellect' (p. 357); inviting us to participate with him in the 'mental fight' to rebuild Jerusalem in 'England's green and pleasant land' (p. 320).

Selections from JERUSALEM[99]
Engraved 1804–(?)1820

Sheep   TO THE PUBLIC[100]   Goats

After my three years' slumber on the banks of the Ocean, I again display
my Giant forms to the Public. My former Giants and Fairies having
receiv'd the highest reward possible, the . . . and . . . of those with whom
to be connected is to be . . . I cannot doubt that this more consolidated
and extended Work will be as kindly received. The Enthusiasm of the
following Poem, the Author hopes . . . I also hope the Reader will be with
me wholly one in Jesus our Lord, Who is the God . . . and Lord . . . to
Whom the Ancients look'd, and saw His day afar off, with trembling and
amazement.

The Spirit of Jesus is continual Forgiveness of Sin: he who waits to be
righteous before he enters into the Saviour's Kingdom, the Divine Body,
will never enter there. I am perhaps the most sinful of men: I pretend
not to holiness; yet I pretend to love, to see, to converse with daily, as
man with man, and the more to have an interest in the Friend of
Sinners. Therefore . . . Reader . . . what you do not approve, and . . me
for this energetic exertion of my talent.

> Reader! . . . of books . . . of Heaven,
> And of that God from whom . . .
> Who in mysterious Sinai's awful cave
> To Man the wondrous art of writing gave;
> Again He speaks in thunder and in fire,
> Thunder of Thought and flames of fierce Desire.
> Even from the depths of Hell His voice I hear
> Within the unfathom'd caverns of my Ear.
> Therefore I print: nor vain my types shall be.
> Heaven, Earth, and Hell, henceforth shall live in harmony

*Of the Measure in which
the following Poem is written.*

We who dwell on Earth can do nothing of ourselves; everything, is
conducted by Spirits, no less than Digestion or Sleep . . .

When this Verse was first dictated to me, I consider'd a monotonous cadence like that used by Milton and Shakspeare, and all writers of English Blank Verse, derived from the modern bondage of Riming, to be a necessary and indispensable part of Verse. But I soon found that in the mouth of a true Orator such monotony was not only awkward, but as much a bondage as rime itself. I therefore have produced a variety in every line, both of cadences and number of syllables. Every word and every letter is studied and put into its fit place; the terrific numbers are reserved for the terrific parts, the mild and gentle for the mild and gentle parts, and the prosaic for inferior parts; all are necessary to each other. Poetry fetter'd fetters the Human Race. Nations are destroy'd or flourish, in proportion as their Poetry, Painting, and Music are destroy'd or flourish. The Primeval State of Man was Wisdom, Art, and Science.

Introduction [101]

This theme calls me in sleep night after night, and ev'ry morn
Awakes me at sunrise; then I see the Saviour over me
Spreading His beams of love, and dictating the words of this
    mild song:
'Awake! Awake! O sleeper of the Land of Shadows, wake! expand!
I am in you, and you in Me, mutual in Love Divine,
Fibres of love from man to man thro' Albion's pleasant land.'

The Reasoning Power [102]

And this is the manner of the Sons of Albion in their strength:
They take the Two Contraries which are call'd Qualities,
    with which
Every Substance is clothèd; they name them Good and Evil.
From them they make an Abstract, which is a Negation
Not only of the Substance from which it is derivèd,
A murderer of its own Body, but also a murderer
Of every Divine Member. It is the Reasoning Power,
An Abstract objecting power, that negatives everything.
This is the Spectre of Man, the Holy Reasoning Power,
And in its Holiness is closèd the Abomination of Desolation!

The Words of Los [103]

I must Create a System, or be enslav'd by another Man's;
I will not Reason and Compare: my business is to Create.

The Builders of Golgonooza [104]

What are those Golden Builders doing? Where was the burying-
place
Of soft Ethinthus? near Tyburn's fatal Tree? Is that
Mild Zion's hill's most ancient promontory, near mournful
Ever-weeping Paddington? Is that Calvary and Golgotha
Becoming a building of Pity and Compassion? Lo!
The stones are Pity, and the bricks well-wrought Affections
Enamell'd with Love and Kindness; and the tiles engraven gold,
Labour of merciful hands; the beams and rafters are Forgiveness,
The mortar and cement of the work, tears of Honesty, the nails
And the screws and iron braces are well-wrought Blandishments
And well-contrivèd words, firm fixing, never forgotten,
Always comforting the remembrance; the floors Humility,
The ceilings Devotion, the hearths Thanksgiving.
Prepare the furniture, O Lambeth, in thy pitying looms!
The curtains, woven tears and sighs, wrought into lovely forms
For Comfort; there the secret furniture of Jerusalem's chamber
Is wrought. Lambeth! the Bride, the Lamb's Wife loveth thee;
Thou art one with her, and knowest not of Self in thy supreme joy.
Go on, Builders in hope! tho' Jerusalem wanders far away
Without the Gate of Los, among the dark Satanic wheels.

A Vision of Albion [105]

I see the Fourfold Man; the Humanity in deadly sleep,
And its fallen Emanation, the Spectre and its cruel Shadow.
I see the Past, Present, and Future existing all at once
Before me. O Divine Spirit! sustain me on thy wings,
That I may awake Albion from his long and cold repose;
For Bacon and Newton, sheath'd in dismal steel, their terrors hang
Like iron scourges over Albion. Reasonings like vast Serpents
Enfold around my limbs, bruising my minute articulations.

I turn my eyes to the Schools and Universities of Europe,
And there behold the Loom of Locke, whose Woof rages dire,
Wash'd by the Water-wheels of Newton: black the cloth
In heavy wreaths folds over every Nation: cruel Works
Of many Wheels I view, wheel without wheel, with cogs tyrannic,
Moving by compulsion each other; not as those in Eden, which,
Wheel within wheel, in freedom revolve, in harmony and peace.

Punishment and Forgiveness [106]

Why should Punishment weave the veil with Iron Wheels of War,
When Forgiveness might it weave with Wings of Cherubim?

The Lament of Albion [107]

O what is Life and what is Man? O what is Death? Wherefore
Are you, my Children, natives in the Grave to where I go?
Or are you born to feed the hungry ravenings of Destruction,
To be the sport of Accident, to waste in Wrath and Love a weary
Life, in brooding cares and anxious labours, that prove but chaff?
O Jerusalem! Jerusalem! I have forsaken thy courts,
Thy pillars of ivory and gold, thy curtains of silk and fine
Linen, thy pavements of precious stones, thy walls of pearl
And gold, thy gates of Thanksgiving, thy windows of Praise,
Thy clouds of Blessing, thy Cherubims of Tender Mercy,
Stretching their Wings sublime over the Little Ones of Albion.
O Human Imagination! O Divine Body, I have crucifièd!
I have turnèd my back upon thee into the Wastes of Moral Law.
There Babylon is builded in the Waste, founded in Human desolation.
O Babylon! thy Watchman stands over thee in the night;
Thy severe Judge all the day long proves thee, O Babylon,
With provings of Destruction, with giving thee thy heart's desire.
But Albion is cast forth to the Potter, his Children to the Builders
To build Babylon, because they have forsaken Jerusalem.
The walls of Babylon are Souls of Men; her gates the Groans
Of Nations; her towers are the Miseries of once happy Families;
Her streets are pavèd with Destruction; her houses built with Death;
Her Palaces with Hell and the Grave; her Synagogues with Torments
Of ever-hardening Despair, squar'd and polish'd with cruel skill.

Jerusalem[108]

Such Visions have appear'd to me,
As I my order'd course have run:
Jerusalem is nam'd Liberty
Among the Sons of Albion.

TO THE JEWS[109]

Jerusalem, the Emanation of the Giant Albion! Can it be? Is it a truth that the learned have explored? Was Britain the primitive seat of the Patriarchal Religion? If it is true, my title page is also true, that Jerusalem was, and is, the Emanation of the Giant Albion. It is true, and cannot be controverted. Ye are united, O ye inhabitants of Earth, in One Religion – the Religion of Jesus, the most ancient, the Eternal, and the Everlasting Gospel. The Wicked will turn it to Wickedness, the Righteous to Righteousness. Amen! Huzza! Selah!

'All things begin and end in Albion's ancient Druid rocky shore.'

Your Ancestors derived their origin from Abraham, Heber, Shem, and Noah, who were Druids, as the Druid Temples (which are the patriarchal pillars and oak groves) over the whole Earth witness to this day.
    You have a tradition that Man anciently contain'd in his mighty limbs all things in Heaven and Earth: this you received from the Druids.

'But now the starry Heavens are fled from the mighty limbs of Albion.'

Albion was the Parent of the Druids, and, in his Chaotic State of Sleep, Satan and Adam and the whole World was created by the Elohim.

The fields from Islington to Marybone,
    To Primrose Hill and Saint John's Wood,
Were builded over with pillars of gold;
    And there Jerusalem's pillars stood.

Her Little Ones ran on the fields,
    The Lamb of God among them seen,
And fair Jerusalem, His Bride,
    Among the little meadows green.

Pancras and Kentish Town repose
  'Among her golden pillars high,
Among her golden arches which
  Shine upon the starry sky.

The Jew's-harp House and the Green Man,
  The Ponds where boys to bathe delight,
The fields of cows by William's farm,
  Shine in Jerusalem's pleasant sight.

She walks upon our meadows green;
  The Lamb of God walks by her side;
And every English child is seen,
  Children of Jesus and His Bride;

Forgiving trespasses and sins,
  Lest Babylon, with cruel Og,
With Moral and Self-righteous Law,
  Should crucify in Satan's Synagogue.

What are those Golden Builders doing
  Near mournful ever-weeping Paddington,
Standing above that mighty ruin,
  Where Satan the first victory won;

Where Albion slept beneath the fatal Tree,
  And the Druid's golden knife
Rioted in human gore,
  In offerings of Human Life?

They groan'd aloud on London Stone,
  They groan'd aloud on Tyburn's Brook:
Albion gave his deadly groan,
  And all the Atlantic mountains shook.

Albion's Spectre, from his loins,
  Tore forth in all the pomp of War;
Satan his name; in flames of fire
  He stretch'd his Druid pillars far.

Jerusalem fell from Lambeth's vale,
  Down thro' Poplar and Old Bow,
Thro' Malden, and across the sea,
  In war and howling, death and woe.

The Rhine was red with human blood;
  The Danube roll'd a purple tide;
On the Euphrates Satan stood,
  And over Asia stretch'd his pride.

He wither'd up sweet Zion's hill
  From every nation of the Earth;
He wither'd up Jerusalem's Gates,
  And in a dark land gave her birth.

He wither'd up the Human Form
  By laws of sacrifice for Sin,
Till it became a Mortal Worm,
  But O! translucent all within.

The Divine Vision still was seen,
  Still was the Human Form Divine;
Weeping, in weak and mortal clay,
  O Jesus! still the Form was Thine!

And Thine the Human Face; and Thine
  The Human Hands, and Feet, and Breath,
Entering thro' the Gates of Birth,
  And passing thro' the Gates of Death.

And O Thou Lamb of God! whom I
  Slew in my dark self-righteous pride,
Art Thou return'd to Albion's land,
  And is Jerusalem Thy Bride?

Come to my arms, and nevermore
  Depart; but dwell for ever here;
Create my spirit to Thy love;
  Subdue my Spectre to Thy fear.

Spectre of Albion! warlike Fiend!
   In clouds of blood and ruin roll'd,
I here reclaim thee as my own,
   My Selfhood – Satan arm'd in gold!

Is this thy soft Family-love,
   Thy cruel patriarchal pride;
Planting thy Family alone,
   Destroying all the World beside?

A man's worst Enemies are those
   Of his own House and Family;
And he who makes his Law a curse,
   By his own Law shall surely die!

In my Exchanges every land
   Shall walk; and mine in every land,
Mutual shall build Jerusalem,
   Both heart in heart and hand in hand.

If Humility is Christianity, you, O Jews! are the true Christians. If your tradition that Man contained in his limbs all animals is true, and they were separated from him by cruel sacrifices, and when compulsory cruel sacrifices had brought Humanity into a Feminine Tabernacle in the loins of Abraham and David, the Lamb of God, the Saviour, became apparent on Earth as the Prophets had foretold! The return of Israel is a return to mental sacrifice and war. Take up the Cross, O Israel! and follow Jesus.

A Female Will [110]

What may Man be? who can tell? But what may Woman be,
To have power over Man from Cradle to corruptible Grave?
There is a Throne in every Man: it is the Throne of God.
This, Woman has claim'd as her own; and Man is no more:
Albion is the Tabernacle of Vala and her Temple,
And not the Tabernacle and Temple of the Most High.
O Albion! why wilt thou create a Female Will,
To hide the most evident God in a hidden covert, even
In the shadows of a Woman and a secluded Holy Place,
That we may pry after him as after a stolen treasure,
Hidden among the Dead and murèd up from the paths of Life?

The Universal Family [111]

Our Wars are wars of life, and wounds of love,
With intellectual spears, and long wingèd arrows of thought.
Mutual in one another's love and wrath all renewing,
We live as One Man: for, contracting our Infinite senses,
We behold multitude; or, expanding, we behold as One,
As One Man all the Universal Family; and that One Man
We call Jesus the Christ. And He in us, and we in Him,
Live in perfect harmony in Eden, the land of Life,
Giving, receiving, and forgiving each other's trespasses.
He is the Good Shepherd, He is the Lord and Master;
He is the Shepherd of Albion, He is all in all,
In Eden, in the garden of God, and in heavenly Jerusalem.
If we have offended, forgive us! take not vengeance against us!

Man's Spectre [112]

Each Man is in his Spectre's power
Until the arrival of that hour,
When his Humanity awake,
And cast his Spectre into the Lake.

The Fury of Los [113]

They saw their wheels rising up poisonous against Albion:
Urizen cold & scientific; Luvah pitying & weeping;
Tharmas indolent & sullen; Urthona doubting & despairing;
Victims to one another & dreadfully plotting against each other
To prevent Albion walking about in the four complexions.

They saw America closed out by the oaks of the western shore,
And Tharmas dashed on the rocks of the altars of victims in Mexico.
'If we are wrathful, Albion will destroy Jerusalem with rooty groves;
If we are merciful, ourselves must suffer destruction on his oaks.
Why should we enter into our spectres to behold our own corruptions?
O God of Albion, descend, deliver Jerusalem from the oaken groves!'

Then Los grew furious, raging: 'Why stand we here trembling around,
Calling on God for help and not ourselves (in whom God dwells),
Stretching a hand to save the falling man? Are we not four,
Beholding Albion upon the precipice ready to fall into non-entity,
Seeing these heavens & hells conglobing in the void? Heavens over hells
Brooding in holy hypocritic lust, drinking the cries of pain
From howling victims of law, building heavens twenty-seven-fold;
Swelled & bloated general forms, repugnant to the Divine
Humanity, who is the only general & universal form
To which all lineaments tend & seek with love & sympathy.
All broad & general principles belong to benevolence,
Who protects minute particulars, every one in their own identity
But here the affectionate touch of the tongue is closed in by deadly teeth,
And the soft smile of friendship & the open dawn of benevolence
Become a net & a trap & every energy rendered cruel,
Till the existence of friendship & benevolence is denied.
The wine of the Spirit & the vineyards of the Holy One
Here turn into poisonous stupor & deadly intoxication,
That they may be condemned by law & the Lamb of God be slain.

And the two sources of life in eternity, hunting & war,
Are becoming the sources of dark & bitter death & of corroding hell.
The open heart is shut up in integuments of frozen silence
That the spear that lights it forth may shatter the ribs & bosom.
A pretence of art to destroy art! A pretence of liberty
To destroy liberty, a pretence of religion to destroy religion!
Oshea and Caleb fight; they contend in the valleys of Peor
 In the terrible family contentions of those who love each other.
The armies of Balaam weep; no women come to the field;
Dead corses lay before them, & not as in wars of old.
(For the soldier who fights for truth, calls his enemy his brother:
They fight & contend for life, & not for eternal death.)
But here the soldier strikes, & a dead corse falls at his feet;
Nor daughter nor sister nor mother come forth to embosom the slain,
But death, eternal death, remains in the valleys of Peor.
The English are scattered over the face of the nations. Are these
Jerusalem's children? Hark! hear the giants of Albion cry at night:

'We smell the blood of the English; we delight in their blood on our altars!
The living & the dead shall be ground in our rumbling mills

For bread of the sons of Albion, of the giants Hand & Skofield!'
Skofield & Kox are let loose upon my Saxons. They accumulate
A world in which man is by his nature the enemy of man,
In pride of selfhood unwieldy stretching out into non-entity,
Generalising art & science till art & science is lost.
Bristol & Bath, listen to my words, & ye seventeen, give ear!
It is easy to acknowledge a man to be great & good while we
Derogate from him in the trifles & small articles of that goodness,
Those alone are his friends who admire his minutest powers.
Instead of Albion's lovely mountains & the curtains of Jerusalem
I see a cave, a rock, a tree deadly & poisonous, unimaginative;
Instead of the mutual forgivenesses, the minute particulars, I see
Pits of bitumen ever burning, artificial riches of the Canaanite
Like lakes of liquid lead; instead of heavenly chapels built
By our dear Lord I see worlds crusted with snows & ice.
I see a wicker idol woven round Jerusalem's children. I see
The Canaanite, the Amalekite, the Moabite, the Egyptian,
By demonstrations the cruel sons of quality & negation,
Driven on the void in incoherent despair into non-entity.
I see America closed apart, & Jerusalem driven in terror
Away from Albion's mountains, far away from London's spires.
I will not endure this thing! I alone withstand to death
This outrage. Ah me, how sick & pale you all stand round me.
Ah me, pitiable ones, do you also go to death's vale?
All you my friends & brothers, all you my beloved companions,
Have you also caught the infection of sin & stern repentance?
I see disease arise upon you. Yet speak to me & give
Me some comfort. Why do you all stand silent? I alone
Remain in permanent strength. Or is all this goodness & pity only
That you may take the greater vengeance in your sepulchre?'

So Los spoke. Pale they stood around the house of death,
In the midst of temptations & despair, among the rooted oaks,
Among reared rocks of Albion's sons.

Fourfold and Twofold Vision [114]

The Visions of Eternity, by reason of narrowèd perceptions,
Are become weak Visions of Time and Space, fix'd into furrows
    of Death;
Till deep dissimulation is the only defence an honest man has left.

The Remembrance of Sin [115]

Come, O thou Lamb of God, and take away the remembrance
    of Sin!
To sin, and to hide the Sin in sweet deceit, is lovely:
To sin in the open face of day is cruel and pitiless; but
To record the Sin for a reproach, to let the Sun go down
In a remembrance of the Sin, is a woe and a horror,
A brooder of an Evil Day, and a Sun rising in blood.
Come then, O Lamb of God, and take away the remembrance
    of Sin!

Rahab is an
Eternal State.

TO THE DEISTS [116]

The Spiritual States of
the Soul are all Eternal.
Distinguish between the
Man and his present State.

He never can be a friend to the Human Race who is the preacher of
Natural Morality or Natural Religion; he is a flatterer who means to
betray, to perpetuate tyrant Pride and the Laws of that Babylon which,
he foresees, shall shortly be destroyed with the Spiritual and not the
Natural Sword. He is in the State named Rahab; which State must be
put off before he can be the Friend of Man.

You, O Deists! profess yourselves the enemies of Christianity, and you
are so: you are also the enemies of the Human Race and of Universal
Nature. Man is born a Spectre, or Satan, and is altogether an Evil, and
requires a new Selfhood continually, and must continually be changed
into his direct Contrary. But your Greek Philosophy, which is a remnant
of Druidism, teaches that Man is righteous in his Vegetated Spectre – an
opinion of fatal and accursed consequence to Man, as the Ancients saw
plainly by Revelation, to the entire abrogation of Experimental Theory;
and many believed what they saw, and prophesied of Jesus.

Man must and will have some religion; if he has not the religion of Jesus, he will have the religion of Satan, and will erect the synagogue of Satan, calling the Prince of this World 'God', and destroying all who do not worship Satan under the name of God. Will any one say: 'Where are those who worship Satan under the name of God?' Where are they? Listen! Every religion that preaches Vengeance for Sin is the religion of the Enemy and Avenger, and not of the Forgiver of Sin, and their God is Satan, named by the Divine Name. Your Religion, O Deists! Deism is the worship of the God of this World by the means of what you call Natural Religion and Natural Philosophy, and of Natural Morality or Self-Righteousness, the selfish virtues of the Natural Heart. This was the religion of the Pharisees who murdered Jesus. Deism is the same, and ends in the same.

Voltaire, Rousseau, Gibbon, Hume charge the spiritually Religious with hypocrisy; but how a Monk, or a Methodist either, can be a hypocrite, I cannot conceive. We are Men of like passions with others, and pretend not to be holier than others; therefore, when a Religious Man falls into sin, he ought not to be call'd a hypocrite: this title is more properly to be given to a player who falls into sin, whose profession is virtue and morality, and the making men self-righteous. Foote, in calling Whitefield hypocrite, was himself one; for Whitefield pretended not to be holier than others, but confessed his sins before all the world. Voltaire! Rousseau! you cannot escape my charge that you are Pharisees and hypocrites; for you are constantly talking of the virtues of the human heart, and particularly of your own; that you may accuse others, and especially the Religious, whose errors you, by this display of pretended virtue, chiefly design to expose. Rousseau thought Men good by nature: he found them evil, and found no friend. Friendship cannot exist without Forgiveness of Sins continually. The book written by Rousseau, call'd his Confessions, is an apology and cloak for his sin, and not a confession.

But you also charge the poor Monks and Religious with being the causes of war, while you acquit and flatter the Alexanders and Cæsars, the Louises and Fredericks, who alone are its causes and its actors. But the Religion of Jesus, Forgiveness of Sin, can never be the cause of a war, nor of a single martyrdom.

Those who martyr others, or who cause war, are Deists, but never can be Forgivers of Sin. The glory of Christianity is to conquer by Forgiveness. All the destruction, therefore, in Christian Europe has arisen from Deism, which is Natural Religion.

I saw a Monk of Charlemaine
Arise before my sight:
I talk'd with the Grey Monk as we stood
In beams of infernal light.

Gibbon arose with a lash of steel,
And Voltaire with a racking wheel;
The Schools, in clouds of learning roll'd,
Arose with War in iron and gold.

'Thou lazy Monk!' they sound afar,
'In vain condemning glorious War;
And in your cell you shall ever dwell:
Rise, War, and bind him in his cell!'

The blood red ran from the Grey Monk's side,
His hands and feet were wounded wide,
His body bent, his arms and knees
Like to the roots of ancient trees.

When Satan first the black bow bent
And the Moral Law from the Gospel rent,
He forg'd the Law into a sword,
And spill'd the blood of Mercy's Lord.

Titus! Constantine! Charlemaine!
O Voltaire! Rousseau! Gibbon! Vain
Your Grecian mocks and Roman sword
Against this image of his Lord;

For a Tear is an Intellectual thing;
And a Sigh is the sword of an angel king;
And the bitter groan of a Martyr's woe
Is an arrow from the Almighty's bow.

Albion's Spectre [117]

But the Spectre, like a hoar-frost and a mildew, rose over Albion,
Saying: 'I am God, O Sons of Men! I am your Rational Power!
Am I not Bacon and Newton and Locke, who teach Humility
    to Man,
Who teach Doubt and Experiment? and my two wings, Voltaire,
    Rousseau?
Where is that Friend of Sinners, that Rebel against my Laws,
Who teaches Belief to the Nations and an unknown Eternal Life?
Come hither into the desert and turn these stones to bread!
Vain, foolish Man! wilt thou believe without Experiment,
And build a World of Phantasy upon my great Abyss,
A World of Shapes in craving lust and devouring appetite?'

The Holiness of Minute Particulars [118]

And many conversèd on these things as they labour'd at the furrow,
Saying 'It is better to prevent misery than to release from misery;
It is better to prevent error than to forgive the criminal.
Labour well the Minute Particulars: attend to the Little Ones,
And those who are in misery cannot remain so long,
If we do but our duty: labour well the teeming Earth. . .
He who would do good to another must do it in Minute Particulars.
General Good is the plea of the scoundrel, hypocrite, and flatterer;
For Art and Science cannot exist but in minutely organised Particulars,
And not in generalising Demonstrations of the Rational Power:
The Infinite alone resides in Definite and Determinate Identity.
Establishment of Truth depends on destruction of Falsehood continually,
On Circumcision, not on Virginity, O Reasoners of Albion!

A Vision of Joseph and Mary [119]

Behold! in the Visions of Elohim Jehovah, behold Joseph and Mary!
And be comforted, O Jerusalem! in the Visions of Jehovah Elohim.

She lookèd and saw Joseph the Carpenter in Nazareth, and Mary,
His espousèd Wife. And Mary said: 'If thou put me away from thee
Dost thou not murder me?' Joseph spoke in anger and fury: 'Should I
Marry a harlot and an adulteress?' Mary answer'd: 'Art thou more pure
Than thy Maker, Who forgiveth Sins and calls again her that is lost?
Tho' she hates, He calls her again in love. I love my dear Joseph,
But he driveth me away from his presence; yet I hear the voice of God
In the voice of my husband: tho' he is angry for a moment he will not
Utterly cast me away: if I were pure, never could I taste the sweets
Of the Forgiveness of Sins; if I were holy, I never could behold the tears
.Of love, of him who loves me in the midst of his anger in furnace of
     fire.'
'Ah, my Mary,' said Joseph, weeping over and embracing her closely in
His arms, 'doth He forgive Jerusalem and not exact Purity from her
     who is
Polluted? I heard His voice in my sleep and His Angel in my dream,
Saying: "Doth Jehovah forgive a Debt only on condition that it shall
Be payèd? Doth He forgive Pollution only on conditions of Purity?
That Debt is not forgiven! That Pollution is not forgiven!
Such is the Forgiveness of the Gods, the Moral Virtues of the
Heathen, whose tender Mercies are Cruelty. But Jehovah's Salvation
Is without Money and without Price, in the Continual Forgiveness
     of Sins,
In the Perpetual Mutual Sacrifice in Great Eternity. For behold!
There is none that liveth and sinneth not! And this is the Covenant
Of Jehovah: 'If you forgive one another, so shall Jehovah forgive you;
That He Himself may dwell among you.' Fear not then to take
To thee Mary, thy Wife, for she is with Child by the Holy Ghost."'

Then Mary burst forth into a song! she flowèd like a river of
Many streams in the arms of Joseph, and gave forth her tears of joy
Like many waters, and emanating into gardens and palaces upon
Euphrates, and to forests and floods and animals, wild and tame, from
Gihon to Hiddekel, and to corn-fields and villages, and inhabitants
Upon Pison and Arnon and Jordan. And I heard the voice among

The Reapers, saying: 'Am I Jerusalem, the lost Adulteress? or am I
Babylon come up to Jerusalem?' And another voice answer'd, saying:
'Does the voice of my Lord call me again? am I pure thro' his Mercy
And Pity? Am I become lovely as a Virgin in his sight, who am
Indeed a Harlot drunken with the Sacrifice of Idols? Does He
Call her pure, as he did in the days of her Infancy, when she
Was cast out to the loathing of her person? The Chaldean took
Me from my cradle; the Amalekite stole me away upon his camels
Before I had ever beheld with love the face of Jehovah, or known
That there was a God of Mercy. O Mercy! O Divine Humanity!
O Forgiveness and Pity and Compassion! If I were pure I should never
Have known Thee: if I were unpolluted I should never have
Glorifièd Thy Holiness, or rejoicèd in thy great Salvation.'
Mary leanèd her side against Jerusalem: Jerusalem receivèd
The Infant into her hands in the Visions of Jehovah. Times passèd on.
Jerusalem fainted over the Cross and Sepulchre. She heard the voice: –
'Wilt thou make Rome thy Patriarch Druid, and the Kings of
    Europe his
Horsemen? Man in the Resurrection changes his Sexual Garments
    at will:
Every Harlot was once a Virgin, every Criminal an infant Love.'

Tirzah [120]

'O thou poor Human Form!' said she. 'O thou poor child of woe!
Why wilt thou wander away from Tirzah, why me compel to
     bind thee?
If thou dost go away from me, I shall consume upon these Rocks.
These fibres of thine eyes, that usèd to beam in distant heavens
Away from me, I have bound down with a hot iron:
These nostrils, that expanded with delight in morning skies,
I have bent downward with lead, melted in my roaring furnaces
Of affliction, of love, of sweet despair, of torment unendurable.
My soul is seven furnaces, incessant roars the bellows
Upon my terribly flaming heart; the molten metal runs
In channels thro' my fiery limbs – O love! O pity! O fear!
O pain! O the pangs, the bitter pangs of love forsaken!'

The Warrior and the Daughter of Albion [121]

Look! the beautiful Daughter of Albion sits naked upon the Stone,
Her panting Victim beside her; her heart is drunk with blood,
Tho' her brain is not drunk with wine; she goes forth from Albion
In pride of beauty, in cruelty of holiness, in the brightness
Of her tabernacle, and her ark and secret place. The beautiful Daughter
Of Albion delights the eyes of the Kings; their hearts and the
Hearts of their Warriors glow hot before Thor and Friga. O Moloch!
O Chemosh! O Bacchus! O Venus! O Double God of Generation!
The Heavens are cut like a mantle around from the Cliffs of Albion,
Across Europe, across Africa, in howlings and deadly War.
A sheet and veil and curtain of blood is let down from Heaven
Across the hills of Ephraim, and down Mount Olivet to
The Valley of the Jebusite . . .
O beautiful Daughter of Albion, cruelty is thy delight!
O Virgin of terrible eyes, who dwellest by Valleys of springs
Beneath the Mountains of Lebanon, in the City of Rehob in Hamath,
Taught to touch the harp, to dance in the circle of Warriors
Before the Kings of Canaan, to cut the flesh from the Victim,
To roast the flesh in fire, to examine the Infant's limbs
In cruelties of holiness, to refuse the joys of love, to bring
The Spies from Egypt to raise jealousy in the bosoms of the twelve

Kings of Canaan; then to let the Spies depart to Meribah Kadesh,
To the place of the Amalekite. I am drunk with unsatiated love;
I must rush again to War, for the Virgin has frown'd and refus'd.
Sometimes I curse, and sometimes bless thy fascinating beauty.
Once Man was occupièd in intellectual pleasures and energies;
But now my Soul is harrow'd with grief and fear, and love and desire,
And now I hate, and now I love, and Intellect is no more:
There is no time for anything but the torments of love and desire:
The Feminine and Masculine Shadows, soft, mild, and ever varying
In beauty, are Shadows now no more, but Rocks in Horeb.

Men and States [122]

As the Pilgrim passes while the Country permanent remains,
So Men pass on, but States remain permanent for ever.

TO THE CHRISTIANS [123]

Devils are False Religions.
Saul! Saul! why persecutest thou me?

I give you the end of a golden string;
Only wind it into a ball,
It will lead you in at Heaven's gate,
Built in Jerusalem's wall.

We are told to abstain from fleshly desires that we may lose no time from the Work of the Lord. Every moment lost is a moment that cannot be redeemed: every pleasure that intermingles with the duty of our station is a folly unredeemable, and is planted like the seed of a wild flower among our wheat. All the tortures of repentance are tortures of self-reproach on account of our leaving the Divine Harvest to the Enemy, the struggles of entanglement with incoherent roots. I know of no other Christianity and of no other Gospel than the liberty both of body and mind to exercise the Divine Arts of Imagination – Imagination, the real and Eternal World of which this Vegetable Universe is but a faint shadow, and in which we shall live in our Eternal or Imaginative Bodies, when these Vegetable Mortal Bodies are no more. The Apostles knew of no other Gospel. What were all their spiritual gifts? What is the Divine Spirit? Is the Holy Ghost

any other than an Intellectual Fountain? What is the harvest of the
Gospel and its labours? What is that talent which it is a curse to hide?
What are the treasures of Heaven which we are to lay up for ourselves?
Are they any other than mental studies and performances? What are all
the gifts of the Gospel? Are they not all mental gifts? Is God a Spirit who
must be worshipped in spirit and in truth? And are not the gifts of the
Spirit everything to Man? O ye Religious, discountenance every one
among you who shall pretend to despise Art and Science! I call upon you
in the name of Jesus! What is the life of Man but Art and Science? Is it
meat and drink? Is not the Body more than raiment? What is Mortality
but the things relating to the Body, which dies? What is Immortality but
the things relating to the Spirit, which lives eternally? What is the Joy of
Heaven but improvement in the things of the Spirit? What are the Pains
of Hell but Ignorance, Bodily Lust, Idleness, and devastation of the
things of the Spirit? Answer this to yourselves, and expel from among you
those who pretend to despise the labours of Art and Science, which alone
are the labours of the Gospel. Is not this plain and manifest to the
thought? Can you think at all, and not pronounce heartily: that to labour
in knowledge is to build up Jerusalem; and to despise knowledge is to
despise Jerusalem and her Builders. And remember: He who despises and
mocks a mental gift in another, calling it pride and selfishness and sin,
mocks Jesus, the giver of every mental gift, which always appear to the
ignorance-loving hypocrite as sins; but that which is a sin in the sight of
cruel Man, is not so in the sight of our kind God. Let every Christian, as
much as in him lies, engage himself openly and publicly, before all the
World, in some mental pursuit for the Building up of Jerusalem.

> I stood among my valleys of the south,
> And saw a flame of fire, even as a Wheel
> Of fire surrounding all the heavens: it went
> From west to east against the current of
> Creation, and devour'd all things in its loud
> Fury and thundering course round Heaven and Earth
> By it the Sun was roll'd into an orb;
> By it the Moon faded into a globe,
> Travelling thro' the night; for from its dire
> And restless fury Man himself shrunk up
> Into a little root a fathom long.
> And I askèd a Watcher and a Holy One
> Its name. He answer'd: 'It is the Wheel of Religion.'

I wept and said: 'Is this the law of Jesus,
This terrible devouring sword turning every way?'
He answer'd: 'Jesus died because He strove
Against the current of this Wheel: its name
Is Caiaphas, the dark Preacher of Death,
Of sin, of sorrow, and of punishment,
Opposing Nature. It is Natural Religion.
But Jesus is the bright Preacher of Life,
Creating Nature from this fiery Law
By self-denial and Forgiveness of Sin.
Go, therefore, cast out devils in Christ's name,
Heal thou the sick of spiritual disease,
Pity the evil; for thou art not sent
To smite with terror and with punishments
Those that are sick, like to the Pharisees,
Crucifying, and encompassing sea and land,
For proselytes to tyranny and wrath.
But to the Publicans and Harlots go:
Teach them true happiness, but let no curse
Go forth out of thy mouth to blight their peace.
For Hell is open'd to Heaven; thine eyes beheld
The dungeons burst, and the prisoners set free.'

England! awake! awake! awake!
Jerusalem thy sister calls!
Why wilt thou sleep the sleep of death,
And close her from thy ancient walls?

Thy hills and valleys felt her feet
Gently upon their bosoms move:
Thy gates beheld sweet Zion's ways;
Then was a time of joy and love.

And now the time returns again:
Our souls exult, and London's towers
Receive the Lamb of God to dwell
In England's green and pleasant bowers.

A Vision of Jerusalem [124]

I see thy Form, O lovely, mild Jerusalem! Wing'd with Six Wings
In the opacous Bosom of the Sleeper, lovely, threefold
In Head and Heart and Reins, three Universes of love and beauty.
Thy forehead bright, Holiness to the Lord! with gates of pearl
Reflects Eternity beneath thy azure wings of feathery down,
Ribb'd, delicate, and cloth'd with feather'd gold and azure and
    purple,
From thy white shoulders shadowing purity in holiness;
Thence, feather'd with soft crimson of the ruby, bright as fire,
Spreading into the azure wings which, like a canopy,
Bends over thy immortal Head in which Eternity dwells.
Albion! belovèd Land, I see thy mountains and thy hills
And valleys, and thy pleasant Cities, Holiness to the Lord!
I see the Spectres of thy Dead, O Emanation of Albion!

Thy Bosom white, translucent, cover'd with immortal gems,
A sublime ornament not obscuring the outlines of beauty,
Terrible to behold, for thy extreme beauty and perfection:
Twelvefold here all the Tribes of Israel I behold
Upon the Holy Land: I see the River of Life and Tree of Life
I see the New Jerusalem descending out of Heaven
Between thy Wings of gold and silver, feather'd immortal,
Clear as the rainbow, as the cloud of the Sun's tabernacle.

Thy Reins cover'd with Wings translucent, sometimes covering
And sometimes spread abroad, reveal the flames of holiness
Which like a robe covers, and like a Veil of Seraphim
In flaming fire unceasing burns from Eternity to Eternity.
Twelvefold I there behold Israel in her Tents;
A Pillar of a Cloud by day, a Pillar of Fire by night
Guides them; there I behold Moab and Ammon and Amalek,
There Bells of silver round thy knees, living, articulate
Comforting sounds of love and harmony; and on thy feet
Sandals of gold and pearl; and Egypt and Assyria before me,
The Isles of Javan, Philistia, Tyre, and Lebanon.

The Worship of God [125]

It is easier to forgive an Enemy than to forgive a Friend.
The man who permits you to injure him deserves your vengeance;
He also will receive it. Go, Spectre! obey my most secret desire,
Which thou knowest without my speaking. Go to these Fiends
      of Righteousness,
Tell them to obey their Humanities, and not pretend Holiness,
When they are murderers. As far as my Hammer and Anvil
      permit,
Go tell them that the Worship of God is honouring His gifts
In other men, and loving the greatest men best, each according
To his Genius, which is the Holy Ghost in Man: there is no other
God than that God who is the intellectual fountain of Humanity.
He who envies or calumniates, which is murder and cruelty,
Murders the Holy One. Go tell them this, and overthrow their cup,
Their bread, their altar-table, their incense, and their oath,
Their marriage and their baptism, their burial and consecration.
I have tried to make friends by corporeal gifts, but have only
Made enemies; I never made friends but by spiritual gifts,
By severe contentions of friendship, and the burning fire of
      thought.
He who would see the Divinity must see Him in His Children,
One first in friendship and love, then a Divine Family, and in
      the midst
Jesus will appear. So he who wishes to see a Vision, a perfect
      Whole,
Must see it in its Minute Particulars, organised; and not as thou,
O Fiend of Righteousness, pretendest! thine is a disorganised
And snowy cloud, brooder of tempests and destructive War.
You smile with pomp and rigour, you talk of benevolence and
      virtue;
I act with benevolence and virtue, and get murder'd time after
      time;
You accumulate Particulars, and murder by analysing, that you
May take the aggregate, and you call the aggregate Moral Law;
And you call that swell'd and bloated Form a Minute Particular.
But General Forms have their vitality in Particulars; and every
Particular is a Man, a Divine Member of the Divine Jesus.

The Cry of Los [126]

I care not whether a man is Good or Evil; all that I care
Is whether he is a Wise man or a Fool. Go! put off Holiness,
And put on Intellect; or my thund'rous hammer shall drive thee
To wrath, which thou condemnest, till thou obey my voice.

Albion upon the Rock [127]

Albion cold lays on his Rock; storms and snows beat round him,
Beneath the Furnaces and the Starry Wheels and the Immortal
   Tomb;
Howling winds cover him; roaring seas dash furious against him;
In the deep darkness broad lightnings glare, long thunders roll.

The weeds of Death enwrap his hands and feet, blown incessant,
And wash'd incessant by the for-ever restless sea-waves, foaming
   abroad
Upon the white Rock. England, a Female Shadow, as deadly
   damps
Of the Mines of Cornwall and Derbyshire, lays upon his bosom
   heavy,
Movèd by the wind in volumes of thick cloud returning, folding
   round
His loins and bosom, unremovable by swelling storms and loud
   rending
Of enragèd thunders. Around them the Starry Wheels of their
   Giant Sons
Revolve, and over them the Furnaces of Los and the Immortal
   Tomb, around,
Erin sitting in the Tomb, to watch them unceasing night and day:
And the Body of Albion was closèd apart from all Nations.

Over them the famish'd Eagle screams on bony wings, and around
Them howls the Wolf of famine; deep heaves the Ocean, black,
   thundering
Around the wormy Garments of Albion, then pausing in
   deathlike silence.

Time was Finishèd!

The Wrath of God [128]

The Breath Divine went forth over the morning hills. Albion rose
In anger, the wrath of God, breaking bright, flaming on all sides
    around
His awful limbs: into the Heavens he walkèd, clothèd in flames,
Loud thund'ring, with broad flashes of flaming lightning and
    pillars
Of fire, speaking the Words of Eternity in Human Forms, in direful
Revolutions of Action and Passion, thro' the Four Elements on
    all sides
Surrounding his awful Members. Thou seest the Sun in heavy
    clouds
Struggling to rise above the Mountains; in his burning hand
He takes his Bow, then chooses out his arrows of flaming gold;
Murmuring, the Bowstring breathes with ardour; clouds roll
    round the
Horns of the wide Bow; loud sounding winds sport on the
    mountain brows,
Compelling Urizen to his Furrow, and Tharmas to his
    Sheepfold, And Luvah to his Loom.

The Divine Image [129]

Jesus said: 'Wouldest thou love one who never died
For thee, or ever die for one who had not died for thee?
And if God dieth not for Man, and giveth not Himself
Eternally for Man, Man could not exist; for Man is Love,
As God is Love: every kindness to another is a little Death
In the Divine Image; nor can Man exist but by Brotherhood.'

The End of the Song of Jerusalem [130]

All Human Forms identifièd, even Tree, Metal, Earth, and Stone; all
Human Forms identifièd, living, going forth and returning wearied
Into the Planetary lives of Years, Months, Days and Hours; reposing,
And then awaking into His bosom in the Life of Immortality.
And I heard the Name of their Emanations: they are namèd Jerusalem.

THE GATES OF PARADISE
Circa 1810

Verses from *The Gates of Paradise* (*c.*1810)   Originally published in
1793, *The Gates of Paradise* was an emblematic picture book for
children, but Blake later retitled it 'For the Sexes' suggesting that it was
addressed to the divided state of humanity, dealing as it does with issues
similar to those explored in *Jerusalem*. As was traditionally the case in
the emblem books on which this was modelled, each of the numbered
lines has an accompanying illustration emblematic of the idea.

Prologue

Mutual Forgiveness of each vice,
Such are the Gates of Paradise,
Against the Accuser's chief desire,
Who walk'd among the stones of fire.
Jehovah's Finger wrote the Law;
Then wept; then rose in zeal and awe,
And the dead corpse, from Sinai's heat,
Buried beneath His Mercy-seat.
O Christians! Christians! tell me why
You rear it on your altars high?

The Keys

The Caterpillar on the leaf
Reminds thee of thy Mother's grief [. . .]

of the Gates

1. My Eternal Man set in repose,
   The Female from his darkness rose;
   And she found me beneath a Tree,
   A Mandrake, and in her Veil hid me.
   Serpent Reasonings us entice
   Of good and evil, virtue and vice,
2. Doubt self-jealous, Watery folly;
3. Struggling thro' Earth's melancholy;
4. Naked in Air, in shame and fear;
5. Blind in Fire, with shield and spear;
   Two-horn'd Reasoning, cloven fiction,
   In doubt, which is self-contradiction,
   A dark Hermaphrodite we stood –

Rational truth, root of evil and good.
Round me flew the Flaming Sword;
Round her snowy Whirlwinds roar'd,
Freezing her Veil, the Mundane Shell.

6. I rent the Veil where the Dead dwell:
When weary Man enters his Cave,
He meets his Saviour in the grave.
Some find a Female Garment there,
And some a Male, woven with care;
Lest the Sexual Garments sweet
Should grow a devouring Winding-sheet.

7. One dies! Alas! the Living and Dead!
One is slain! and One is fled!

8. In Vain-glory hatcht and nurst,
By double Spectres, self-accurst.
My Son! my Son! thou treatest me
But as I have instructed thee.

9. On the shadows of the Moon,
Climbing thro' Night's highest noon;

10. In Time's Ocean falling, drown'd;

11 In Aged Ignorance profound,
Holy and cold, I clipp'd the wings
Of all sublunary things,

12. And in depths of my dungeons
Closed the Father and the Sons.

13. But when once I did descry
The Immortal Man that cannot die,

14. Thro' evening shades I haste away
To close the labours of my day.

15. The Door of Death I open found,
And the Worm weaving in the ground:

16. Thou'rt my Mother, from the womb;
Wife, Sister, Daughter, to the tomb;
Weaving to dreams the Sexual strife,
And weeping over the Web of Life.

Epilogue

To the Accuser who is The God of this World

Truly, my Satan, thou art but a dunce,
And dost not know the garment from the man;
Every harlot was a virgin once,
Nor canst thou ever change Kate into Nan.

Tho' thou art worship'd by the names divine
Of Jesus and Jehovah, thou art still
The Son of Morn in weary Night's decline,
The lost traveller's dream under the hill.

THE GHOST OF ABEL
Engraved 1822

The Ghost of Abel – Blake's only drama other than *King Edward III* (in *Poetical Sketches*) is a variation on Byron's *Cain, a Mystery* (1821).

A REVELATION IN THE VISIONS OF JEHOVAH SEEN
BY WILLIAM BLAKE

To Lord Byron in the Wilderness:

What doest thou here, Elijah?
Can a Poet doubt the Visions of Jehovah? Nature has no Outline,
But Imagination has. Nature has no Tune, but Imagination has.
Nature has no Supernatural, and dissolves: Imagination is eternity.

SCENE – *A rocky Country.* EVE, *fainted, over the dead body of* ABEL, *which lays near a Grave.* ADAM *kneels by her.* JEHOVAH *stands above.*

Jehovah.	Adam!
Adam.	I will not hear Thee more, Thou Spiritual Voice Is this Death?
Jehovah.	Adam!
Adam.	It is in vain: I will not hear Thee Henceforth. Is this Thy Promise, that the Woman's seed Should bruise the Serpent's head? Is this the Serpent? Ah! Seven times, O Eve! thou hast fainted over the Dead. Ah! Ah!

EVE *revives.*

Eve.	Is this the Promise of Jehovah? O! it is all a vain delusion, This Death, and this Life, and this Jehovah!
Jehovah.	Woman, lift thine eyes!

A Voice is heard coming on.

Voice.	O Earth, cover not thou my blood! cover not thou my blood!

Enter the Ghost of ABEL.

Eve.   Thou visionary Phantasm, thou art not the real Abel.

Abel.   Among the Elohim, a Human Victim I wander: I am
their House,
Prince of the Air, and our dimensions compass Zenith
and Nadir.
Vain is Thy Covenant, O Jehovah! I am the Accuser and
Avenger
Of Blood. O Earth! cover not thou the blood of Abel.

Jehovah.   What Vengeance dost thou require?

Abel.   Life for Life! Life for Life!

Jehovah.   He who shall take Cain's life must also die, O Abel!
And who is he? Adam, wilt thou, or Eve, thou do this?

Adam.   It is all a vain delusion of the all-creative Imagination.
Eve, come away, and let us not believe these vain delusions.
Abel is dead, and Cain slew him. We shall also die a death,
And then – what then? be, as poor Abel, a Thought; or as
This? O! what shall I call Thee, Form Divine, Father of
Mercies,
That appearest to my Spiritual Vision? Eve, seest thou also?

Eve.   I see Him plainly with my Mind's Eye. I see also Abel living,
Tho' terribly afflicted, as we also are; yet Jehovah sees him
Alive and not dead. Were it not better to believe Vision
With all our might and strength, tho' we are fallen and lost?

Adam.   Eve, thou hast spoken truly: let us kneel before His feet.

They kneel before JEHOVAH.

Abel.   Are these the sacrifices of Eternity, O Jehovah – a broken
spirit
And a contrite heart? O! I cannot forgive: the Accuser hath
Enter'd into me as into his house, and I loathe Thy
Tabernacles.
As Thou hast said, so is it come to pass. My desire is
unto Cain,
And he doth rule over me; therefore my soul in fumes of
blood
Cries for Vengeance, Sacrifice on Sacrifice, Blood on Blood!

Jehovah.   Lo! I have given you a Lamb for an Atonement, instead
Of the transgressor, or no Flesh or Spirit could ever live.

Abel.   Compellèd I cry, O Earth! cover not the blood of Abel.

ABEL *sinks down into the Grave, from which arises* SATAN,
armed in glittering scales, with a Crown and a Spear.

Satan.   I will have Human blood, and not the blood of bulls or
                goats,
             And no Atonement, O Jehovah! The Elohim live on
                Sacrifice
             Of Men: hence I am God of Men! Thou human, O
                Jehovah!
             By the rock and oak of the Druid, creeping mistletoe, and
                thorn,
             Cain's city built with human blood, not blood of bulls
                and goats,
             Thou shalt Thyself be sacrificed to Me, thy God! on
                Calvary.
Jehovah.   Such is My Will – (*Thunders*) – that thou thyself go to
                Eternal Death.
             In Self-Annihilation, even till Satan, self-subdu'd, put off
                Satan
             Into the Bottomless Abyss, whose torment arises for ever
                and ever.

On each side a chorus of Angels, entering, sing the following:

The Elohim of the Heathen swore Vengeance for Sin! Then Thou
     stood'st
Forth, O Elohim Jehovah! in the midst of the darkness of the
     Oath, all clothèd
In Thy Covenant of the Forgiveness of Sins. Death, O Holy! Is
     this Brotherhood?
The Elohim saw their Oath Eternal Fire: they rollèd apart,
     trembling, over the
Mercy-seat, each in his station fixt in the firmament by Peace
     Brotherhood, and Love.

                    The Curtain falls.

NOTES

Anyone wishing to follow the complex detail of Blake's poetry needs to consult *Blake – The Complete Poems*, ed. W. H. Stevenson (second edition). The following notes do not pretend to be exhaustive and have been kept to a minimum particularly for the prophetic books as the introductory essays provide a starting point for each work.

Poetical Sketches (1783)

To Winter

1 (p. 5) *Hecla*   a volcano in Iceland, although there is also a Mount Hecla in the Outer Hebrides

To the Muses

2 (p. 13) *Ida*   mountain in Greece associated with the classical Gods

An Island in the Moon (1784)

3 (p. 49) *I–III*   sung by quid the Cynic, who is based on Blake himself

4 (p. 52) *X*   sung by Obtuse Angle, a Blakean parody of the scientist

5 (p. 53) *XI*   sung by the Lawgiver and anticipating the ironic satire of *Songs of Innocence and Experience*. The 'Holy Thursday' poem from *Innocence* also appears in *An Island in the Moon*, sung by Obtuse Angle.

Songs of Innocence and Experience (1789–94)

SONGS OF INNOCENCE

Holy Thursday

6 (p. 67) *Holy Thursday*   From 1782 some six thousand children from charity schools for the poor and destitute were annually marched to St Paul's Cathedral for a service to honour their patrons and supporters. The 'innocent' view here is savagely challenged by the later poem in *Experience* (p. 81).

The Chimney Sweeper

7 (p. 68) *The Chimney Sweeper*   The true plight of these children and their enslavement by brutal masters was brought to the attention of Parliament in 1788.

The Divine Image

8 (p. 69) *The Divine Image*   The opening is an ironic reworking of Song 6 from Isaac Watts's *Divine Songs attempted in Easy Language for the Use of Children* (1715): 'Lord I ascribe it to thy Grace,/ And not to Chance, as others do,/ That I was born of Christian Race,/ And not a Heathen, or a Jew' (ed. J. H. P. Pafford, Oxford University Press, London 1971, p. 157).

SONGS OF EXPERIENCE

The Schoolboy

9 (p. 87) *The Schoolboy*   Like some of the other *Songs*, this was transferred from *Innocence* to *Experience* in later copies.

London

10 (p. 88) *charter'd*   Charters originally functioned to grant liberties and rights, but ones which were often limited in their extent to the privileged; but the word also had overtones of contracts and companies, and was beginning to mean 'to limit' or 'to hire'. See also, 'Why should I care for the men of Thames', in the *Rossetti Manuscript* poems (p. 99).

11 (p. 88) *ban*   prohibition

The Rossetti Manuscript (1793–1811)

Blake's notebook was eventually owned by Dante Gabriel Rossetti (1828–82), the Pre-Raphaelite poet and painter; hence the name.

To Nobodaddy

12 (p. 100) *Nobodaddy*   The name is a Blakean pun on 'nobody' and 'daddy' to invoke a figure similar to Urizen.

Lafayette

13 (p. 103) *Lafayette*   Untitled in the notebook, as were many of the fragments and drafts. Marie Joseph, Marquis de Lafayette (1757–1834), a liberal aristocrat, was a hero of the American War of Independence against the British, but after presenting the draft of the Rights of Man in 1789 he became hated by the Jacobins for being too moderate and fled to Austria. Here, he epitomises a figure compromised

by his compassion for the superficial gloss of monarchy behind which lies the tyranny of Nobodaddy.

My Spectre around me night and day

14 (p. 105) *My Spectre around me night and day*   Like many of the poems in the notebook, this poem was left unfinished, with deleted and additional stanzas. The arrangement presented here includes three additional stanzas (marked a, b, c) within the numbered sequence which Blake seems to have approved. Various editors have used speech marks to indicate sections of the poem as being spoken by the narrator, the Spectre or the Emanation; but as Blake did not use any speech marks, it is probably better for readers to make up their own minds.

15 (p. 105) *Spectre*   In Blake's mythic psychology, the spectre is the aggressive, domineering ego or selfhood, masculine in gender and associated with rationalism and law.

16 (p. 105) *Emanation*   The emanation is female, empathetic, but in danger of being self-willed and domineering like the spectre, both being contentious elements of a divided psyche or lapsed human state.

When Klopstock England defied

17 (p. 107) *Klopstock*   Friedrich Gottlieb Klopstock (1724–1803) was a German religious poet who, although inspired by Milton, attacked English poetry, and Jonathan Swift in particular, for what he saw as its crudity. Blake's response is both Swiftian and Rabelaisian in its bawdy satire.

Mock on, mock on, Voltaire, Rousseau

18 (p. 108) *Mock on, mock on, Voltaire, Rousseau*   French philosophers Voltaire (1694–1778) and Jean Jacques Rousseau (1712–78), Greek scientist Democritus (*c*. 460–370 BC) and English physicist Sir Isaac Newton (1642–1727) are all associated by Blake with the limits of rationalism.

I saw a Monk of Charlemaine

19 (p. 109) *Gibbon*   Edward Gibbon (1737–94), the famous historian of the Roman empire, is associated here with the institutional schools and academies of learning which Blake attacks elsewhere.

If it is true what the prophets write:

20 (p. 112) *Bezaleel and Aholiab*   craftsmen who undertook to act out Moses' vision from Mount Sinai (Exodus 31:2,6)

I will tell you what Joseph of Arimathea

21 (p. 113) *Joseph*   alleged to have visited Britain, bringing information about Jesus

22 (p. 113) *Pliny and Trajan*   a Roman scholar and a Roman emperor, epitomising a despised empire

The Caverns of the Grave I've seen

23 (p. 115) *The Caverns of the Grave I've seen*   a poem as a dedication for the painting *A Vision of the Last Judgement*, done for the Egremonts

To the Queen

24 (p. 116) *To the Queen*   a dedication to Queen Charlotte to accompany Blake's drawings for an edition of Blair's *The Grave*

The Everlasting Gospel

25 (p. 117) *The Everlasting Gospel*   a fragmentary sequence of variations scattered through the notebook. The selection is numbered with Greek characters; but the correct order remains highly speculative. In the manuscript there is a prose passage which begins:

> There is not one moral virtue that Jesus inculcated but Plato and Cicero did inculcate before him: what then did Christ inculcate? – Forgiveness of Sins. This alone is the Gospel, and this is the life and immortality brought to light by Jesus.
>
> (Stevenson, pp. 854–5)

26 (p. 117) *Socrates . . . Meletus*   Socrates was accused of corrupting young minds with his philosophy and put to death; Meletus was one of his accusers.

27 (p.117) *Caiaphas*   the High Priest who interrogated Christ (Matthew 26; John 18)

28 (p. 117) *Sinai*   mountain in Exodus in the Old Testament of the Bible where Moses had his vision of God and received the Ten Commandments; hence a source of religious law

29 (p. 120) *Dr Priestly and Bacon and Newton*   Joseph Priestley (1733–1804), a deist Unitarian minister and scientist who discovered oxygen; Francis Bacon (1561–1626), the author of *The Advancement of Learning* (1605), which promoted scientific method against the obscurities of scholasticism; Sir Isaac Newton (1642–1727), the epitome of scientific rationalism

The Pickering Manuscript (circa 1801–1803)

Auguries of Innocence

30 (p. 135) *Auguries of Innocence* Blake's copy is clear but there remains doubt as to the best order of the couplets.

Poems from Letters (circa 1800–1803)

The letter poems date from Blake's period at Felpham in a cottage lent by William Hayley (1745–1820), a prolific and popular poet as well as Blake's friend and patron, and show a sense of optimism at a new start for Blake's career after the dark period of the later 1790s.

To my dearest friend, John Flaxman

31 (p. 143) *Flaxman* John Flaxman (1755–1826), a sculptor and engraver who recommended the Blakes to Hayley and is the subject of warm feelings of friendship during this period which were later to turn sour

32 (p. 143) *Fuseli* Henry Fuseli (1741–1825), a painter, famous for his painting 'The Nightmare' and Blake's neighbour for a time

33 (p. 143) *Ezra* The Book of Ezra in the Bible deals with a return from exile.

34 (p. 143) *Paracelsus and Behmen* Paracelsus (1493–1541) and Jacob Boehme (1575–1624) were mystical writers of the Renaissance (Behmen was the eighteenth-century spelling for Boehme).

To my dear friend, Mrs Anna Flaxman

35 (p. 143) *To my dear friend, Mrs Anna Flaxman* from a letter dated 14 September 1800

36 (p. 144) *The bless'd Hermit* William Hayley

To Thomas Butts

37 (p. 144) *To Thomas Butts* from a letter dated 2 October 1800. Thomas Butts (1757–1845), one of Blake's most consistent friends and patrons, amassed a large collection of Blake's works which gradually took over his house and greenhouse; he employed Blake to teach his son, Master Thomas Butts Jnr.

To Thomas Butts

38 (p. 146) *To Thomas Butts* from a letter dated 22 November 1802

39 (p. 146) *Robert* Robert was Blake's favourite brother and died in 1787 after Blake had cared for him intensively.

40 (p. 146) *John* There is no clear information about Blake's other brother.

41 (p. 147) *Theotormon*   a character-name from *Visions of the Daughters of Albion*

42 (p. 147) *Enitharmon*   the name of Los's female partner and emanation

43 (p. 147) *Los*   The embodiment of the creative imagination, Los becomes a highly significant figure in the prophetic poems. Appearing here as the sun, he fulfils the possible anagram in his name, 'sol'.

44 (p. 148) *Beulah*   a region associated with sexuality in other poems

To Thomas Butts

45 (p. 149) *To Thomas Butts*   from a letter dated 16 August 1803, in which Blake describes the circumstances which led to his trial for treason and, before transcribing the poem, concludes: 'Give me your advice in my perilous adventure [. . .] I have been very much degraded and injuriously treated; but, if it all arise from my own fault, I ought to blame myself' (Keynes, p. 828).

Gnomic Verses, Epigrams and Short Satirical Pieces

Gnomic Verses

46 (p. 150) *Gnomic Verses*   All these pieces are taken from the *Rossetti* notebook.

On Art and Artists

47 (p. 155) *On Art and Artists*   A number of these derive from Blake's marginal annotations to his copy of Reynolds's *Works*; others are from the notebook.

48 (p. 155) ii *On the great encouragement . . . Doodle*   The names are all of painters, except for 'Dilberry Doodle' which is a sarcastic swipe at supposed artists.

49 (p. 155) *Colonel Wardle*   launched a Commons attack in 1809 on the corruptions of the Duke of York and the army, achieving great popularity

50 (p. 157) xi *English Encouragement of Art*   Blake felt that the publisher Cromek had betrayed him by cheating him over a design commission as well as stealing some of his ideas.

51 (p. 158) xiv *On Sir Joshua Reynolds's disappointment . . . Raphael*   Sir Joshua Reynolds (1723–92) was probably the most famous establishment painter of the late eighteenth century, being President of the Royal Academy, and epitomised much that Blake rebelled against.

On Friends and Foes

52 (p. 163) *On Friends and Foes* All taken from the *Rossetti* notebook, these refer to an unhappy period when Blake felt himself to be the victim of a conspiracy and became alienated from many of his friends after being treated badly by Cromek and being attacked by Leigh Hunt (1784–1859) in the journal *The Examiner*; the failure of his 1809 exhibition led *The Examiner* review to describe Blake as 'an unfortunate lunatic' (O'Neill, pp. 12–13).

53 (p. 167) *xxviii* a fragment lacking an opening line and probably composed soon after the review. The 'he' of the opening lines is Cromek, the 'me' is Stewhard, a variation on the name of artist Thomas Stothard; Chichester was the scene of Blake's trial for treason; 'Death' is a nickname for Blake himself; Felpham Billy is Hayley; Assassinetti is a punning name for the fashionable engraver Schiavonetti who had been employed by Cromek to do work Blake had been asked to do; Screwmuch is Cromek.

54 (p. 169) *Macklin, or Boydell, or Bowyer* publishers for whom Blake engraved

55 (p. 169) *Bartoloze* Bartollozi(1727–1815) was a fashionable Italian engraver whose style was soft-lined as opposed to Blake's own preference for the unfashionable hard-line drawing.

Miscellaneous Epigrams

56 (p. 170) *Miscellaneous Epigrams* all taken from the *Rossetti* notebook except for xi, which comes from Blake's Reynolds marginalia

57 (p. 171) *Johanna Southcott* Joanna Southcott (1750–1814), a Christian mystic from Dorset who claimed divine revelations as well as to be carrying the new Messiah – she died soon after the supposed birth

The Four Zoas (1797–1804)

58 (p. 302) *Selections from The Four Zoas (1797–1804)* The manuscript of *The Four Zoas* is full of deletions and additions which make some sections very difficult to order. The selections follow the ordering and lineation to be found in *Blake – The Complete Poems*, ed. W. H. Stevenson (second edition), details of which are listed here to allow the interested reader to put them in context. The titles to the passages are editorial in order to give the reader some focus.

59 (p. 302) *Introduction to Night the First* Night I, lines 1–8

60 (p. 302) *The Wanderer* deleted passage, Night I, following line 127

61 (p. 302) *A Vision of Eternity*   Night II, lines 105–12
62 (p. 303) *The Song sung at the Feast of Los and Enitharmon*   Night II, lines 128–43 – the opening clause was changed later to the more symbolic 'Ephraim called out to Zion'
63 (p. 303) *The Song of Enitharmon over Los*   Night II, lines 551–86
64 (p. 305) *The Wail of Enion*   Night II, lines 597–628
65 (p. 306) *Winter*   Night V, lines 30–5
66 (p. 306) *The Woes of Urizen in the Dens of Urthona*   Night V, lines 190–241
67 (p. 308) *Los in his Wrath*   Night VII, lines 366–74
68 (p. 308) *The War-Song of Orc*   Night VII, lines 469–83
69 (p. 309) *Vala's Going Forth*   Night VII, lines 594–610
70 (p. 309) *Urizen's Words of Wisdom*   Night VII, lines 109–29
71 (p. 310) *The Shade of Enitharmon*   Night VII, lines 173–6
72 (p. 310) *The Serpent Orc*   Night VIII, lines 57–9
73 (p. 311) *The Last Judgement*   Night IX, lines 5–23, 33–66
74 (p. 312) *The Lament of Albion*   Night IX, lines 97–120
75 (p. 313) *Accuser and Accused*   Night IX, lines 263–9
76 (p. 313) *The Tillage of Urizen*   Night IX, lines 289–305
77 (p. 314) *Song of the Sinless Soul*   Night IX, lines 385–451
78 (p. 316) *Vala in Lower Paradise*   Night IX, lines 468–81

Milton (1804–9)

79 (p. 319) *Selections from Milton (1804–9)* The selections here list the lineation to be found in *Blake – The Complete Poems*, ed. W. H. Stevenson (second edition) to allow the interested reader to put them in context. The titles to the passages are editorial in order to give the reader some focus.
80 (p. 320) *The Invocation*   First Book, Plate 2, lines 1–15
81 (p. 320) *The Mills of Satan*   First Book, Plate 11, lines 6–14
82 (p. 321) *The Sin of Leutha*   First Book, Plate 133, lines 10–11
83 (p. 321) *Milton's Journey to Eternal Death* First Book, Plate 14, lines 10–41
84 (p. 322) *The Nature of Infinity*   First Book, Plate 15, lines 21–35
85 (p. 322) *The Sea of Time and Space*   First Book, Plate 15, lines 36–46
86 (p. 323) *The Mundane Shell*   First Book, Plate 17, lines 21–7
87 (p. 323) *A River in Eden*   First Book, Plate 21, lines 15–19
88 (p. 323) *Los*   First Book, Plate 22, lines 15–25
89 (p. 324) *Swedenborg*   First Book, Plate 22, lines 50–4

90 (p. 324) *Whitefield and Wesley*   First Book, Plate 22, line 61; Plate 23, line 5

91 (p. 324) *The Forge of Los*   First Book, Plate 24, lines 51–66

92 (p. 325) *The Wine-Press of Los*   First Book, Plate 25, lines 1–41

93 (p. 326) *The Building of Time*   First Book, Plate 28, line 44; Plate 29, line 3

94 (p. 327) *The Heavens and the Earth*   First Book, Plate 29, lines 4–16

95 (p. 327) *The Birds and the Flowers*   Second Book, Plate 31, lines 28–63

96 (p. 328) *Love and Jealousy*   Second Book, Plate 33, lines 1–24

97 (p. 329) *Reason and Imagination*   Second Book, Plate 40, line 34; Plate 41, line 28

98 (p. 340) *The Song of the Shadowy Female*   Extra Plates, Plate 18, lines 5–25

Jerusalem (1804–20)

99 (p. 334) *Selections from Jerusalem (1804–20)*   The selections here list the lineation to be found in *Blake – The Complete Poems*, ed. W. H. Stevenson (second edition) to allow the interested reader to put them in context. The titles to the passages are editorial in order to give the reader some focus.

100 (p. 334) *To the Public*   The following are editorial suggestions for the gaps in the text, which indicate places where Blake erased his text. These are derived from D.V. Erdman (see Stevenson, p. 632): [love] [friendship] [blessed] [no reader will think presumptuousness or arrogance when he is reminded that the Ancients acknowledged their love to their deities, to the full as enthusiastically as I have who acknowledge mine for my Saviour and Lord, for they were wholly absorbed in their gods.] [of Fire] [of Love] [dear] [forgive] [love] [lover] [lover] [all books are given] [To note the last words of Jesus, Εδοθη μοι παζα εξουσια εν ουρανω̃ και επι γη̃ζ.]

101 (p. 335) *Introduction* Chapter 1, Plate 4, lines 3–8. The Chapter is headed with the following statement of the theme:

> Of the sleep of Ulro, and of the passage through
> Eternal Death, and of the awakening to Eternal Life.
>
> (Stevenson, p. 634)

102 (p. 335) *The Reasoning Power*   Chapter 1, Plate 10, lines 7–16

103 (p. 336) *The Words of Los*   Chapter 1, Plate 10, lines 20–1

104 (p. 336) *The Builders of Golgonooza*   Chapter 1, Plate 12, lines 25–44

INDEX OF POEM TITLES

INDEX OF FIRST LINES